THE YEAR OF FEAR

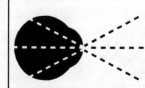

This Large Print Book carries the
Seal of Approval of N.A.V.H.

THE YEAR OF FEAR

MACHINE GUN KELLY AND THE MANHUNT THAT CHANGED THE NATION

JOE URSCHEL

THORNDIKE PRESS

A part of Gale, Cengage Learning

GALE
CENGAGE Learning·

Farmington Hills, Mich • San Francisco • New York • Waterville, Maine
Meriden, Conn • Mason, Ohio • Chicago

GALE
CENGAGE Learning·

Copyright © 2015 by Joe Urschel.
Thorndike Press, a part of Gale, Cengage Learning.

ALL RIGHTS RESERVED
Thorndike Press® Large Print Crime Scene.
The text of this Large Print edition is unabridged.
Other aspects of the book may vary from the original edition.
Set in 16 pt. Plantin.

LIBRARY OF CONGRESS CATALOGING-IN-PUBLICATION DATA

Urschel, Joe, author
  The year of fear : Machine Gun Kelly and the manhunt that changed the
nation / by Joe Urschel. — Large print edition.
    pages cm. — (Thorndike Press large print crime scene)
  Includes bibliographical references.
  ISBN 978-1-4104-8521-2 (hardcover) — ISBN 1-4104-8521-8 (hardcover)
  1. Kelly, Machine Gun, 1897-1954. 2. Criminals—United States—Biography.
3. Outlaws—United States—Biography. 4. Crime—United
States—History—20th century. 5. Law enforcement—United
States—History—20th century. 6. United States—History—1933-1945. I. Title.
HV6248.K414U77 2016
364.152'3092—dc23
[B]   2015031718

Published in 2016 by arrangement with St. Martin's Press, LLC

Printed in Mexico
1 2 3 4 5 6 7 20 19 18 17 16

To Donna,
Liz and Eric

CONTENTS

AUTHOR'S NOTE

In 1982, shortly after I'd moved to Washington, DC, I went to visit the Library of Congress's Jefferson Building, one of the city's most gorgeous landmarks, which contains, it is said, the greatest collection of knowledge in the world. The LOC had just recently converted its famed collection cataloging system (the one J. Edgar Hoover had learned during his brief stint there as a clerk early in his career) into a searchable, computerized database, something that was quite novel and innovative at the time. Out of curiosity, I went to the keyboard and typed in my last name. A simple Google search today would now reveal hundreds of hits, but back then, in the early days of the digital revolution, the LOC's computer index turned up only one: Charles Urschel, kidnapping victim. And there was one book in which he was noted prominently. It was E. E. Kirkpatrick's firsthand account,

Crime's Paradise: The Authentic Inside Story of the Urschel Kidnapping published in 1934. I immediately requested the book, and when the librarian pulled it from the stacks, I sat in the LOC's stately reading room and read it cover to cover. (Only members of Congress and staff can actually check a book out of the LOC.)

I was, of course, transfixed by Kirkpatrick's rendering of a story that could have been the blueprint for a Dashiell Hammett novel. But I was also bewildered that I — and most other Americans — had never heard of the main character. This was especially embarrassing for me in that I shared his rather uncommon last name, and I'd believed all the Urschels in the United States were related. Everyone seemed familiar with the name of Urschel's kidnapper, the notorious George "Machine Gun" Kelly even if they knew nothing about his biggest crime.

My research ultimately found no American familial connection with Charles Urschel. Our relationship dates back centuries to Germany. My interest in his story, however, continued to grow as the years passed and the historical exploration into the crime wave of the '30s shed more and more light on the period and the fascinating men and women who made it so infamous.

The year of the crime, 1933, saw an extraordinary confluence of events in the country. With unprecedented dust storms inflicting further misery on a population mired in the Great Depression, Franklin Delano Roosevelt swept into office warily eyeing the almost simultaneous election of Adolf Hitler in Germany while telling his fellow Americans they had nothing to fear, but "fear itself." And while he was constructing a big, activist federal government to address the nation's ills, another national industry was being launched to celebrate it. With national radio news networks starting up and wire services and huge regional daily newspapers growing, the "mass media" as we know it today were bringing the sprawling, unwieldy country together in ways it had not experienced earlier.

The Urschel kidnapping provided a captivating scenario that dominated the headlines and airwaves from New York City to San Francisco. There were those, like Roosevelt and J. Edgar Hoover, who quickly learned how to use and exploit this pervasive new national megaphone to their own great benefit.

There were others, like Charles Urschel, who shunned and reviled it. Nevertheless, the decisions Urschel made, and the actions he took, had a profound effect on the course of history, just like the other, more famous and infamous men of his time. Had he not chosen the course of action he did — standing up to the threats of his captors and co-operating with the federal authorities — J. Edgar Hoover would have been denied the spectacular trial on which he launched his career, and George Kelly most likely would have remained in anonymity as a relative bit player in the saga of America's gangland.

But that is not the way it happened. It happened like this . . .

INTRODUCTION:
THE CALL

As J. Edgar Hoover lay asleep in his home in the early morning hours of July 22, 1933, he was fitfully aware of the tentative hold he had on the job he had come to know and love. He was Director of the United States Department of Justice's Bureau of Investigation. At age thirty-six, he was thought by most to be too young, too inexperienced and too politically unconnected for the job most people in government considered to be barely more than a political patronage appointment. And, lately, he'd been proving them right.

His team's investigation of the Charles Lindbergh baby kidnapping had been a laughable failure. The case had dragged on with no resolution or notable progress in the sixteen months since then-President Herbert Hoover had tapped him to lead the federal efforts to solve the case and find the kidnappers. His initial efforts to get involved in the investigation had been rebuffed by the New Jersey State Police, who flat out refused to share information, and dismissed his men as inept federal glory hunters. Lindbergh himself was barely cooperative.

His overreaching in the capture and arrest of an escaped federal prisoner had resulted in the mass murder of four law enforcement officers, including one from his bureau, and the prisoner himself. The machine gun assault had taken place in the parking lot of Kansas City's busy Union Station in full view of the train station's bustling crowds.

Not only was his competence being called into question by the national press, but his masculinity was, as well. The new president's wife was said to loathe him, and he'd just barely escaped a sacking by Franklin Delano Roosevelt's first choice for attorney general.

But Hoover was about to receive a phone call that would turn his fortunes around. The call would deliver to Hoover the most effective and cooperative witness in the history of the agency's war against crime. It would set into motion the biggest manhunt in the nation's history and lead to a spectacular trial that would transfix the country and transform the Bureau.

The events would unleash a cavalcade of

publicity that would ultimately put the beleaguered director on course to become not only the most powerful lawman in the nation's history, but the most admired, as well. Within ninety days, Hoover would go from a man whose head had been on the political chopping block, to the star performer of the new administration's ambitious plans.

Hoover could not have realized all of this as his bedside telephone rang on that Sunday at 2:00 a.m. But his life was about to change, and history was about to be made.

Just weeks earlier, Hoover had established the country's first national crime hotline, a special telephone number that anyone could call to be put through immediately to the Justice Department headquarters in Washington, DC. It was intended to be used for reporting kidnappings, a heinous crime that was occurring with alarming regularity throughout the country. Hoover hoped his hotline would tip his agents off quickly so they could get on the scene without delay and get control of the investigation before the local authorities could lock things up and freeze them out. So eager was he to get news quickly that he instructed the telephone operators at the Bureau to put calls through to a special line he had installed in his home.

It was now ringing.

Hoover roused himself awake and sat in his pajamas on the side of the bed, clearing his head and lifting the receiver from its cradle.

"National 7-1-1-7," he intoned.

"This is Mrs. Charles F. Urschel in Oklahoma City. I wish to report a kidnapping."

"This is J. Edgar Hoover, Mrs. Urschel. Give me every detail you can."

1
GEORGE AND KATHRYN
GO TO WORK

On a warm morning in 1932, George and Kathryn Kelly were getting dressed for work in their comfortable Fort Worth home.

George loved watching his wife get dressed almost as much as he liked watching her undress. She was a stunner with the kind of frame that fine clothes were just made to adorn. She assembled herself into a brown silk blouse that draped off her shoulders and breasts as if it had been constructed specially for her by the finest seamstress in Dallas.

The gentle friction of the beige wool skirt she pulled up over her silk slip purred slightly as it glided over her hips. When she was finished tucking and smoothing, she snapped the waistband closed with a definitive click, like the sound of a .38 slug sliding into its chamber.

She plucked a weighty diamond brooch off the dresser and pinned it near her throat.

Its sparkle drew George's eye to the lovely little pool of flesh at the base of her throat, where the exquisite lines of Kathryn's neck joined the frame of her shoulders. She slipped her arms into the beige suit jacket and tugged gently at it, pulling it into place. She set a smart beige cloche hat atop her head and tilted it ever so slightly to the right. It sat on her auburn hair like the crown on a European monarch and warmed her brown eyes into a deceptive look of coquettishness.

She turned gently to her husband, seeking the fawning approval that he was always eager to provide.

George, too, looked sharp. Tall and muscular, he knew how to polish the image with just the right amount of fashion-savvy style and masculine panache. Today he was wearing a custom-made brown English wool suit, with a creamy linen shirt. His tie was a ballet of greens and browns. His shoes, brown wingtips, were polished like brass. When he gazed at Kathryn, his hazel eyes looked as green and seductive as a cat in heat.

They were in the banking business and they were about to begin their twelve-hour commute to Boulder, Colorado, to go to work.

They nestled into the warm leather seats of their sixteen-cylinder Cadillac convertible roadster and headed north with smiles on their faces and Lucky Strikes glowing between their fingers.

George loved his Cadillac almost as much as he loved Kit. The car was the pride of General Motors and the envy of carmakers around the world. When GM introduced it in 1930, the company boasted: "the sixteen-cylinder Cadillac initiates a new trend in motor car design." It was "designed for enormous acceleration, unheard of hill-climbing ability, and more speed than perhaps any man will care to use."

In short, the perfect vehicle for a man in George's line of work.

Off the assembly line it could cruise easily at eighty-five miles per hour. But after George's mechanics got finished customizing it, the car would race along at more than one hundred miles per hour on the paved roads of the nation's state highway system. They'd also reinforce the suspension to handle the heavy loads of liquor George would haul and the extra cans of gasoline he'd pack in the trunk because the monster engine would barely eke out eight miles a gallon.

And it looked like a dream, with billowing

oval fender skirts, teardrop headlamps, glistening chrome-spoked wheels and white-wall tires. It turned as many heads as Kit.

They arrived in Denver slightly after 9:00 p.m. and pulled up to the garage next to a small bungalow on the outskirts of the city.

"Kit, come on baby, move over to the driver's seat," said George. "We've got to change cars."

Albert Bates, who'd rented the bungalow and the garage, walked out of the house and greeted the couple in the yard.

"You sure took your time getting here, George," said Al. "It was dark over an hour ago. The coast was clear."

George was moving gear from the Cadillac to a nondescript Buick they would use in the morning. "We stopped for a leisurely dinner, Al. You know how Kit likes candle-light and wine. No rush anyway, you've got the job all laid out."

Bates poured them all a glass of whiskey, the finest contraband in the country, and spread out a hand-drawn map of the neigh-borhood on the table. He marked the major streets, the stop signs, the police patrol route. He outlined the best approach to the bank and where Kit would need to park the getaway car. They then went over the layout of the bank's interior — the teller locations, the vault, the president's office — and the guard's routine. He showed them the ideal escape route and several others in case something unexpected should happen.

"How far away is the police station?" George asked.

"It's far enough away to make getting there difficult for the cops. Nine, ten blocks. We can be out of town before anyone can get them on the phone."

George had spent a lifetime as a bootlegger. He knew how to elude the law and he knew the roads and highway system as if he had designed them himself. He knew his cars and how to race them around the back roads, avoiding bottlenecks, bridges and areas where a roadblock might slow his escape. Once he was in the car and moving, there was no way he'd get caught from behind. Hell, he'd be out of the county before the cops were done cranking up their pathetic Model As.

After a few hours' sleep, George and Al threw on some cheap gray suits and waited impatiently while Kit primped in the house's single bathroom. She emerged in a silk navy-blue dress and carried a wide-brimmed hat. She also carried a men's suit that had been tailored to fit over the dress. Al took the wheel of the car and Kit lay across the backseat in case there were any early-morning looky-loos, who'd see only two men heading out for work.

Along the way, they stopped briefly so Kit could don her masculine garb and take over the driving duties. George looked on admiringly. Best looking wheelman he'd ever worked with.

She backed expertly into an open parking spot in front of the bank, positioned perfectly for a quick getaway.

"Good luck, fellas," she said as she pulled a revolver from under the seat.

As the two entered the bank and headed toward the tellers, Al pulled a sawed-off shotgun from under his coat.

"It's a holdup!" he announced. "Hands to heaven, and no yelling!"

George tossed a canvas bag over the counter to each teller. "Fill 'em up, girls. And be quick!"

As he did, the bank's elderly guard was moving warily in George's direction. Al yelled out a warning and George turned his .38 in the guard's direction. The guard was fumbling to remove his sidearm from its holster. George fired off a single round, clipping the guard in the arm and dropping him to the floor as the panicked tellers stuffed stacks of wadded-up bills into the bags.

"You stupid son of a bitch! I warned you! Do what you're told!"

He grabbed the bags from the tellers and the two jogged quickly back to the car and jumped in as Kit sped away.

"What happened?" she asked. "You scared the hell out of me when I heard that shot."

"The old bank guard wanted to be a hero, so George shot him," said Al. "Nothing serious. He'll survive."

"Could have shot the old guy in the heart," said George, "but I've never killed anyone and don't intend on starting."

Al could not make a similar claim. He'd shot an earlier partner who he thought had been cheating him. He wouldn't have to worry about that with George, though. George was all business and he played it straight. He had a reputation going all the way back to his bootlegging days as the most honest thief you'd ever meet. But although it was true he'd never killed anyone, the fact was he didn't need to. There were plenty experienced killers among the members he'd assemble into bank-robbing teams. If he needed a shooter, he could get one with a single phone call.

Yet another rural western bank had been relieved of its deposits — $15,000 in this case. The handsome couple in the front seat of the nondescript Buick were heading back to pick up their shiny new Cadillac roadster and were busy making bigger plans.

First, off to Mexico to lie low and spend some of their recent earnings. George spoke fluent Spanish and, along with his extravagant tips, he was a popular customer at the lavish beach resorts that Kit favored.

Since his release from Leavenworth Penitentiary in February 1930, Kelly had been on a tear, robbing banks at the rate of nearly one a month. The jobs were getting to be almost routine, but with the Depression dragging on, the take was getting smaller and smaller. Banks had less and less money in their vaults, and some were simply closing up shop and going out of business as panicked customers pulled out their cash. George had a feeling his real good thing was not going to last forever. Worse, the couple's lucrative sideline — running booze — looked like it would be drying up if the Democrats won the upcoming election and their gin-sipping candidate made good on his promise to bring the era of Prohibition to an end.

From their R & R vacation spot, they would begin the planning for a series of jobs that would set them up for life — an audacious scheme that Kit had dreamed up. It involved a series of kidnappings of high-net-worth individuals in the lawless Southwest that would — if everything went according to plan — bring them $1 million in cash and set them up for permanent retirement in the luxury lifestyle they had grown so accustomed to. They were about to graduate into the burgeoning Snatch Racket that was about to become the latest calamity to afflict the country.

When Franklin Delano Roosevelt took office in March 1933, he inherited a surreal and almost unimaginable American nightmare. The country had become a cauldron of poverty, starvation and environmental disaster. A pervasive lawlessness infected nearly every city, town and godforsaken outpost in the forty-eight states he would need to rescue.

Since the Stock Market Crash of 1929, almost 90 percent of its value had been lost. Much of the nation's upper class was wiped out. The ripple effects of those losses decimated the middle class and those less fortunate, as well. Average household incomes dropped by a third. Thousands of banks closed. Local and community banks foreclosed on nearly one million homeowners. Business failures and the collapsing real estate market deprived cities and states of tax revenue, which resulted in draconian cuts in the few social services that existed. Municipal workers, police and teachers were laid off or went unpaid. Thousands of schools closed or reduced hours. Millions of students dropped out.

The gross national product (GNP) had fallen to half its 1929 level. Industrial investment dropped by 90 percent. Automobile production was down nearly 70 percent, as were iron and steel production and nearly every other industry that provided work for Americans. Sixteen million jobs had evaporated. The per capita income was lower than it was in the early 1900s.

John L. Lewis, head of the United Mine Workers of America, was not engaging in hyperbole when he asserted that the diets of most members of his union had sunk "below domestic animal standards."

The national unemployment rate, which was as low as 3 percent before the market crashed, pushed north of 25 percent. For non-farm workers it was almost 40 percent. In many cities it stretched as high as 80 percent. But those numbers masked the reduced hours and trimmed wages of the workers who managed to hang on. Those who couldn't walked the city streets in a daze looking for work, food or hope. And there just wasn't any.

Proud men and women who populated the nation's cities — from the architects and engineers who designed them to the iron-workers and carpenters who built them — stood in breadlines for hours. Occasionally, they would form up into a mob and attack the food trucks that passed by making their deliveries. At night, a desperate few would organize raids on local grocery stores, kicking in windows and looting them dry before the police could arrive.

The misery was even greater on the farms and ranches of the Midwest and Plains, where the Great Depression had arrived years earlier. The droughts that started in the late '20s continued unrelentingly into the '30s. During the war years, as Europe's farmland was incinerated and destroyed, American farmers had stepped up, increased production, expanded their acreage and fed the world. After the war ended and the verdant fields in Europe returned, the price of everything produced in America plummeted.

Overproduction from the war years had stripped much of the land of its fertility. The drought dried it up and it simply began to blow away — slowly at first, but eventually in dust clouds so thick they would choke cattle and blacken the sky at noon. American farm production had dropped 60 percent from 1929 to 1932.

That was the state of the nation that Roosevelt was elected to rescue: bankrupt, starving, without hope and growing increasingly violent.

Just months before he was to take office, Roosevelt himself had narrowly escaped an assassin's bullet. Attending a celebration rally in Miami after returning from a cruise aboard his friend Vincent Astor's yacht, an assassin fired five times in his direction, fatally wounding Anton Cermak, the mayor of Chicago, who was standing next to him. And while the violence that day was deemed a national disgrace, it was indicative of the kind of nation the President governed. In major cities, particularly Chicago, large, entrenched criminal empires had been established essentially by providing to the citizenry the very things that the government had outlawed: liquor, gambling, prostitution and a small collection of lesser vices. To protect their business operations, these organized crime families set up their own codes, laws and accepted business practices. They hired their own enforcement operators and bribed the local cops to either look the other way or lend a hand for an accepted price.

In the '20s and '30s, law enforcement was primarily a local affair. Law officers were beholden to area politicians, many of whom were beholden to the local mob. The untrained, underfinanced web of law enforcement in 1933 consisted of a mere collection of four thousand county sheriffs, eleven state police forces and a handful of big city operations — all with conflicting degrees of cooperation, political affiliations and corruption. (Currently, there are more than eighteen thousand law enforcement agencies and nearly one million law enforcement officers.) In many towns it was not too much of a stretch to say that the local mob not only ran the criminal activities, but the government and law enforcement, as well.

The New York Times lamented that "the criminal courts of this nation have become in effect a protection to the criminal through the web of technicalities, objections to evidence, delays, appeals, straw bond, parole, and pardon at the disposal of unscrupulous criminal lawyers." The 1931 editorial noted that since the declaration of war in 1917, the number of murders associated with the crime wave in the United States was greater than three times the

50,280 deaths caused by World War I. (The murder rate in the '30s was twice that of contemporary times, and the vast majority went unsolved.)

The banking collapse and FDR's pledge to end Prohibition were putting the squeeze on a particular brand of outlaw plying his trade in the middle of the country. These men, who operated in loosely organized small units or on their own, were viewed by the local populace as the direct descendants of the legendary Western outlaws who roamed the West robbing trains, banks and wealthy ranchers. The modern equivalents in the '20s and '30s were highwaymen, bootleggers and bank robbers. But the Depression and the impending legalization of liquor sales were wiping out their lucrative businesses. There was little money left in the banks, and there was no money on the road. But there were plenty of wealthy fat cats at the top of the food chain who still had plenty of cash in their pockets and in their vaults. If your business is thievery, you go where the money is. And, in 1933, there were precious few places to raid. But if you could snatch a member of the moneyed class, ransom them off and get away with the cash, you could get rich.

Out of this state of criminal desperation,

the Snatch Racket was born.

An accelerating scourge of kidnapping was about to envelop the nation, and it had almost no means of combatting it. The bootleggers and bank robbers who operated with virtual impunity out West were well aware that fleeing county and state lines left the local law without the authority to give chase, and that handing off that authority to another county or state was a coordination nightmare. Outlaws, with their fast cars, superior weaponry and the tacit support of the locals, were agonizingly hard to chase and capture. It would be the same for those who turned to kidnapping.

FDR, who was hatching plans to expand the federal government to combat the Depression, recognized the need to create a national law enforcement arm to combat the rampant criminality that was bleeding the country.

What Roosevelt wanted was a national force that would be small, well-trained and largely invisible to the public. But, most importantly, it would be beholden to no state or local politician. It would be the law enforcement arm of the federal government. But national police forces were perceived by many as the stuff of dictators and European potentates. In the United States, with its aversion to concentrated federal power and big government, there had been no appetite for one.

But in the hot summer of 1933, as Roosevelt completed his ambitious first 100 days in office, those big-government fears would begin to abate. An unlikely confluence of criminal events would soon put the need for a national police force on center stage.

George Kelly's road to criminal notoriety was unlike those of his contemporaries. Most of the other gangster types roving the South and Midwest were the charmless products of tough or impoverished backgrounds. George was the son of well-to-do parents in Memphis, Tennessee. Born George Francis Barnes Jr. on July 18, 1900, he grew up comfortably middle class, attending Catholic schools and getting by on his innate intelligence rather than applying himself to any serious scholastic pursuits. He worked as a caddy at the local country club and, when he was old enough to drive, he began smuggling liquor into the dry state of Tennessee from over the state line in nearby Arkansas.

George was the product of a loveless marriage. His mother suffered constantly from the inattention of her husband and his distant relationship with his children.

When George got wind of a rumor that his father was carrying on a relationship with another woman across town, he staked out the house and, when he got evidence of the tryst, he confronted his father by barging into his office the next day. George agreed to keep the information from his mother in exchange for a hefty increase in his allowance and liberal use of the family car.

George used the car and his cash to expand his liquor-running business. He found willing customers among the members of the country club where he worked, and soon they were setting him up with so many patrons he no longer needed to hump clubs around the course for measly tips. When the enterprising high school entrepreneur would get busted by the local police, his father would dutifully bail him out and use his influence to get the charges dropped.

George fled his home life the way most middle-class kids do, by going off to college. Even though he'd dropped out of high school, he managed to pass the college entrance exam and enrolled at Mississippi A&M (now Mississippi State University) as a probationary student. But he spent most of his time and money on the co-eds he charmed and the parties they attended. By the beginning of his second semester, he'd run up some 55 demerits — which he famously tried to reduce by climbing to the top of the school's flagpole to fix a broken pulley. Ultimately, he dropped out and returned to Memphis and the business he'd started, which would later expand to great profit when the Volstead Act brought in the Prohibition era in 1919.

Back in the gentleman bootlegging business, he set his sights on the beautiful daughter of a wealthy businessman, Geneva Ramsey. But Ramsey's father, George, was well aware of the young lothario's reputation, criminal and otherwise, and he forbade his daughter from seeing him. He sent her away to boarding school when George persisted in his romantic pursuits.

Eventually, they eloped and got married in Mississippi, assisted by none other than the governor's daughter, whom Geneva had met while at school.

On their return, Ramsey relented and took George into the family with reluctant acceptance that eventually grew into genuine affection. He gave him a job at his construction company and George worked with great enthusiasm, adopting Ramsey as the "father I never had." The couple had two kids, and Ramsey was naturally taken with his grandchildren, just as he was with his new assistant. But tragedy struck in 1925, when a dynamite charge exploded prematurely and killed Ramsey. His widow, Della, was forced to sell the company, and she generously set George up in various businesses, from selling cars to goat farming, but George was not the businessman that his father-in-law had been and he failed at all of them.

Eventually, George returned to the life of a bootlegger, wearing fashionable suits and snap-brimmed fedoras as he hauled his liquor in fast cars with his golf clubs cohabitating with the contraband in the trunk. Geneva hated the new life with George, gone so frequently, alternately getting chased by police or rivals and ending up in jail in all sorts of places. When she'd had enough, she took the kids and left him.

With Geneva gone, George took off for the wilds of Kansas City, an open city for criminality of all measures and styles. He changed his name to George Ramsey Kelly, using Ramsey as his middle name in deference to his departed father-in-law. He got serious about the business of bootlegging, which was growing increasingly profitable as the Prohibition era dragged on.

He was arrested a number of times in connection with his criminal exploits. In Santa Fe on March 14, 1927, in Tulsa on July 24 and then again in Tulsa in January 1928. But bootlegging in the rural Southwest was a well-tolerated crime, and if the right people were paid off and the right protection acquired, the penalties were light from the local authorities. But he made the foolish mistake of getting caught selling liquor on an Indian reservation, a minor crime, but because it was on federal land, it was a federal offense. On January 13, 1928, he was convicted and sent to Leavenworth Federal Penitentiary, where he was thrown in with a bunch of hard cases with long rap sheets — the type of men who really did belong there. It was there he would meet the people who would change his life forever, most notably a tight group of professional bank robbers: Francis "Jimmy" Keating, Tommy Holden and the legendary Frank "Jelly" Nash.

Kelly used his math and accounting skills to work his way into a cushy job in the prison's records office. With access to all of the inmates' personal statistics and fingerprints, Kelly was able to expertly fabricate fake IDs for Keating and Holden that allowed them to walk out with a work crew of less notorious inmates assigned to farm labor. Once out, they ditched the work crew, changed into civilian clothing and simply walked away. (Nash, the wily veteran, didn't need any help. He walked out in a similar fashion a short time later.) The three had told Kelly that if he was looking for work once he got on the outside, he should come by the Green Lantern tavern in St. Paul, Minnesota, and look them up. When Kelly was released two years later on good behavior, he was tougher, smarter and had a whole cadre of experienced criminal pals he was looking to reconnect with. And he knew exactly where to find them.

The Green Lantern was a major clearinghouse for underworld activities of all sorts run by an Orthodox Jew named Harry "Dutch" Sawyer, who had St. Paul's notoriously corrupt police department in his pocket. At the Green Lantern, Dutch could put you together with big-time criminal gangs who might be in need of an additional player for a bank heist, burglary, safecracking, shakedown, extortion or whatever other kind of racket you were into. If things didn't go as planned, he could lead you to a friendly auto body repair shop where they wouldn't ask questions about the bullet holes in the fender or the shattered back window. If you needed to arm up, he could get you the kind of weapon you desired. Suffer an unfortunate injury on the job? He could get you the best treatment from a skilled, no-questions-asked member of the medical profession. In need of female companionship? He could arrange that, too. And if you needed to unload some marked bills, government bonds or any other hard-to-fence item, he could get you the best rate going.

In 1930, the Green Lantern was a very popular spot. Dutch arranged for employees at the Prohibition-crippled Schmidt Brewery to provide him with beer through a tunnel system. St. Paul Police Chief Tom Brown drank at the bar and worked his various "business deals" with Dutch. In the areas of the country bordered by Chicago, St. Louis, Kansas City and the Canadian border, there were few significant criminal activities that didn't have a connection to the Green Lantern. It was "big time," but you needed an entrée to get in. And when George got out of prison, he had one.

Dutch was running what was commonly referred to around St. Paul as the "O'Connor System." From the turn of the century to 1920, Police Chief John O'Connor ran the crime and law enforcement operations of St. Paul. O'Connor was both a law enforcement officer and a criminal enforcer. He was known as the "Smiling Peacemaker," both for his Irish charm and his ability to keep trouble out of his town by accommodating and protecting those who would ply their trades outside of it. The equation was simple; it didn't matter what kind of criminal you were, you were protected in St. Paul as long as you didn't commit any crimes within the city limits. It was a system that worked well for the banks and citizens of the city. The city fathers were happy to live in ignorant bliss and enjoy the crime-free environs of their proud state capital.

On the other side of the river, in Minneapolis, a similar system was run by a tall, affable Irishman named Edward G. "Big Ed" Morgan. It was a perverted form of law enforcement, but it worked particularly well, as long as you lived in the Twin Cities. However, once you got outside the city limits, the countryside was ravaged by the criminals that the O'Connor System protected.

By the early '30s, fully 20 percent of the bank robberies in the nation occurred within an easy drive of St. Paul. In 1933 alone, forty-three bank robberies had drained $1.4 million from regional coffers (approximately $20 million in contemporary value). The pillaging teams that formed at the Green Lantern hit small community banks in little towns virtually unknown to the rest of the nation: Hugo, Sandstone, Elk River, Cushing, Savage, Shakopee and on and on. They hit the banks in neighboring North and South Dakota, as well. The county sheriffs and amateur guards hired by the local banks were unprepared and ill-equipped for the marauding robbers who would swoop in carrying machine guns, sawed-off shotguns and pistols stuck in their belts. And even if they were lucky enough to have a squad car, they would be left in the dust as gangsters sped away in fast Cadillacs and Packards, back to the safety and comfort of St. Paul.

This was the fraternity Kelly was able to join with Keating and Holden and Nash as his sponsors. He would begin his on-the-job training almost immediately after leaving prison from the guys who were the very best in the business. Nash was the old-timer with a criminal résumé that stretched back more than a decade. Nash was part of the team that robbed the Katy Limited on August

20, 1923 — the last successful horseback-mounted train robbery in American history. Nash's charm and erudition were noted by the Associated Press when reporting on the robbery: "Four men under the leadership of a suave outlaw, who chatted amiably with his victims about the merits of a certain well-known political writer and discussed current questions of the day, held up the Missouri, Kansas & Texas train 123 southbound near Okesa, Okla., early today and robbed the express and mail cars of packages," the story noted.

Nash had spent so much time in prison libraries that he'd become something of a Shakespeare scholar, quoting liberally from his works for comic effect when the time was right — jokes that went right over the heads of his thuggish compadres. When he walked out of Leavenworth, he'd taken the library's copy of the Bard's collected works with him.

Nash worked frequently with another Green Lantern denizen by the name of Harvey Bailey. Bailey was thought to be the most successful bank robber in the country. He had basically invented the modern form of bank robbery — one that emphasized meticulous planning, precise timing and hasty escapes over country roads using the finest and fastest of Detroit's products. He'd study road maps, often at the county surveyor's office, and drive them ahead of time for practice, always plotting alternative routes in case things didn't go according to plan. He knew where the traffic cops were stationed and when the patrolmen walked their beat. There wasn't a cop in the country that could catch Bailey when he was fleeing a job. He'd be flying down back alleys in speedy escape cars before the local lawmen even knew their town had been hit.

Bailey would study a bank for weeks or months before he would pull a job. He could judge the health of a bank by the commercial activity of its city and county. He knew when payroll deposits were made and the cash on hand would be greatest. There was no point in risking your life to rob a bank that was low on money.

Bailey robbed his first bank in 1920, and by the end of the decade his successful plunders included the Denver Mint and Lincoln National Bank, which netted him and his crew a cool million in cash and bonds, which he then laundered through Sawyer at the Green Lantern. The losses suffered by the Lincoln Bank were so severe that it closed its doors a short time later. Bailey had stolen so much money in fact, that in the late '20s he quit the business and went straight, investing in real estate and opening a group of gas stations and car washes in Chicago. But when the market crashed in 1929 and his bank failed, Bailey's legitimate businesses were wiped out and he had to return to the kind of work he did best.

Keating and Holden had been incarcerated so long they needed a couple of jobs to retrain for the modern era. So Dutch assigned them and Bailey, along with their rookie friend Kelly, to assist Sammy Silverman and Robert Steinhardt from Chicago on a job planned to knock over the bank of Willmar, Minnesota. For George, the amiable bootlegger who'd never been in on a bank robbery, it was baptism by fire.

Bailey brought in his longtime partner and legendary gunman, Verne Miller. Miller was a former county sheriff from South Dakota and a combat-hardened army marksman who'd served in World War I. He'd taken his talents over to the criminal side after the county fathers had sent him to prison on an embezzlement charge. If there was the risk of gunplay on a job, Verne Miller was the kind of man you would want on your team. Bailey was uneasy about the Willmar raid because he had not participated in the plan-

ning and in his view it was poorly planned
— in fact, not really planned at all. Steinhardt and Silverman were going to take the
place by force and surprise. This was not
the way Bailey liked to work, but, not wanting to disappoint Dutch, he agreed to go
along.

On the day of the job, the group assembled, each grabbing a tommy gun or
sawed-off shotgun and a sidearm out of the
trunk of the assault cars. Kelly was assigned
to guard the bank's front door while the
others went inside to empty the vaults and
cover the customers.

The group sped into Willmar, jumped
from the cars with guns drawn and burst
into the lobby. There were sixteen employees and nine customers milling about.

"Lay down or we'll blow the hell out of
you!"

The crowd dove for the floor. Steinhardt
covered them as Bailey went to work on the
tellers and the vault, filling satchels with
cash and bonds. When the bank's vice
president was slow to comply with the order
to hit the floor, Steinhardt clubbed him with
his gun and kicked him into compliance.

But the bank had done some planning. A
silent alarm switch had been installed under
the counter to alert the police and a group

of unofficially deputized neighbors. As Bailey leapt the counter, he noticed a teller lift his leg, tripping the silent alarm.

"I'll kill you for that," snarled Bailey as he pushed the teller to the floor. Steinhardt and Silverman were having trouble getting the vaults opened and valuable time was wasting away as a small crowd, alerted by the alarm, began to assemble outside as Kelly tried to keep them at bay waving his weapon from side to side and threatening to shoot.

Inside, Bailey and Steinhardt grabbed the bank's vice president and threatened to kill him if he didn't give them the safe's combination.

"Then shoot," he replied stoically. "I don't know it."

Another teller was not so defiant and finally got the door open after a sizeable delay. With their satchels full, they headed for the door. Bailey put his gun on the cowering teller who had tripped the alarm.

"Stand up, I'll need you," he said, grabbing him by the collar and forcing him to the door as a shield. Bailey's compatriot grabbed a woman off the floor and did the same. When they burst outside, Kelly let loose a volley of machine-gun fire to scatter the crowd as the escape car approached.

But the crowd was returning fire and a bullet whizzed past the head of Bailey's shield. As it did, the teller ducked violently, getting free of Bailey's grip. Bailey clubbed him to the ground with a swift blow from his rifle's butt and the kid crawled along the ground back into the bank and reached up to lock the door as the frightened employees were jumping out the rear window to flee the scene.

The female hostage was doing little to dissuade the townsfolk from returning fire in her direction. Bullets tore past her head until she was finally released as the gang jumped inside the escape car and started returning fire into the crowd.

Mrs. Emil Johnson was standing on the corner holding her two-and-a-half-year-old granddaughter, Annette Ruth, in her arms when a bullet tore into her. Her daughter screamed. As she tried to drag her mother and daughter into the safety of a doorway, she, too, was hit. A third round hit the bag the child was holding.

As the cars sped away back to St. Paul, they were peppered with gunfire from the vigilantes strategically positioned along the way. One round shattered the rear window of one of the getaway cars and hit Steinhardt in the back of the head. He slumped forward and passed out as blood splattered the car's interior and sent shards of glass shrapnel into the other occupants.

Still, the gang eluded their pursuers and fled back to the Twin Cities with $142,000 in cash and securities.

The next edition of the *Minneapolis Journal* was topped with bold headlines reporting the raid:

MACHINEGUN BANDITS
RAID WILLMAR
STREETS SPRAYED WITH BULLETS, 3 SHOT

Citizens Held at Bay Before Machinegun While Gangsters Scoop Up Currency — Townspeople Fire Upon Fleeing Auto

"The robbery," said the *Journal,* "was one of the most daring in the history of the Northwest. The outlaws used a modernized version of the Jesse James practice of half a century ago to shoot up the town after the holdup."

"The bandits certainly were thorough in their work," one eyewitness noted. "They were not amateurs. I just saw one of them. He appeared about 35 or 40 years old and was fairly well dressed."

The *Journal* noted that the Willmar raid

was the thirteenth successful holdup on Minnesota banks since the beginning of the year. And at $142,000, it was the biggest theft to date.

To Bailey it was totally botched. He vowed to only work on jobs he planned himself in the future. He'd taken the job as a favor to Dutch, but it seemed every time he agreed to help someone out, there was trouble. And he hated trouble. Trouble brought notoriety and notoriety brought the law. Bailey liked to keep a low profile, and stay as anonymous as possible. Other people had often been suspected of pulling the jobs he'd executed. But Bailey didn't care who got the credit as long as he got the money.

In the Willmar robbery, nobody had cased the place. Nobody had staged it, nobody had mapped out alternative escape routes, so everybody got confused once they got inside. It took eight minutes to get in and get out, and that was way too long. (By contrast, when Bailey and company robbed the Denver Mint, it took all of ninety seconds.) Worse, there was gunplay and people got hurt. That was something the cops could not ignore, no matter how well they were being paid off.

Within days of the Willmar job, the Bankers Association of Minnesota and the Dakotas began urging county officials to band their sheriffs' departments together into a unified police force and join with citizens' groups to arm up and fight the gangster scourge. The Saint Paul *Pioneer Press* announced the initiative with a banner headline.

3 N.W. STATES MAP
WAR AGAINST BANDITS

"Preparing for the greatest crime drive in the history of the northwest, organizations in three states have evolved plans by which they hope bank bandits will be an expression of the past."

At a special meeting of county officials, E. F. Riley of the North Dakota School of Science urged the arming of special deputies with machine guns and high-powered rifles in every town, city and farm community in the state.

"We are going to war on bandits and meet them with the same poison they use in staging their holdups — machine guns, high powered rifles, special automobiles with mounted guns and airplanes," he declared. "Every garage and filling station along main highways will be equipped to meet the invasion of bank robbers." He also suggested that machine guns be mounted in second-story offices across the street from local banks.

Dutch Sawyer did not like the heat that the Willmar job was bringing. Still, in the northern Plains states, crippled by drought and the Depression, he knew there were precious few funds available to supply the states with the kind of armaments they would need for their grand plans.

Silverman had gone to the Green Lantern to get Dutch to provide him with a team and Dutch had obliged, for his usual cut of the proceeds. He knew Silverman was a trigger-happy hothead who shot a policeman and four bystanders when he robbed a bank during the Republican National Convention in Kansas City in 1928. But that was not something that concerned Dutch. What did concern him, however, was his discovery that Silverman had cheated Dutch's team out of their fair share of the take from the Willmar job. He sent Verne Miller out to square things up.

On August 14, a double-deck, seven-column headline in the *Saint Paul Dispatch* announced the end result of that misguided slight.

Verne Miller tracked down Silverman and two of his hoodlum buddies near a resort at Lake Minnetonka, popular among the gangster crowd for R & R unmolested by local law enforcement. Miller killed all three and hung their bodies from a tree near a desolate road that was popular as a trysting spot for young couples visiting a nearby amusement park.

George Kelly was getting quite an education in the way banks were robbed and business was conducted in the new Wild West. Although the murderous gunplay terrified him, robbing banks was a lot less work than running booze, and the payout was exponentially better.

Following the Willmar fiasco, Bailey took Kelly under his wing and taught him how to rob banks without all the drama and fireworks of the Willmar job.

Two months later, Bailey took Kelly, Miller, Holden and Keating to hit the Ottumwa Savings Bank in Iowa. It went off without a hitch. With one in the getaway car and one on the door, Holden, Keating and Bailey burst through the door and Bailey jumped the counter to grab a clerk who was going for his gun.

"We won't hurt anyone, but do as we say," he explained.

Holden grabbed the bank's vice president, H. L. Pollard, and put a gun to his temple.

"Open the vault door and don't stall, or it goes through your head."

They were out the side door, into the getaway car and on their way before the alarm even sounded.

Kelly continued to team up with members of the group throughout the year and into the next until his education was complete. Then he started branching out on his own, and turning his criminal pursuits into a family affair. In doing so, he would be breaking one of the cardinal rules of the Bailey bank-robbing system. "Don't ever work with women," Bailey had told him. "They can't keep their mouths shut."

At Leavenworth, Kelly had been introduced to a comely young Texan who'd come to the prison to visit her incarcerated uncle. She'd caught his eye and he bulldozed an introduction. She responded in the way that women had always responded to the rakish George Kelly. From prison, they struck up a pen pal relationship, and once he got out and established himself with his new bank-robbing buddies, Kelly decided to take it to the next level.

At that time, Kathryn was shacking up with a bootlegger named "Little Steve" Anderson in Oklahoma City, sharing in both his affections and his business. Kelly, who'd managed a successful multi-state liquor-running business before his little misstep on the Indian reservation, offered his expertise and assistance to the duo, and in no time he was sharing in their profits and Kathryn's affections, as well.

She was smitten with the smooth-talking ex-con. In almost every way, Kit was the classic gangster moll. The hardscrabble Texan was a schemer who'd spent her life getting by on good looks and bad attitude.

Kathryn was born in Saltillo, Mississippi, as Cleo Brooks in 1904. At age 15, she married a field hand named Lonnie Frye and gave birth to a daughter, Pauline. Soon after, she divorced Frye and took off with Pauline.

She then changed her name to Kathryn because it had more of a movie-star sound to it than the frumpish Cleo. She married again, but left her new husband right about the time her mother, Ora, extricated herself from Kathryn's father, J. E. Brooks. With no love lost between Kathryn and her father, she was thrilled when her beloved mother finally left him.

Ora remarried a connected Texas county politico named Robert Shannon, who preferred to go by his nickname "Boss." Boss owned a farm in Paradise, Texas, where Kathryn soon relocated, set up a little bootlegging business and started renting out space at the farm to criminal associates who were on the run or needed to lie low. She continued trading up husbands, and the next rung on her ladder was a bootlegger and small-time crook named Charlie Thorne.

For a woman with so many husbands and the occasional foray into the "escort" business, Kathryn was an insanely jealous wife.

While she was away on business, she discovered that Charlie was cheating on her. She headed back home, telling one of her associates, "I'm bound for Coleman, Texas, to kill that god-damned Charlie Thorne."

When she confronted Charlie with accusations of his philandering, an enormous row ensued and Charlie ended up dead on the floor with a bullet through his head.

Kathryn called the police, and when they arrived there was a neatly typed suicide note next to the illiterate bootlegger. If the police were suspicious, they didn't bother to investigate. Why investigate the murder of a man most people wouldn't miss and wanted dead anyway?

Kathryn, who'd seen her share of tough, charmless gangsters, had never met a man like George Kelly. He was classy, smart and he dressed like a million bucks. Better yet, he had money in his pocket and connections with a lot of big shots up north.

One September afternoon when Steve was out of town, George invited Kit out to dinner. Over drinks, he interrupted the small talk with a startling proposal.

"Let's get married!" he blurted.

Kit didn't miss a beat. "All right, big guy. When?"

George grabbed his fiancée and hustled her out of the restaurant in a delirious rush. They sped back to Anderson's house, where Kit picked up her belongings — along with Anderson's prized bulldog, whom she loved — and headed up to St. Paul, where Kelly's connections could arrange the hasty nuptials without all the bothersome paperwork, legal documents and irksome questions about all those outstanding warrants for his arrest.

After the nuptials, they drove down to Dallas for a short honeymoon and some long days of shopping. George wanted his bride wearing a brand-new wardrobe of the latest fashions. Kit was an absolute clotheshorse, and she was never happier than when she was acquiring new baubles and adornments. And when Kit was happy, George was happy.

George often told people he was in the banking business when they asked what he did for a living. So on their honeymoon Kit and George played the roles of a banker and his wife on a shopping spree. They'd spend their way through the finest stores in town and dine at the best eateries while pounding down shots in gulps from George's flask and the bottles in their room.

They were madly in love — with each other, with money, with booze, with cars and with the kind of lifestyle that could be yours if you were a successful criminal in Depression-era America.

2
A MASSACRE IN KANSAS CITY

On the evening of June 16, 1933, an enterprising reporter walking through the train station in sleepy Fort Smith, Arkansas, noticed something curious — two neatly dressed men in suits, ties and snap-brimmed hats standing beside a disheveled, older, mustachioed man in casual clothes wearing shackles and a cheap wig.

He identified himself to the dapper men and inquired about the man in their custody. He feigned nonchalance as the two suits boasted about their prisoner.

After gleaning enough details, he wished them luck, excused himself and hustled to the nearest pay phone to dictate the elements of a story that would be racing across the regional Associated Press wires within minutes.

FT. SMITH, ARK. June 16 (AP) Frank Nash, one of the last surviving members of the notorious Al Spencer gang of bank and train robbers that operated a decade ago, was recaptured today at Hot Springs, Ark., by three Department of Justice agents — who "kidnapped" him on the streets of the resort city.

Nash had been at liberty since his escape from the federal penitentiary at Leavenworth, Kansas, in October 1930. He was serving a 25-year term for robbing a mail train at Okesa, Okla., with Spencer and five others of the gang.

The Department of Justice men moved with utmost secrecy after rushing Nash out of Hot Springs in their automobile. They revealed the identity of the prisoner for the first time here, although they were stopped by officers at Little Rock following a report from Hot Springs that three men had kidnapped a man known there as "Doc."

The agents left their automobile here and boarded a train for Leavenworth shortly after their arrival here from Little Rock tonight in an effort, they said, to block a possible attempt at rescue by Nash's confederates. Nash was heavily manacled and the agents were armed with rifles.

The secret service men refused to discuss details of how Nash was trailed to

Hot Springs. They said they "kidnapped" him because of the danger of a clash with Nash's men in making an open capture.

It was indicated the agents had been "shadowing" Nash for some time, waiting for an opportunity to capture him when he was alone.

The wire story hit the AP offices and newspaper newsrooms throughout the South and Midwest late that evening, and editors snapped to attention. But as fast as the news moved across the wires, it couldn't match the speed with which information sped across the telephone tree of the criminal network that stretched across the western United States, from Dallas, Texas, to St. Paul, Minnesota.

Even as editors were ripping the bulletin off their wire machines and preparing stories for insertion into their next editions, plans were being made in the opulent Fred Harvey restaurant in Kansas City's Union Station to "snatch" Nash back and hide him away in Chicago, or St. Paul or some other city where the underworld hospitality was impervious to incursions from the feds and the few stoolies in law enforcement who were dumb enough to work with them.

Late that evening, Verne Miller sat down

for drinks at Fred Harvey's with Johnny Lazia, the underworld fixer for the notorious Kansas City political machine of Tom Pendergast. Except that Verne Miller didn't drink. He didn't curse either. Neither did he whore around, gamble or partake in any of the other vices that his tablemate, Johnny Lazia, was paid to protect. What Verne Miller did was kill people. He'd kill people who would stupidly try to stop him from robbing a bank. He'd kill people who double-crossed him. He'd kill people for money when Al Capone's mob in Chicago needed a mess cleaned up or if the Jews running the Purple Gang in Detroit wanted somebody to disappear after a deal gone bad. Or he'd kill people who ran afoul of his twisted form of chivalry, which dictated that all women were to be treated with utmost respect and none of his friends or trusted criminal associates were to be harmed in any way.

Miller had a penchant for knocking off other hired killers who had the misfortune to be hired to rub out one of the members of his tight circle of friends. This had earned him the title of "Assassin of Assassins."

Miller was smart enough to know he needed Lazia's blessing before pulling any kind of caper on Lazia's turf. With time so short, though, he also needed Lazia's help. Miller didn't have time to recruit his own muscle for the job. He'd need some backup, and he was hoping Lazia could provide it. Nash's pretty young wife, Frances, had called Miller the previous night in tears and explained that Frankie had been snatched at gunpoint out of the White Front Tavern in Little Rock, a place that was supposed to be safe.

The White Front was a cigar store and pool hall used as a social club by gangland elements from around the Midwest. It was a place where they would hook up to plan jobs, grab a beer, gamble and relax. It was owned and operated by the city's crime lord, Richard Galatas, and it was protected by his top enforcer, the city's Chief of Detectives, Dutch Akers.

Frances pleaded with Miller to get Frank back. She couldn't stand the thought of him going back to prison.

"Don't carry on like that," said Miller. "You'll see Jelly again soon."

Lazia sat across from Miller and offered up the names of local shooters who could provide backup for Miller in case somebody got trigger happy — but that was unlikely, since federal agents travel unarmed, relying on the local law for armed support, and Lazia could virtually guarantee that no cop on the Kansas City police would interfere with one of his sanctioned operations. He suggested two out-of-towners who had checked in earlier, Charles Arthur "Pretty Boy" Floyd (also known as "Choc") and his partner, Adam Richetti. Miller didn't think much of the hayseed Floyd. And Richetti was an unreliable drunk. Miller went off hoping to persuade a couple of Lazia's men to help him out, and Lazia phoned in instructions to his inside men at the cop shop.

In the morning, when Kansas City police officers W. J. "Red" Grooms and Frank Hermanson reported for the early shift, they were given what sounded to them like a routine, though somewhat incongruous, assignment: go down to the train station and assist two federal officers in the transfer of a prisoner from the Missouri Pacific, arriving at 7:15 a.m., to Leavenworth prison. Assist the feds? Since when did the Kansas City police start working for Washington? And weren't the feds supposed to assist local law enforcement?

Whatever the case, Grooms and Hermanson got into their "war wagon," a specially fitted, armored vehicle the Kansas City police used to quell riots and other disturbances that might spring up among the labor groups, unions, communists, blacks or disenchanted farmers who were going broke and getting thrown off their farms across the state. Curiously, the machine guns that normally were mounted in the car were missing. They drove to the station, parked and went inside to meet up with federal agents from the Department of Justice, Reed Vetterli, a 29-year-old, strait-laced Mormon, and Ray Caffrey, his young charge, who'd just arrived from Nebraska.

They would also meet two other federal agents, Joe Lackey and Frank Smith, and McAlester, Oklahoma, Police Chief Otto Reed, the veteran cop who'd gone along with the federal agents to assist in snatching Nash and make the arrest, since the federal agents lacked the legal authority to do that on their own.

Union Station was crowded that Saturday morning. Nearly a dozen trains were arriving between 7:00 and 8:00 a.m., and the parking lot was filling up with people and cars.

The bright prairie sun was climbing in the eastern sky and the temperature was rising right along with it. The lawmen flanked their captive as they hustled him through the station. The curious crowd parted as the group moved toward Caffrey's car like a "flying wedge" down a football field.

Miller and his two backups had taken their places in the parking lot, strategically aligned to close in on the agents when they got to the Chevrolet that was parked facing south in front of the station.

As Miller edged along a row of cars, shielding himself and getting a better angle, he saw the large group of men hustling out of the station and he did not like what he was seeing. Not only were the men armed, but they had their weapons drawn.

Grooms and Hermanson, stripped of their automatic weapons, had their .38-caliber handguns in plain view. One federal agent carried a .45. Lackey and Reed carried shotguns. Miller watched as Lackey and Reed climbed in the backseat and Nash climbed in beside them. But then Lackey told Nash to get up front, where he could watch him. Smith then climbed in the back between Lackey and Reed. Nash got in the front seat and Caffrey closed the door and began walking toward the front of the car to get into the driver's seat.

It was time for Miller to move. With most of the agents' firepower now bottled up in the car, Miller and a second machine gunner began closing in from two angles. With the clear advantage of firepower and surprise, it should have been easy enough to grab Nash and go without ever having to fire a shot.

Miller set his machine gun across the hood of the car he was using for cover and aimed directly at the lawmen while his partner inched closer, setting up the crossing fire line.

"Put 'em up! Up! Up!" he screamed.

Lackey pulled up the riot gun that had been nestled between his seat and the car door and furiously began trying to cock the unfamiliar weapon without releasing its triggering mechanism. When he finally stumbled on the release, the gun discharged unexpectedly, blowing off half of Nash's head, killing him instantly. The blast shattered the car's windshield and hit Caffrey in the back of the head as he stood near the front of the car.

The panicked Lackey jerked the gun to the left as it discharged again, hitting Hermanson in the head before tearing into the Plymouth parked in the adjacent space.

Reactively, the machine gunners unleashed a fusillade of return fire. Two bullets hit Grooms in the chest as he attempted to return fire, killing him. Vetterli, who had ducked to the ground for cover after taking a bullet in the arm, sprang to his feet and ran toward the station with a spray of machine-gun fire following him and slamming into the station's granite walls.

Miller trained his sights on Lackey, hitting him three times.

Chief Reed, hit by multiple rounds, crumbled to the floor.

The furious firefight was over in less than ninety seconds.

With his gun trained on the car, Miller approached cautiously. Hermanson and Grooms lay in an expanding pool of blood on the passenger side of the car. Caffrey was sprawled next to the driver's door with half his head blown away.

Miller peered in at the blood-soaked front seat and the body of his longtime friend.

"He's dead," he said to his partners. "They're all dead."

With that he reached into the backseat, pulled Lackey's gun from his hands and threw it to the ground. The unharmed Smith lay on the floor next to Lackey, playing possum.

Miller and company ran back to the getaway car and sped off as the early morning crowds at Union Station looked on in horror.

Patrolmen in the station raced to the parking lot, guns drawn. Flashbulbs popped as news photographers, who were at the station in force, having been tipped off by the wire story, went to work. In no time, they were rearranging the scene, moving people and evidence to get more graphic shots, as their polished leather shoes soaked up blood from the pavement and splashed it onto the cuffs of their trousers.

Bedlam had broken out among the bystanders, some of whom fled screaming, while others ghoulishly picked up spent shells and casings from the ground for souvenirs.

The Kansas City police began rounding up witnesses to the shooting. There were nearly sixty in all. All, it seemed, had wildly different stories about what they had just seen.

News of the shootout reached J. Edgar Hoover, within minutes. Hoover was an obsessive workaholic who was never really off the clock. "Married to his job," is how his colleagues would describe the young bachelor. He preferred agents who had a similar relationship with their work and drove them to work harder, faster and better.

The Bureau had just received a telegram from Kansas City.

Director, United States Bureau of Investigation, Wash DC — Ott Reed Chief Police McAlester Oklahoma special agents Frank Smith and Lackey with Frank Nash were met at Union Station this morning, seven fifteen by agents Vetterli and Caffrey and two local detectives. Nash was taken to Caffrey's automobile in front Union Station when unknown parties believed four altho definite number unknown opened up with submachine guns killing two local police officers Chief Reed Frank Nash and shooting agents Caffrey in head fatally. Lackey shot right side not believed fatal. Frank Smith escaped uninjured Vetterli nipped in left arm license number of shooting car obtained doing everything possible. Vetterli.

Hoover had set the whole debacle in motion when he'd offered a reward for information leading to the arrest and capture of Nash, who had "escaped" from the Federal penitentiary in Leavenworth, Kansas, nearly three years earlier. His escape was an embarrassment and an outrage to Hoover, who blamed the bleeding hearts and social reformers who ran the nation's prisons for their lax security.

In the three years since, Nash had re-teamed with his old St. Paul gang and had been plundering banks throughout the upper Midwest.

When Hoover offered a cash reward for information about his whereabouts, there was the usual flood of tips from all manner of chiselers and hustlers looking to scam their way to the reward money. But one tip had the feel of authenticity to it. It came from a corrupt cop in Hot Springs, Arkansas, who claimed Frank Nash was vacationing there. Hoover was leery of any police officer in the mobbed-up city of Hot Springs. He could be setting a trap, or he could be looking to make some easy money.

Hot Springs in the '20s and '30s was the destination of choice for the nation's criminal class. Gambling had been the town's chief industry since the end of the Civil War, along with its famous "healing waters." The city's strongman was Leo Patrick McLaughlin, who'd come to power in 1926 running on the promise that if elected, Hot Springs would be run as an open city, and for the next twenty years it was. In the '30s, Hot Springs boasted more than a dozen high-end casinos, brothels, race tracks, pool halls, spring training facilities for major league baseball teams, off-track betting — in short, a functional service industry for any vice you might enjoy. The money flowed from the underworld, to the police that protected it, to the political structure that allowed it. Al Capone maintained a year-round suite at the Arlington Hotel. Chasing down Nash in the Hot Springs environment was a grand, but dangerous, play. No one on the local police force could really be trusted, and that made Joe Lackey and Frank Smith in the Bureau's Kansas City field office a little uneasy, but, nevertheless, they had wanted to pursue the tip.

Hoover was even itchier to make something happen. He had a tenuous hold on his job and needed something to show the new administration's architects, who were pushing to replace him with a political appointment, that he was up to the job.

The precocious and ambitious Hoover joined the Justice Department in 1917 after working his way through law school as a clerk at the Library of Congress. The job at Justice had a draft-exempt status, a designation Hoover appreciated because his father had recently suffered a nervous breakdown and lost his job. The young J. Edgar felt he could not afford to serve because he had become his family's breadwinner and his mother was desperately in need of his support. In less than a year's time, Hoover had been promoted twice and, at the age of twenty-two, found himself in charge of the Bureau's Enemy Alien Registration Section. During and immediately after World War I, the country learned to hate all things German, all things alien and anything that smacked of radicalism, socialism or communism.

Hoover found himself a busy man, helping to stage raids on organizations suspected of radical or socialist ideals and labor unions of almost any stripe, all the while compiling a master list of suspected radicals, terrorists and draft dodgers that would expand to include hundreds of thousands of names.

After the war, with new Attorney General, A. Mitchell Palmer, Hoover established the General Intelligence Division, which expanded his antiradical operations to include more general intelligence gathering at home and abroad, as well as work to prevent labor disputes and strikes. Under Palmer's tutelage, Hoover became an early architect of "Red Scare" propagandizing, and helped his attorney general stage coordinated raids that resulted in as many as ten thousand arrests of suspected radical aliens and suspected communists in a single day — most of whom were not aliens or communists or guilty of anything whatsoever. Hoover made himself the country's leading authority on communist activities and how to fight them.

When Warren G. Harding took office in 1921 he appointed his campaign manager, Harry Daugherty, as Attorney General. Daugherty purged the department of the hangers-on from the previous administration and peopled it with a collection of political appointments and partisans who were eager to do the administration's dirty work, as long as there was good money in it. Daugherty found Hoover's lists handy material for political blackmail, so Hoover managed to keep his job. Before long, the Bureau had succumbed to the corrupting influences of the Harding administration and was jokingly referred to as the "Department of Easy Virtue" — much to the chagrin of the prim and moralistic Hoover, who nevertheless found himself up to his neck in the nefarious practices that Daugherty allowed the Bureau to engage in. In fact, those activities he undertook during the Harding administration nearly torpedoed his career when Roosevelt was swept into office.

Just months after the election, Hoover was in the crosshairs of FDR's first choice for Attorney General, Montana Senator Thomas Walsh.

Walsh had a long history with Hoover, and it wasn't a good one. When Walsh and his fellow Montana senator Burton Wheeler were investigating corruption in the Harding administration, Hoover, then second in command at the Bureau, organized a campaign to discredit them on orders from the Bureau's director. Hoover's tactics included tapping their phones, intercepting their mail, tailing their family members and breaking into their offices. He tried to lure Wheeler into a hotel room with a comely female, but the ploy failed, Wheeler having been forewarned. Walsh made no secret of the fact that upon taking over as attorney general, one of his first official acts would be to clean house and fire that miserable son of a bitch J. Edgar Hoover.

Before heading to Washington, though, the seventy-two-year-old Walsh, a widower for sixteen years, married a young Cuban debutante. On the train ride from Miami to Washington, the young bride woke up in North Carolina, but her new husband didn't. The old civil libertarian may have died a happy man, but he never got his revenge on Hoover.

FDR's next selection for Attorney General was Homer Cummings. With both a Ph.D. and a law degree from Yale, the sixty-three-year-old former mayor of Stamford, Connecticut, was one of FDR's intellectual and political heavyweights. Originally tapped to become ambassador to the Philippines, FDR put him in the Justice Department as an emergency replacement for Walsh after his untimely death. It was a fortuitous choice. Cummings had big ideas for raising the profile of the Justice Department, which at the time, in 1933, was but a minor player in the small government world of Washington, DC. FDR was articulating a vision for his administration. He was going to war against the forces of the Depression. Cummings liked that positioning. He would prosecute a "war on crime" to raise the profile of his adopted department and make it a major player in the new administration's ambitious efforts to federalize the nation's governance. He crafted a plan to merge the Prohibition Bureau's 1,200 investigators, who would soon have diminished responsibilities with the end of Prohibition in sight, with the Department of Justice's Bureau of Investigation and Bureau of Identification. With that as a start, he hoped to begin crafting the kind of national police force the public and the President were clamoring for. He also began to craft a major crime bill that would give that force greater powers and tough federal laws to enforce. And he started zeroing in on his first targets.

In the hellish landscape of the drought-plagued and Dust Bowl–afflicted states out West, gangsters plied their trade with virtual impunity. In that part of the country, bank robbers and bootleggers enjoyed not only the popular support of the citizenry, but the tacit support of the local government and police forces, as well. In many cities and towns, it would not be too much of a stretch to say that the local mob not only ran the criminal activities, but the government and law enforcement, too.

Closer in time to the Civil War than the present, the rural areas of the "criminal alley" that stretched from Texas to North Dakota had evolved only marginally in political and social attitudes. The Ku Klux Klan (KKK) was so enmeshed in parts of Oklahoma that the governor was forced to declare martial law to fight its influence. Race riots proliferated. Socialists and communists spread anti-government paranoia in their attempts to organize farmers. Anarchists spread terror in cities and towns with random bombings and assassination attempts.

The gangland elements that worked the West were a breed apart from the organized mobs that built their empires in the big cities in the eastern states. Those rackets were built on an organized — though violent — business model. In the West, criminals largely mirrored the political attitudes of their environment — they were fiercely independent, roguish and tough. They were loosely organized when they had to be, but preferred the go-it-alone life of a freelancer whenever it was possible. They didn't want to take orders from a boss — criminal or otherwise — just as the states they roamed through did not want to take direction from the federal government in Washington. The Western gangster had more in common with the outlaws of the Old West than he did with his modern big-city brethren back East.

This was the enemy Cummings wanted to confront. He was well aware of how entrenched and protected the criminal empires were in Chicago and along the East Coast, his home. You would need an army and the authority of martial law to take them down. But with a few good men, the West might be tamed. It was the soft underbelly, and it was there that he would go first. Cummings and FDR believed the country needed its own national law enforcement agency, patterned after Britain's skillful and sophisticated Scotland Yard. A force that could sidestep the local police forces with their political and criminal connections and obligations. A force with the legal ability to cross city, county and state lines in its pursuit of lawbreakers. Cummings was enough of a political operative to know he needed to move fast, lest his agency be left, as always, sitting on the sidelines. Could he count on this controversial autocrat who was running the Bureau of Investigation to bust some crooks, grab some headlines and move the Justice Department out front in the rush to nationalize police work? The odds didn't favor it.

Hoover was an entrenched Washington bureaucrat in an age when that was the last thing anyone with marketable skills wanted to be. He had no police or military experience. He had a law degree, but he had never prosecuted a case or assisted anyone who had. He dressed like a dandy, had an effeminate gait so extreme it had been mocked in the press and lived with his mother. *Collier's* magazine had scoffed at his efforts to train his "college boy" gumshoes and noted with sarcasm that he was a stylish dresser who favored "Eleanor blue" socks and walked with "a mincing step." Wags around town noted with raised eyebrows the handsome bachelor he dined with daily and traveled with frequently. To top it off, the President's wife despised him for his "red-baiting" and obsession with smearing anyone he suspected of communist sympathies. (She would later accuse him of running an American Gestapo. They maintained a lifelong antipathy toward one another.) But Hoover had cleaned up the notoriously corrupt Bureau after his appointment as acting director during the Herbert Hoover administration and remade it with a bunch of guys in his mirror image: well-dressed, clean-cut accountants and lawyers who knew how to organize files to his exacting standards and build reasoned, science-based cases for prosecution. He ran the Bureau as a puritanical dictator who demanded blind loyalty, conformity and a scandal-free performance devoid of political chicanery. Was this the guy to take on machine gun–toting mobsters and bomb-throwing anarchists? Probably not, but he was in place, desperate and willing to do anything to save his job.

So, Cummings decided to stick with Hoover. But he wanted results and he wanted them fast. Hoover, eminently disdainful — and fearful — of politicians, heard the message loud and clear and desperately began looking for a card to play. Snatching Nash out of gangland's playground could have been it. Instead, Nash, three lawmen and one of his own agents were lying dead in a Kansas City parking lot.

Hoover didn't realize it, but they were dead not as the result of unprovoked gangland violence, but because of his own agent's ineptitude with an unfamiliar weapon.

What he did realize was that the whole operation was technically illegal. Hoover's agents were not authorized to make arrests. In addition, they were not authorized to carry weapons, although that was an admonition they willfully ignored on many occasions. Many agents, especially in the dangerous Southwest, where violent crime was rampant and the murder rate was four to five times higher than even the most dangerous cities up north, would purchase their own weapons and train themselves how to use them.

The Bureau's agents had turned to Chief Reed for help. Reed had been chasing Nash for years and wanted desperately to be there when an arrest was made. Reed really had no authority in Hot Springs either, but he knew Nash, and he knew there was no one in Hot Springs who'd make the arrest. So the three lawmen hatched a plan for their own "snatch job." Go in, grab Nash, get him out of the city, out of the state and back to some neutral ground where an arrest could be made. Not very neat and lawyerly, but there really was no other way to get the job done.

At the end of day, Hoover wrote back to Vetterli.

Confirming my several telephonic conversations with you today, it is my desire that every effort and resource of this bureau be utilized to bring about the apprehension of the parties responsible for the killing of Special Agent R.J. Caffrey and the injuring of Special Agent Lackey and yourself, as well as the killing of police officers who were assisting us in this assignment. I cannot too strongly emphasize the imperative necessity of concentrating upon this matter, without any let-up in the same until the parties are taken dead or alive.

Hoover knew he would have to meet this challenge to his authority head-on. He had wanted to build an army of agents molded from the same cast he had set for himself: businesslike investigators who wouldn't have to get their hands dirty with the nasty elements of real police work. But now, experienced police professionals were the very types he would need. Fortunately, he'd hung on to a number of old-time lawmen who were running the Bureau's field offices in the wild outposts of Texas, Oklahoma and the crime-infested Midwest. But out of a force of more than three hundred agents, in eighty-eight field offices across the country, he found less than a dozen who had the experience and training to go up against the type of machine gun–toting murderers who had massacred the lawmen in the Union Station parking lot. By 11:30 that morning Hoover had assembled a special task force of agents from that veteran staff to descend on Kansas City and bring the murdering outlaws to justice.

To head the task force he turned to Agent Gus "Buster" T. Jones who was in charge of the Bureau's Texas office in San Antonio. Jones was not modeled on Hoover's image of the modern agent. Jones was old school, a career lawman whose biography was the stuff of legends. Jones had worked as town marshal, deputy sheriff, customs agent and Texas Ranger. Unlike Hoover's East Coast agents, who dressed in fashionable suits, starched shirts and polished wingtips, Jones would most often be found wearing a 10-gallon hat, cowboy boots and a holstered sidearm on his hip.

Jones was born in the Texas frontier town of San Angelo in 1881. His father had died when a Comanche arrow went through his chest as the Frontier Battalion, as the Texas Rangers were formerly known, were furiously fighting to evict the tribe from the barren landscape that they had inhabited for centuries.

On his twelfth birthday, his mother gave Jones his father's cedar-handled, .45-caliber Colt — "the gun that won the West." He then adopted the town sheriff, Rome Shields, as his substitute father. Shields had molded him into an expert marksman and an adoring student of how the law was administered, Texas style. At sixteen, he ran off and joined the Texas militia to fight in the Spanish-American War. When the malaria-weakened teenager returned to San Angelo, he had little interest in returning to high school. Instead, he took a job with Shields as an undercover agent spying on members of Black Jack Ketchum's gang, which included several members from San Angelo. Ketchum was making a fine living robbing trains and mail carriers across the Southwest. Evidence gathered by Jones helped lead to the arrest and capture of much of the gang. When the remnants of the gang joined up with Butch Cassidy's Wild Bunch, Jones continued his work and helped capture three of its key members. In 1901, Cassidy fled to South America with his longtime associate, Harry Alonzo Longabaugh, the Sundance Kid.

By then San Angelo was beginning to sink under the weight of its success as a trading center and transfer point for cattlemen who drove their herds into town and onto the railcars for their journey north. To entertain the visiting businessmen, cowboys and drovers, the town had developed a bustling saloon, prostitution and gambling business that was getting out of hand. The town fathers were growing fearful of venturing out at night and were looking for someone who could keep a lid on the nighttime revelry but not screw the lid down so tightly that the profitable wages of sin would dry up.

Jones was soon walking the darkened streets, Wyatt Earp–style, with pistols on his hips, as the town's night watchman and building a reputation as a quick draw and an expert marksman. Stints with the Texas Rangers and U.S. Customs and Border Patrol soon followed. In 1916, he joined the Justice Department as Special Agent in Charge of the El Paso office, which he quickly populated with a crew of like-minded pals from the Texas Rangers, men who were familiar with the ways of the underworld and who knew when to get involved or, more importantly, look the other way. When he was promoted to the San Antonio office, he brought even more of his old law enforcement buddies into the Bureau.

By putting Jones in charge of the investigation, Hoover was making a conscious decision to sideline his sycophantic pets in favor of the hard-drinking, hard-charging, gun-toting Western toughs who'd been living in and outside the law for their entire careers. Jones's knowledge of the underworld was expansive. He knew every thief, bank robber, gangster and hit man west of the Mississippi and south of the border. Jones's network was so wide that when things were going poorly for Pancho Villa, it was to Jones he turned for help negotiating a truce. He also knew the legitimate cops and reliable politicos he could trust in an emergency. Chief Otto Reed had been one of those. Now, he was a gangland victim lying dead in the Kansas City morgue.

Hoover knew that if he allowed gangsters to get away with the murder of federal agents, none of his men would be safe. He told Jones in no uncertain terms that he wanted the Kansas City killers brought to justice by any means necessary.

Jones was on a plane to Kansas City by 11:30 the morning of the massacre. On his arrival, he studied the collected evidence, most of it from eyewitnesses whom he knew to be unreliable even in the best of circumstances. This was a 30-second volley of gunfire in which hundreds of bullets were spent, and any sensible witness would have been ducking for cover. The accounts all differed.

Even the number of shooters was in doubt. People reported seeing from two to seven machine gunners, men and women.

A month earlier, on Memorial Day, there had been a spectacular escape from the nearby Kansas State Penitentiary in Lansing led by Harvey Bailey. Bailey, Keating and Holden had been recaptured while playing golf in a foursome with Nash. Nash eluded capture by slipping off into the woods. He aided Bailey from the outside by smuggling guns into the prison for the break, in which the escapees had kidnapped the warden and fled over the prison walls. Bailey had been shot in the leg during the escape. His picture, along with the other escapees', had been all over the Kansas City papers.

Several witnesses said one of the machine gunners was limping and believed him to be Bailey. Another identified Pretty Boy Floyd. When Jones got to Kansas City, there were more than fifteen names on the list.

The crime scene didn't yield much evidence either.

With not much to go on, Jones was playing his hunches. The job had the markings of a professional operation. Any one of the Lansing prison escapees could have pulled this off, and Bailey was a close friend of Nash's. But the rest of Bailey's profile didn't fit the crime. Bailey was all about planning and stealth. Gunplay, murder, innocent victims? Those things brought the heat. Bailey never wanted to be associated with anything violent. Why bother? In most cases it was so unnecessary. And when it was necessary, he'd pin it on somebody else.

Despite the identification from several witnesses noting the limping gunner, Jones didn't like Bailey for this one.

"The Kansas City Massacre was a stupid crime, committed by stupid criminals — and nobody would ever accuse Harvey Bailey of being stupid," Jones told the agents.

"Besides, Bailey is no killer. A thief, yes — but never a killer. The men who pulled this job were killers, first and foremost. They could never have expected to take Nash away from those officers without killing some of them. They came to kill. Harvey Bailey would never in the world have had any part of a job like that."

Still, Jones really wanted to bring Bailey in. And his hunch told him that it was members of the escaped crowd that had gone to free Nash as payback for his help springing them. But why waste a crisis? Bailey would remain a suspect, as would everyone else from the prison break: Bob Brady, Jim Clark, Ed Davis, Wilbur Underhill and Frank Sawyer. Any one of those hard cases could have done it and not thought twice.

Similarly, Jones doubted Pretty Boy Floyd had anything to do with it. Floyd was a loner and an outlier. He never worked with the Keating-Holden crowd. He didn't owe Nash any favors. But if Washington wanted his name on the list, no harm in that. George Kelly was often misidentified as Pretty Boy Floyd, perhaps because of his good looks. Kelly had served time at Leavenworth with Nash, and had helped Keating and Holden escape. But Kelly's tough-guy image was largely the creation of his clever wife, newspaper reporters and pulp fiction writers. He'd robbed a lot of banks and run a lot of gin, but had never been clearly identified in anything murderous. Kelly, a handsome charmer, rarely needed to even pull a gun on a bank job. He could talk money right out of the vault and many a female teller was left smitten by the dreamy clotheshorse who'd relieved them of all the cash in their drawer. Kelly had learned the trade from his good friend Harvey Bailey. Kelly had never been charged with anything violent. Jones wouldn't waste any time trying to tie him to the shootout. Instead, he turned to his mental Rolodex of underworld fixers and operators. If the crime started in Hot Springs, Arkansas, Dick Galatas would be involved one way or the other. Fly out to Hot Springs, he told his agents. Follow Galatas. Backfill his movements. Get his phone records. Where was he when they grabbed Nash? Where did he go afterward? If somebody sent shooters to spring Nash, Galatas would have to be involved. He'll lead us to him.

Jones also knew that nothing happened in Kansas City without the blessing of the Pendergast machine's underworld fixer, Johnny Lazia. Nobody would have the nerve to walk into Kansas City and pull a caper like this without Lazia's blessing. But getting information from Lazia would be all but impossible, and the notorious Kansas City police would be of no help either. In one way or another most worked for or with Lazia. In fact, the Kansas City police director, Eugene Reppert, who'd been a golf partner of Bailey's and whose photograph with him on the course at Mission Hills had touched off the raid that sent Keating and Holden back to prison, flat out told the federal agents that, despite the death of two of his officers, it was up to the feds to solve the case. The feds were an annoyance. In his opinion, they had brought this disaster to Kansas City through their ineptitude and their failure to work through the well-established system in the city that could have prevented it. And now that system was going under a national microscope, which was making things uncomfortable for people like Reppert and the men he worked for. The bumbling feds would get no help from the Kansas City Police Department. Such was the level of police professionalism in Kansas City in 1933. And such was the weakness of Hoover's Bureau and its agents that they were powerless to do anything about it.

But the sleuthing by Jones's men turned up a solid connection between Nash and Miller in the days before the massacre.

Phone records showed Frances Nash had called Miller several times immediately after Nash's arrest. After some intense interrogation by Bureau agents, Frances gave Miller up, but said she had no idea where he had gone after the shooting.

When the story hit the press that one Verne Miller was the primary suspect in the Union Station massacre, it got the attention of a Fort Worth detective named Ed Weatherford.

Weatherford had been watching Kathryn Kelly for years, suspicious of her extravagant lifestyle and the fancy cars she and her husband would park in front of their home on East Mulkey Street. Weatherford had duped Kathryn into thinking he was a crooked cop who'd help her out if she and her gregarious husband should ever get in a jam.

Weatherford would run into Kathryn when she made her rounds of the local taverns and speakeasies, where she was constantly boasting about her husband, saying he could shoot walnuts off a fence line with his machine gun and write his name with it on the sides of barns. She'd brag about all the big-shot gangsters he worked with. The notorious Verne Miller was a name she had constantly bandied about.

Weatherford passed his information to agent Frank Blake in the Bureau's Dallas office, who moved it along to Jones in Kansas City, noting that George Kelly was reputed to be an expert machine gunner, who could "write his name with bullets discharged from such a gun."

Harvey Bailey, it turned out, was right. Kathryn's loose lips had just put her husband's name on the list of the most wanted men in the country.

3
THE KIDNAPPING SCOURGE

Organized crime in the major cities of the country had used kidnapping for decades as they built their empires. They did it to filch money from rival gangs. They did it to get inconvenient characters off the street at appropriate times. They used it to threaten or intimidate balky cops and politicians who might not otherwise play along with the racketeers who needed their protection and cooperation. But as long as the kidnappings, payoffs and murders were confined to the underworld, few really cared. But in the '30s, it was happening to good citizens and national heroes. Anybody with money was growing uneasy, especially as the national press reported stories of "kidnapping syndicates" that were operating around the nation and compiling lists of prospective victims and their families.

When they took office in the spring of 1933, President Roosevelt and Attorney

General Homer Cummings inherited the kidnapping case that newspaper columnists were calling the greatest story "since the resurrection": the Lindbergh case. For more than a year it had lingered on, with no end in sight and no good leads to pursue.

In the '30s, Charles Lindbergh was about the most famous and revered American in the nation, and perhaps around the world.

On May 20, 1927, when Lindbergh took off from New York and landed thirty-three and a half hours later in France, he had successfully set the record for sustained flight by flying over the Atlantic Ocean and winning the $25,000 Orteig Prize after six other better-known aviators had died trying.

His accomplishment transformed the nation — and the very idea of winged flight. When Lindbergh boarded his plane that rainy morning, much of the nation thought the very idea of flying was an affront to the Almighty. In that year, European airlines were flying hundreds of thousands of passengers. The United States had virtually none. But after Lucky Lindy set down in Paris, greeted by a crowd of 150,000 joyous fans, the irreligiosity of aviation melted away. Superiority in the sky became a national aspiration as an industry was launched on Lindy's accomplishments, and the nation became transfixed by the possibilities of flying. It was the '20s equivalent of "Man Walks on Moon," and Lindbergh became its standard-bearer.

President Herbert Hoover awarded Lindbergh the Medal of Honor, and New York went wild with ticker-tape parades. The previously unknown U.S. Air Mail pilot had, in a matter of hours, become arguably the biggest celebrity in the world.

Lindbergh flew the *Spirit of Saint Louis* around Europe, mesmerizing crowds and promoting the idea of air travel.

Back in the States, he took to the air and the lectern to add his promotional gravitas to the infant aviation industry, which was trying to launch itself in the sparsely populated, wide-open spaces Lindy called home.

President Hoover appointed Lindbergh to the National Advisory Committee for Aeronautics, and he embarked on a cross-country tour paid for by the Guggenheim Fund for the Promotion of Aeronautics. The 1927 "Lindbergh Tour" was the country's first truly national celebrity tour — bigger and bolder than even those of men campaigning for president. It hit every state and virtually every major city. Lindbergh delivered speech after speech and rode in hundreds of parades. At the conclusion of the tour, Lindbergh spent a month penning a book about his transatlantic flight titled *We*, and it became an instant bestseller.

The massive publicity surrounding him and his flight boosted the aviation industry and made a skeptical public take air travel seriously. Within a year of his flight, an estimated 30 million Americans personally saw Lindbergh and the *Spirit of Saint Louis* as he and his flying machine toured the country. The effects of his accomplishments were transformative. Over the remainder of 1927, the number of licensed aircraft quadrupled. The number of U.S. airline passengers grew by an estimated 1,000 percent per year for the next three years, and investment in American aviation topped $100 million. Air travel was beginning to shrink the vast nation, pulling it together like nothing since the final spike was pounded into the transcontinental railroad. Lindbergh's exploits spawned an explosion in the number of daredevil pilots trying to set new records for distances traveled and heights achieved. Their exploits gave the national media one of the few upbeat stories to follow to leaven their coverage of crime, Depression and loss.

But on the evening of March 1, 1932, even Lucky Lindy's story would become part of the nation's nightmare.

Around 9:30 p.m., Lindbergh was sitting in his library and thought he heard a noise. Half an hour later, his panicked family nurse told him that his infant son, Charles Jr., was gone.

Lindbergh grabbed his gun, searched the house and found a white envelope on the windowsill in the baby's room. It was a ransom note demanding $50,000 for the return of his son.

On March 3, 1932, two days after the Lindbergh kidnapping, the normally reserved *New York Times* ran a deck of headlines that would have been right at home on the pages of any of its more sensational rivals.

KIDNAPPING WAVE SWEEPS THE NATION

Lindbergh Crime Is Climax of Development of Abductions Into Major Racket Ring's Center in Midwest Leading Citizens in Chicago Are Compelled to Band for Self-Protection

The kidnapping of Charles A. Lindbergh Jr. topping a long list of kidnappings in recent years serves to emphasize the fact that abduction for ransom has become a "big money crime," taking its place beside the liquor, vice and drug traffic among the prominent "rackets" of the country.

Authorities pointed out yesterday that there had been a big wave of kidnappings during the past two years, when more than 2,000 persons were abducted for ransom. During these two years kidnapping syndicates have arisen and have extorted millions of dollars from their victims or their relatives and friends by means of torture or terrorization.

It is estimated that in Illinois alone during 1930 and 1931 there were 400 kidnappings, according to Alexander Jamie, chief investigator for the "Secret Six," a Chicago organization devoted to fighting organized crime.

By 1933, the Snatch Racket and the abductions of prominent citizens had grown so widespread that companies began marketing a new product — kidnapping insurance. Wealthy businessmen hired bodyguards and private security details. In Hollywood, celebrities traveled in bulletproof limos with armed guards in the passenger seats. A national paranoia had hatched among the nation's fragile moneyed class, and it was pressuring its new president to do something about it.

In June 1932, just weeks after the decomposed body of Lindbergh's son had been discovered in a field near his house, Congress rushed through an emergency piece of legislation, the Federal Kidnapping Act, which made it a federal felony to take a kidnap victim across state lines. Known as the "Lindbergh Law," it allowed federal judges, upon conviction, to impose any penalty, up to life in prison — the only federal statute to allow such discretion. J. Edgar Hoover's Bureau had gained relevance overnight. Unlike local law enforcement, his agents, and his agents alone, would have the authority to pursue kidnappers across state lines to bring them to justice. He was eager to put his new power into play at the first opportunity.

Cummings put Hoover in charge of coordinating all federal and state agencies involved in the investigation. But, despite the law's authority, Hoover and his men failed to make any inroads, further enhancing their reputation for ineffectiveness and incompetence. From prison, Al Capone offered to solve the case for them in exchange for a reduced sentence. Though there were many in the country who thought that was the only hope for a successful resolution, the Justice Department rejected it.

The hunt for the Lindbergh kidnapper dragged on for nearly a year, and by 1933 Hoover no longer had a convenient excuse for why he had not solved it. In short order, a string of additional kidnappings of prominent Americans would land on his desk, and the Bureau's response would prove equally inept.

On the snowy night of February 13, Charles Boettcher II, thirty-one, the playboy son of one of Denver's leading families, was snatched away as he and his glamorous wife were returning to their expansive mansion after a night of partying.

As Boettcher and his wife got out of their car, a man stepped out of the dark.

"Come here, Charlie, and stick up your hands. Do what you are told and everything will be all right."

He then handed an envelope to Boettcher's wife, Anna Lou, and hauled Charlie away.

When Anna Lou opened the envelope, she discovered a note with odd fill-in-the-blank spaces and misspellings. It read:

Do not notify the police. If you do, and they

start making it hot for us, you will never see _____ alive again. We are holding _____ for Sixty Thousand Dollars. We are asking you to get this money in Ten and Twenty dollar bills and they must be old bills only. When you get this money ready and are willig *[sic]* to pay as above for the safe return of _____, then insert the following ad in the Denver Post, personal items . . .

(please write, I am ready to return) SIGN (Mabel) . . .

We will not stand for any stalling thru advice that police may give you. You are smart enough to know what the results will be if you try that. You know what happened to little Charles Lindbergh through his father calling the police. He would be alive today if his father had followed instructions given him. You are to choose one of these to *[sic]* courses, Either insert add and be prepared to pay ransom, Or forget it all.

The Boettchers were friends of the Lindberghs, and Charles had stayed at their home in Denver during his victory lap after his historic transatlantic flight.

Within hours of the abduction, *The Denver*

Post was on the street with a special edition.

CHARLES BOETTCHER II HELD
FOR RANSOM OF $60,000

Charles Boettcher II, 31, prominent broker and scion of one of the west's wealthiest families, was kidnapped from his fashionable home, 777 Washington Street, late Sunday night by dapper desperadoes who are holding him for $60,000 ransom.

Young Boettcher and his beautiful wife, Anna Lou Boettcher, an expectant mother, had just driven into the driveway of their home when the abductors suddenly appeared, forced Boettcher into their machine and whisked away after handing Mrs. Boettcher a note demanding the ransom.

Anna Lou had immediately gone to her father-in-law, Claude Boettcher, who, despite the kidnappers' warning, called the Denver police, who mobilized immediately, stopping every black sedan that matched Anna Lou's description, but to no avail.

With no evidence to go on, Denver Police Chief Albert Clark announced that the prime suspects in the case were a couple of

Chicago gangsters who'd recently been seen in Denver: Louis "Diamond Jack" Alterie and Mike "Bon Bon" Allegretti. He boasted that the perpetrators of the crime would be in custody within forty-eight hours.

But Alterie and Allegretti weren't even in Denver at the time of the abduction.

Boettcher had been kidnapped by successful bootlegger and occasional bank robber Verne Sankey. Sankey began his bootlegging career hauling fine Canadian liquor over the border into the Dakotas and St. Paul, Minnesota. Sankey made a fortune in the mid- to late '20s, most of which he gambled away or lost speculating in the commodities market. He owned a farm in South Dakota that he used as a base for his liquor business and a convenient hideout after bank jobs. With both of his main sources of income getting pinched, he hatched a plan to pull a snatch job with his partner, Gordon Alcorn.

By researching public records, he had come up with a list of thirty potential victims in and around Denver, the closest city to his Dakota farm with any real wealth. He rented a house in Denver to prepare for the job. He had pared the list down to five top prospects, which included Boettcher and beer brewer Adolf Coors. Sankey and

Alcorn were casing the Boettchers when a fortuitous opportunity presented itself and they grabbed Charlie. Because they hadn't been expecting to execute the kidnapping at that moment, Sankey hadn't had the chance to fill in the blanks on his ransom note. Nevertheless, the job came off flawlessly, and Boettcher was effortlessly spirited out of Denver to Sankey's farm 570 miles away in South Dakota.

Two days later, Sankey sent a letter to Claude Boettcher:

> So far you have not done as I requested. If you are ready to keep this a secret and pay the $60,000 in small bills as I wrote you first then insert this ad in the Post. Charles is very nervous and frightened, he often asks if we will release him if you pay and I keep telling him we will, but he lives in fear of being bumped off.

But Claude was not willing to pay the ransom unless his son was returned first. He believed that Lindbergh's son had been killed because Lindbergh complied with the kidnappers' demands and thus lost his leverage. Meanwhile, Claude conducted his negotiations through the press, and Denver's newspapers were eating it up. However,

Sankey was not about to release his captive without the payment.

The frustrated Denver police arrested dozens of innocent suspects, who made for a continuous stream of stories for Colorado's daily papers. With no good leads to go on, the hysteria spread, garnering interest even from the European press, which was fascinated with America's lawlessness and criminality. At the *Post*'s suggestion, vigilante groups were forming to hunt down the kidnappers and string them up as they'd done in the town's not-too-distant past. The state, realizing that the maximum punishment for the crime was a mere seven years in prison, rushed through legislation making kidnapping a capital offense punishable by life in prison. A string of other states did likewise.

Within forty-eight hours of the news of the kidnapping, Hoover had sent in his Denver agents to assist. He put his favorite special agent, Melvin Purvis, who was heading up the Chicago office, in charge of the case. With so many headlines flying around, Hoover was desperate to grab a few of his own.

Charlie Boettcher had become the most written about crime victim in the nation. In the words of the *Rocky Mountain News,* he was hunted by the "police of every city from coast to coast." But with no results.

The Denver Post condemned the ineptitude of the local law enforcement:

> Absolutely nothing has been accomplished by the police to restore (Charles Boettcher II) to his distracted family, apprehend his kidnappers and avenge their monstrous crime. They don't know any more about this case than they did when it was reported to them.

Ultimately, Claude Boettcher dismissed the police and took charge of the proceedings himself, eventually securing Charles's release and paying the $60,000 ransom. But even though Claude had tipped the police off to the time and location of the payoff, Sankey and Alcorn slipped away after dropping off their prisoner and headed back to the safety of Sankey's South Dakota farm.

The Boettcher kidnapping did not escape the attention of Kathryn Kelly. She liked the big dollar amounts involved and pushed George to get back in the game. Kelly had teamed up with a small-time bank robber named Eddie Doll in January 1932 to snatch the son of an Indiana banker named Howard Woolverton. They grabbed him from his car while he was on the way home from the theater with his wife, Florence. They gave her a note with instructions demanding $50,000 and let her go.

They kept Woolverton hostage for two days, but when his wife couldn't raise the money, they let him go, telling him to go home and find some cash or they'd come back and kill him. He couldn't, and they didn't and the whole thing just faded away as they went back to robbing banks.

Back in Fort Worth, George and Kit made plans to kidnap Guy Waggoner, the son of a wealthy local oilman. But two local cops, Ed Weatherford and J. W. Swinney, got wind of the job when Kathryn tried to recruit them to help out if anything went wrong. They tipped off the feds, and Kelly had to back off because it became obvious that Waggoner was under constant surveillance.

Undeterred, Kathryn started a list of potential victims. She'd learned her lesson with Woolverton. Never again would she snatch a low-life piker without the wherewithal to meet the ransom demand. Her next victims would have verifiable fortunes and easy access to them. Her plan was to go through them one by one until they had collected a million dollars in ransom. That, she thought, just might be enough to set her up for life in the lifestyle to which she'd become accustomed. Four jobs at $250,000 apiece. *That ought to do it,* she thought. And she had a name at the top of her list.

She also thought that her charming husband's reputation needed a little hardening up.

She bought George a Thompson submachine gun at a Fort Worth pawnshop and began spreading stories about how good he had gotten with it.

At every bar, speakeasy and dive she frequented — and she frequented plenty — she'd leave behind spent shells and handsome tips and more details about the legend she was building.

The national kidnapping spree continued unabated. At the Green Lantern, Dutch Sawyer was drawing up lists of potential kidnap victims based on their net wealth, their accessibility and the willingness of their companies or families to come to their aid. The perfect victim would be easy to grab, easy to hide and, most importantly, someone too fearful to go to the authorities and pursue his kidnappers in order to seek justice or get his money back. The threat of retribution to the victim and his family needed to be understood and appreciated.

Otherwise, the job was too risky. Choosing the victim to be kidnapped was just as important as choosing the bank to be robbed.

With the Boettcher case still unsolved, the feds were bringing the heat to every known criminal establishment in the Midwest — and that included the Green Lantern. St. Paul's new "reform-minded" police chief, Thomas Dunhill, announced a "drive against hoodlums" and "gun-toters," vowing to do "everything in our power to drive them out." The St. Paul Police Department created a special Kidnap Squad and appointed Detective Tom Brown to head it up.

Dunhill wanted to serve notice on Sawyer, so he arrested two of Harry's patrons on a minor charge. The next day, Sawyer confronted Detective Fred Raasch and let him know that the delicate balance of the O'Connor System had been violated. If the cops were going to bring heat to him, he would bring it to the cops.

"I wonder how Dunhill would like a couple of snatches in this town?" asked Sawyer. And with that, he began putting the team together to kidnap one of St. Paul's leading businessmen.

Around lunchtime on the afternoon of June 15, William Hamm Jr., president of St. Paul's Hamm Brewing Company, was walking home for lunch, as was his usual practice. Things were going well for the handsome millionaire. He sat on the boards of several successful corporations and was the president of a local department store. But the real source of his riches, the business he inherited from his grandfather, was back in business minting money after a twelve-year downturn during the Prohibition years. The Hamm Brewing Company was back doing what it did best: brewing, distributing and selling one of the most popular beers in the nation.

If Hamm had any idea that his every move had been studied for weeks as he was followed and tracked by some of St. Paul's most nefarious criminals, he didn't show it as he crossed the street in front of his downtown brewery.

He was approached by a well-dressed elderly man who extended his right hand.

"You are Mr. Hamm, are you not?" he asked.

Hamm extended his hand to the stranger

and said, "Yes."

With that, the man grabbed Hamm's hand tightly and seized his elbow with his left. A second man grabbed Hamm from the other side and pushed him roughly toward the curb.

"What is it you want?" cried Hamm.

A car sped to the curb, its rear door open, and the two men pushed Hamm inside. A pillowcase was dropped over his head and his assailants shoved him to the floor of the car as it sped away. They told him to keep his mouth shut and everything would be all right.

Hamm realized he was being driven around on unpaved dirt and gravel back roads. After about an hour, they stopped and met a second group of men in another car. They forced him to sign a series of ransom notes, put him back in the car and drove him out of state to a house in Bensenville, Illinois.

The Hamm kidnapping was organized by Jack Peifer, Sawyer's partner in crime. He ran the Twin Cities' finest gambling casino, the Hollyhocks Inn. He also ran a loan sharking operation and a makeshift bank for the gangsters who frequented his casino and were loath to keep their money in a commercial bank. With underworld connections like Peifer's, the money was a lot safer sitting in his second-floor safe than in any real bank, vulnerable as they were to marauding thieves. He used a couple of Green Lantern regulars, Fred Barker and Alvin Karpis, to pull the kidnapping off. Karpis recruited two of Capone's shooters who had taken part in the St. Valentine's Day Massacre, George "Shotgun" Ziegler and Monty Bolton, along with Fred's brother, Doc, and Chuck Fitzgerald.

Peifer knew Hamm from his visits to the Hollyhocks, and also knew that with Prohibition ending, the Hamm brewing company was flush with cash now that real beer could be manufactured once again. Brewers and distillers immediately became a target of underworld kidnappers. During Prohibition, many had made unholy alliances with criminals and bootleggers to keep their companies afloat by supplying the ingredients that could be easily remixed by bootlegging operations to create quality intoxicants that could then be resold to the high-end hotels, resorts and other establishments that demanded them. Once freed of the governmental restraints on their trade, brewers and distillers no longer saw the need to include the underworld in their lucrative endeavors. Those who were being cut out felt they had legitimate reasons for finding another way to get their share.

The Barker-Karpis gang was able to extract a cool $100,000 for Hamm's release and disappear seamlessly back into the St. Paul underworld, aided in no small part by their inside man at the police department, none other than Tom Brown, head of the police department's Kidnap Squad.

Two weeks after the Hamm abduction, John Factor, the brother of cosmetics king Max Factor, was kidnapped as he walked to his car late at night after visiting a gambling casino in the Chicago suburbs. After his release twelve days later, he told police his family had paid $70,000. Factor had been abducted near the Des Plaines, Illinois, headquarters of Roger Touhy's operations. Touhy had been battling with Capone's operatives, who were trying to make inroads on Touhy's territory. Factor was a shady businessman who was wanted in Britain on embezzlement charges and was fighting extradition. So the whole thing looked to the local authorities like it was a gang kidnapping or shakedown, and they never showed much interest in solving it. Instead, they kicked it over to Melvin Purvis at the Chicago office of the Justice Department's Bureau of Investigation. Purvis was trying to learn the ropes in Chicago, and the mild-mannered Southern gentleman was having a tough time of it. But he'd been watching the Touhys — the "Terrible Touhys" — as the newspapers called them — a gang of six brothers, sons of a corrupt Chicago police-man, who were alleged to have successfully staged some thirty kidnappings in Chicago.

So when the Factor kidnapping came his way, Purvis immediately suspected the Touhys. "We assumed from the start, with no material evidence, that the Touhy gang was responsible," Purvis said.

Within days, Purvis got a call from the chief investigator for the Illinois state's at-torney in Chicago, Dan Gilbert. Gilbert told Purvis that he had information that the Touhys were behind the kidnapping of Fac-tor, and also had orchestrated the kidnap-ping of William Hamm, the wealthy brewer up in St. Paul. Not only that, but Gilbert also told him that Roger Touhy had just been jailed in Elkhorn, Wisconsin, on a weapons charge.

Touhy and his men were up in Wisconsin vacationing when they lost control of their car and knocked out a telephone pole. When police arrived to investigate, they discovered the trunk was full of expensive fishing gear and equipment, but it also contained a goodly supply of rifles, handguns and ammunition.

Purvis pounced on the tip and dispatched two of his agents to Wisconsin, who did some kidnapping of their own: without bothering with an extradition hearing, they brought Touhy and his men back to Chicago for questioning.

They led Roger Touhy in shackles to Purvis's office, where he was questioned by Purvis himself. But the veteran gangster just laughed at the questions or refused to answer. Finally, Purvis accused him of the Hamm kidnapping.

"What do you mean by *ham,* Mr. Purvis?" he scoffed. "A ham sandwich? Or did I kidnap a ham steak?"

Purvis put Touhy and his three associates behind one-way glass and brought in Factor and Hamm to see if they could make an identification.

Factor identified one of the four, William Sharkey, as being among those who'd kidnapped and tortured him. But Hamm didn't recognize anybody. Nevertheless, Purvis shipped his evidence off to prosecutors and had the group tried for both kidnappings. The rash move was indicative of Purvis's desire to please his demanding boss in Washington, who was increasingly emphatic about the need to successfully solve an important case and bring some glory to his beleaguered Bureau.

The jury failed to convict any in the group of the Hamm kidnapping because the evidence was so slim and shoddy.

By the time Factor's trial came around, he'd become emboldened. He identified the remaining three as being among his kidnappers, as well. A parade of other witnesses also came forward to falsely tie Touhy to the job. After one hung jury, the second voted to convict, and the judge sentenced the three to ninety-nine years in prison. Touhy's lawyers appealed the case to the Illinois Supreme Court, which upheld the conviction. (Touhy maintained his innocence as he languished in prison for nearly twenty-five years. After a retrial, he was acquitted and released in 1959. Less than a month after his release, he was standing at the doorway to his sister's home, where he'd been staying. Two men, identifying themselves as Chicago policemen, pulled shotguns out of their coats and fired five times into Touhy, who died a short time later.)

In fact, Touhy's crew had nothing to do with the Hamm kidnapping. Touhy had been set up by Factor and Gilbert. Touhy was Capone's main rival for control of

Chicago's labor unions and their fat pension funds, and they wanted him out of the way. Touhy controlled large portions of the criminal scene in the north and western Chicago suburbs, and he'd been successfully fighting off Capone's Chicago boys from moving in. It had been Touhy who Chicago Mayor Anton Cermak had recruited to help him fight the Capone mob in the city. The mayor couldn't trust his own police force, the majority of whom had ties to Capone. So when Cermak needed reinforcements to his own private force, he hired them out from Touhy. That effort ended when Cermak was assassinated in Miami. There were many at the time, including the President himself, who believed Cermak had been the target all along, the victim of a Capone-orchestrated hit.

Gilbert, who was known around Chicago as the "richest cop in the world," was the Capone mob's inside man at the prosecutor's office. During his tenure there, he had managed to stave off conviction of any of Capone's men who came before the courts.

Purvis had nailed the wrong men in the Hamm and Factor kidnappings. In fact, he'd been played for the fool in the prosecution of Touhy by the Chicago mob. And he was getting nowhere with the kidnapping case that really mattered, the one which, other than Lindbergh, was generating public hysteria and garnering the biggest headlines throughout the country and in Europe. Charlie Boettcher's kidnappers had gotten away clean, and no one had a clue where they had gone.

Purvis could not have known it, but another sensational abduction of an even more prominent and moneyed citizen was about to knock the Boettcher case off the front pages and relegate its significance to a historical footnote.

4
THE ABDUCTION

On the evening of July 22, 1933, the air in Oklahoma City was hot and lifeless. During the day, the winds would blow the furnace-like air off the plains surrounding the city, but did nothing to relieve the discomfort that permeated everything. Heat records were being broken on an almost daily basis. *The Daily Oklahoman* had taken to running a graphic of a thermometer on its front page, and the mercury was regularly sitting above the 100° mark.

Occasionally, the wind would ease and the humidity would build to such a level that even the simplest movement or task would produce a rolling sweat that would bind wet clothing to the body and bleed bodily fluids and caused the elderly and infirm to pass out and die as they sought relief sitting in front of pathetic electric fans. Oklahoma City's destitute and desperate citizens were leaving their "community camps" in ambulances bound for the hospital or the morgue. The humidity was baffling — and frustrating. It would hang in the air, but rarely turn into rain. For three years, the stubborn drought had wrung Oklahoma, and all of the Great Plains, dry.

Charles Urschel's oil empire, divided among a variety of names and partnerships, had nearly five hundred thousand acres of that land locked up in oil leases, and in 1933, oil was about the only thing that the land was producing. The worldwide Depression had driven the price of wheat so low that farmers were no longer even putting seeds in the ground.

Having grown up in Ohio and Indiana, Urschel was well aware of what hard times were like on a farm. But the misery that surrounded him now was unprecedented. More than a third of the farmers in the Southwest had lost their land to foreclosure. Many were left huddling in shacks, grinding wheat for cereal and bracing themselves against the increasingly violent dust storms that would stop cars in their tracks and blow so much fine silt through the cracks and windows of their wood-frame houses that cribs needed to be covered in wet sheets to protect sleeping infants from choking. With the blowing dust stinging their faces, farmers would wander their formerly lush lands carrying shotguns and revolvers, shooting squirrels, prairie dogs and any other surviving rodents to put food on the table for their families, who were wasting away before their eyes.

Those were the farmers who still had land to hunt on. Or a shack to live in. As the Depression wore on, banks, desperate for cash, collateral — anything — were foreclosing on farmers with a vengeance and chasing them off the land. With nowhere else to go, some families remained on the land in the deteriorating wood-frame homes that no one else would want. But the cruelty would continue. The squatters would often discover a bank-dispatched tractor attaching cables to its framework and pulling it down while the wife and kids cried in the yard and Dad and Grandpa held their hunting rifles exercising every degree of restraint they had left to keep from shooting as the sheriff eyed them warily.

It was an American nightmare that pitted one proud citizen against the next in county after county, state after state, from one shore to the other, like nothing else had since the Civil War.

Things had gotten so desperate in Iowa, which suffered more farm foreclosures than any other state, that a group of farmers broke into a courthouse in Le Mars and demanded the judge not allow any more so that they could at least hold on to their land until better times rolled around. They were proud men. They'd fed the nation, and when war broke out in Europe, they'd fed the rest of the world, too. They did not want to be put out on the road like a bunch of homeless vagrants.

When the indignant judge refused, the men dragged him out to the county fairgrounds and threw a rope around his neck before coming to their senses.

It was no wonder people cheered when gangsters blew up bank vaults and shot up their lobbies. Out West, a popular sentiment prevailed: "The government stole my money with taxes and the banks stole my land in court."

A sense of anarchy was in the air. Unions threatened revolt and state legislatures debated secession. Farmers plowed under crops and dumped milk in the ground rather than sell at a loss. Meanwhile, back East, people stood in breadlines, picked through garbage and still starved. The head of the American Farm Bureau told Congress that unless something was done to help the American farmer there would be "revolution in the countryside."

A revolution of sorts had begun with the election of Franklin Delano Roosevelt. In his inaugural address, he lashed out at the banking industry. Millions of Americans sat around radio sets and cheered as loudly as those in Washington, DC, as FDR gripped the podium and scolded the moneychangers who had "failed through their own stubbornness and their own incompetence."

"They have no vision, and where there is no vision, the people perish," he intoned. "There must be an end to a conduct in banking and in business which too often has given to a sacred trust the likeness of callous and selfish wrongdoing."

On March 9, his first day in office, FDR rammed the Emergency Banking Act through both houses of Congress and signed into law strict new regulations. A month later, he signed the Federal Emergency Relief Act, the Agricultural Adjustment Act and the Emergency Farm Mortgage Act for the refinancing of farm mortgages. Two weeks later, it was the Truth-in-Securities Act, which required full disclosure of facts in all stock issues. Then he abandoned the gold standard and signed the National Industrial Recovery Act with a $3.3 billion public works program; the Glass–Steagall

Banking Act, which separated commercial and investment banking and guaranteed all bank deposits; the Farm Credit Act; the Emergency Railroad Transportation Act and the Home Owner's Loan Act.

The era of an activist, aggressive federal government had arrived in a flash, and its scope surprised even its most ardent supporters. The legislative accomplishments of the first 100 days of the Roosevelt administration would set the standard for all presidencies to follow. "It's more than a New Deal," said Interior Secretary Harold Ickes. "It's a New World."

Urschel was an ardent Democrat and strong Roosevelt supporter, just like almost everybody else in Oklahoma and Texas. But Urschel had a particular interest in the New Deal apart from hoping it could lift the country out of the desperate state it had sunken into. Urschel needed Roosevelt to help bring some control and conservation to the nation's booming oil business before the ruthless competitors who drove it pushed the price so low that nobody could make any money. Urschel and his companies had been leaders in the push for self-regulation, as was the legendary oilman by whom Urschel's operations had been built, Thomas B. Slick, who discovered Oklahoma's Cushing oil field and owned the Prairie Oil and Gas Company.

But Urschel and his competitors in Texas and Oklahoma were finding so much oil that the price per barrel was going through the floor. From 1932 to spring 1933, the price of oil had fallen from eighty-seven cents a barrel to forty-four cents. Then, big oil companies, in an attempt to drive independents like Urschel out of the market, escalated their over-production to bring the price down to a quarter, and then a dime. The independents needed FDR to step in and establish price controls and production quotas. The President eventually would come to Urschel's aid, but not in the way he was hoping, or even imagining.

Tom Slick was the best thing that had ever happened to Charles F. Urschel, a poor farm boy from Ohio who worked his way out of the Midwest by translating his love of numbers into accounting skills and a number of jobs that allowed him to polish his craft and save enough money to leave the farming life behind. Barely twenty years old, he packed what little he had, boarded a southbound train and headed to Oklahoma to make his fortune in the oil business. There he found a job with oilman Charles B.

Shaffer, with whom Slick had also gone to work.

Slick was coming off a string of spectacular failures and had teamed up with Shaffer, who was about the only other oilman who believed in the potential of the Cushing oil fields. Slick was buying up leases and drilling as secretly as it is possible to drill, hoping to strike gold and buy up the surrounding land before the competition could get word of the find. When he hit a gusher in the middle of winter in the middle of the night in 1912, he capped it off quickly and told his crew to hold tight and spread the word that the well was proving a disappointment. But the shroud of secrecy could only hold for so long, and when word leaked out the industry pounced.

However, when they got to Cushing they found they'd been stymied. Typical was the note that Harry Ford Sinclair's man wrote to his boss, the founder of Sinclair Oil:

Slick and Shaffer roped off their well on the Wheeler farm and posted guards and nobody can get near it . . . I got a call yesterday at the hotel in Cushing from a friend who said they had struck oil out there. A friend of his was listening in on the party line and heard the driller call Tom

125

Slick at the farm where he's been boarding and said they'd hit. Well, I rushed down
to the livery stable to get a rig to go out
and do some leasing and damned if Slick
hadn't already been there and hired every
rig. Not only there, but every other stable
in town. They all had the barns locked and
the horses out to pasture. There's 25 rigs
for hire here in Cushing and he had them
all for ten days at $4.50 a day apiece, so
you know he really thinks he's got something. I went looking for a farm wagon to
hire and had to walk three miles. Some
other scouts had already gotten the wag-
ons on the first farms I hit. Soon as I got
one, I beat it back to town to pick up a
notary public to carry along with me to get
leases — and damned if Slick hadn't hired
every notary in town, too.

Slick had leased everything solid . . .
except some Indian leases. I've been
checking the records and you have to get
the Interior Department to put them up for
sale.

Slick had locked everything up at one dollar per acre. By the time the Indian leases
became available, Sinclair and others were
paying $200 per acre.

The gusher that Slick tapped that night in

Cushing eventually set off one of the greatest oil booms in American history. Within a few short years, Cushing made Oklahoma the leading producer of oil in the nation. Slick had found gold in the red dust of the Oklahoma soil, and Charles Urschel had found the man he wanted to work for. It was a partnership that blossomed into a friendship that would last for life.

Within a few years of painting the skyline black with belching wells, Tom Slick had acquired the title that would stick for life: King of the Wildcatters.

Cushing sat atop the richest field in the history of the oil business. When Urschel joined him, Slick was putting so many wells in the ground and finding so much oil that it overwhelmed the technology available to contain it. The landscape that Urschel found himself surrounded by was otherworldly and bizarre.

Farmers were eager to lease their lands to Slick because, in many cases, it was the only way they could stay on their land. Slick was a man of the people and always dealt generously with his leaseholders and others from the lower ranks. Farmers knew that Tom Slick was a man of his word and that if he struck oil on their land, they'd be paid their share — and maybe more. And that was true whether they were white, black or Indians on the reservation.

So they cared little about the devastation brought to their land when Tom hit a gusher. Natural gas would spew into the air with little opportunity or system to contain it. Lest it collect in low-lying areas and choke people to death, in many cases it was ignited and allowed to burn off in fires that would last weeks. Inspectors from the Bureau of Mines estimated that in some of the fields drilled by Slick more than a billion cubic feet of natural gas was escaping into the air or being burned off in low-lying fires that gave the landscape a numinous glow that could be seen for miles. Oil would pool up in farmers' fields, creating shallow black lakes. The escaping natural gas would blow geysers of oil into the air, where the winds would carry the slimy clouds for miles.

When the wind wasn't blowing punishing brown dust clouds, it carried black rain, spreading a slick and stinking blanket over once-rich farmlands as the gas-powered rigs thumped and clanged and steam hissed and belched, adding a deafening soundtrack to the appalling scene.

One newspaper reported that "oil runs in the ditches; escaping gas shimmers in the sunshine, and on the hills are brown patches where the oil has gushed over the top of the derrick and come down in a golden torrent at the rate of 76 cents a barrel until the well has been choked into submission."

The oil flowed into creeks and rivers. The oilmen built dams in an attempt to contain it, but the dry heat would cause the oil to partially evaporate into an unusable lake of stinking slime. Creeks and rivers turned black, running so thick with oil that Slick's competitors would pump it out downstream into storage tanks. This set up bitter fights over who owned the oil, the company that pumped it out of the ground or the company or farmer with the surface rights to the land through which the spewing oil flowed. As inadequate as the technology was to capture and contain Slick's wells, the law was equally undeveloped in interpreting who it belonged to after it had escaped the well.

And, despite the environmental devastation that an oil strike might create, there wasn't a town, city, hamlet, burg or farm that wouldn't welcome — or pray for — a strike on their land. In a matter of months, oil could not only lift an entire region out of the Depression — it could bring riches to the formerly destitute.

Like most of the country, Oklahoma was

a bitter cauldron of racial division and hatred. In fact, to fight the Klan's influence, Governor John Calloway put the entire state under martial law in 1923 and called out the National Guard to keep the peace. Yet, in the impoverished, segregated black country towns, signs were often posted stating, "White men not welcome after dark — except Tom Slick." Such was the appeal and the legend of the King of the Wildcatters.

When Urschel left the lush green landscapes of the Midwest to find his fortune in the Oklahoma-Texas oil boom, he found himself in the polluted and acrid world of a largely unregulated business that was inflicting an environmental nightmare on the countryside. He was also time-traveling back to a world that closely resembled the locale's Wild West past.

When Slick or one of his competitors would find oil in some lost corner of the countryside, the word would spread and throngs of entrepreneurs, dreamers, schemers and crooks would rush in, hoping to ride Tom's coattails to the riches a boom town might bring. First the roustabouts, rig workers, miners and carpenters would flood in to build the derricks, assemble the drills and plumb the wells. With no housing, often for miles, they'd live in tents or hastily constructed shacks and cook their meals on open fires until the get-rich-quick business sharks would flood in to erect cheap shanty-towns with lumberyards, blacksmiths, brick masons and all the attendant services to support the oilmen in the field. And in no time at all there were a multitude of saloons, pool halls, gambling dens and whorehouses supporting the men in town who were supporting the men in the field.

In a matter of months, a formerly quiet corner of the countryside would revert back in time some fifty years, and the Wild West was reborn in the Oklahoma Plains. With very little governance and no law enforcement to speak of, the denizens of the new towns would stick a revolver in their belts or grab a shotgun off the shelf for their own protection as they set off into the night as it came alive with the kind of adventurous entertainment that a man who'd labored fourteen hours in the sweaty stench of an untamed oil field could most enjoy.

In 1920, Slick and his partner, Joseph Frates, attempted to bring some order and discipline to the land developing around their oil fields, essentially by building their own towns, the first of which they named Slick. They advertised it as "a mecca for wide-awake businessmen who are ever on the lookout for better locations for their business," boasted that it was surrounded by a "great forest of oil derricks" and claimed that it would swell to a population of five thousand within weeks.

On the first day of the land rush to Slick, hundreds of lots were sold and businesses started popping up like weeds in the barren wheat fields. Frates routed his railroad in and facilitated the flow of supplies and people to fuel Slick's growth. Within a year, the town boasted not only the usual oil-supporting supply stores and businesses, but a fine hotel, train station and a small hospital. Slick built a baseball park and an outdoor boxing ring for the men of the town to let off steam in a more gentlemanly manner than was the custom in the "less civilized" boom towns. He also installed streetlights, natural gas and water lines.

But some people just don't want to be civilized. In short order, Slick had the usual collection of rowdy saloons, houses of prostitution and gambling dens feeding on the after-hours desires of the oil workers with fresh money in their pockets and sidearms on their hips.

Within a year of its establishment, the *Tulsa Tribune* reported that "The old west, unfettered by law and conventionalities lives again in Slick."

In some ways, the town was a little more advanced than the typical boom town in that it had its own underworld enforcer, Whitey Payne, a law enforcement officer who was supposed to keep a lid on things. But the lid just didn't stay on.

On Christmas evening in 1920, a bunch of drunken roustabouts started firing their weapons randomly into businesses and the various enterprises around town. Amid the confusion, the town's meager security force fled. A thirty-six-hour gunfight played out over December 26 and 27, and Slick's main street was transformed into a shootout scene only Hollywood could imagine. Stores and patrons were robbed, cars were hijacked and several people were shot before the merriment subsided and additional police support arrived from the county.

Urschel had not imagined that the oil business would transport him so far back in time, but it didn't matter. In Urschel, Slick found a man he could trust like a brother.

By 1916, Slick's business empire was so sprawling and internecine that even he couldn't keep track of it. So he brought on Urschel, a born numbers man, to help him out. Urschel could work numbers in his head nearly as fast as he could on paper.

And he forgot nothing. In no time he was saving the company thousands and building a fast friendship with Slick, who took to him almost immediately. The two were perfectly complementary personalities. The chain-smoking, hyperactive, risk-taking gambler paired up with the stoic, methodical German. Together they were making millions, and Urschel was even able on occasion to pull Tom away from his workaholic ways for a round of golf or a trip into the country for some hunting and fishing. Urschel couldn't match Slick on the links, but he was impressive with a rifle in his hands.

The two traveled the vast acreage of Slick's oil fields in Oklahoma, Texas and Kansas and continued to find oil and earn millions until most in the business considered him the largest independent oilman in the country. But the pace and the pressures of the business were killing him. Slick had worked himself into hospital-inducing exhaustion several times in his career, and doctors continually advised him that he could not live long at that pace. By 1929, he was wasted and frail and, conceding to the pleas of his family, agreed to get out of the business and rest until his health returned.

He arranged for his good friend Urschel

to sell most of his oil-producing wells, and when Urschel completed the deal, the grateful wildcatter handed his numbers man a little bonus — a check for $2 million — and headed off for some extensive R & R.

The deal drew the attention of even *The New York Times,* which detailed the transaction under the headline:

TOM SLICK, EX-MULE DRIVER, SELLS HIS WELLS TO THE PRAIRIE OIL COMPANY FOR $30,000,000

The largest transfer of oil-producing properties in recent years was made known yesterday in the announcement that the Prairie Oil and Gas Company had bought all the Mid-Continent holdings of Thomas B. Slick, who is called the world's greatest individual operator.

The story went on to note how Slick had begun his oil career as a teenage mule-driver, roustabout and driller in the oil fields of southern Illinois before discovering huge deposits in Oklahoma, Kansas and North Texas. The story said he planned to take a year off and tour Europe.

But relaxing was something that Slick was just not good at and, within a matter of weeks after the sale, he was back in the business. In April he established the Tom Slick Oil Company and named Urschel as his first vice president and treasurer. The two chased Tom's latest hunch and began drilling for oil on leases in Oklahoma City itself. Characteristically, nearly every well that the company dug began producing record amounts. However, city folk were not quite as enamored of Slick's handiwork as were the impoverished residents of the countryside, where the income from the oil leases was keeping them afloat. As the wind blew the oil spray across cars, businesses and city parks, and lakes of sludge belched from the ground, Slick Oil was battered with dozens of lawsuits. Slick lived in fear that an errant fire would ignite the combustible fumes blowing through the dry city and burn it down in an untamable conflagration. Still, he could not stop. The Oklahoma City discovery was turning out to be the biggest deposit since the Cushing fields, and it was feeding some of the most productive wells that Slick had ever drilled. But the yearlong pursuit of the Oklahoma City claim only accelerated the decline in his health.

On June 27, 1930, he checked himself into Johns Hopkins Hospital in Baltimore. Two weeks later, he began writing his will. A month later, after twenty-seven years in the frenetic oil business, he suffered a massive stroke and cerebral hemorrhage and died. He was forty-seven.

His obituary ran in newspapers from New York to Kansas City. Just as notable, though, were the letters from readers that flooded into newspapers after Slick's death. Readers praised him for his honesty and success at helping them survive the drought and the Depression by finding oil on their land and sharing in the profits, allowing them to not only stay on their land, but pay off their mortgages and survive the repossession efforts of the banks. Slick managed to be the most inexplicable combination of characteristics: a rich oilman and populist hero.

Urschel had lost his best friend and business partner.

Slick had shunned publicity all his life, in part because it was part and parcel of his business, but also because he hated the attention and scrutiny it brought. Slick knew how hard it was to amass a fortune and how quickly that fortune would attract schemers, con men and thieves bent on taking it away by any means necessary. So he lived his life without ostentation and as far out of the spotlight as possible.

Urschel understood that sense of secrecy

as well, perhaps even better. But he was about to inherit a third of Slick's fortune and the lion's share of the nightmare of publicity that the news of that wealth would bring.

On August 27, the Associated Press moved a story on their national wire stating that "The will of a former teamster was revealed today as leaving a fortune of between $75,000,000 and $100,000,000 . . . The will was that of Thomas B. Slick, whose independent operation in Illinois and the Southwest led to his being known as the wealthiest independent oil operator in the world."

Within weeks, Oklahoma newspapers began speculating that the inheritance taxes on the Slick estate would bring enough cash into the state's coffers that its burgeoning debt would be erased and budget cuts in response to the lingering Depression eliminated.

All of the publicity about the Slick-Urschel fortune was making Charles extremely uncomfortable. Slick, a bit paranoid by nature, lived in fear that someone would kidnap him or a member of his family to extort the money he'd worked so hard to earn. He had passed that fear along to Charles, who now had the onus of protecting his family and Tom's, as well. Charles, a widower, had become legal guardian of Tom's children since his death. Two years later, he married Tom's widow, Berenice, and set off a new round of publicity about the marriage of the two fortunes. All of this did not escape the attention of Kathryn Kelly, who found it to be most interesting reading. Urschel's worst fears about the dangers of his family's high-profile fortune were about to be realized.

On Saturday, July 22, 1933, Charles and Berenice were preparing for a night of socializing and a few rounds of bridge with some neighborhood friends. Charles, though, was finding it hard to relax. His son, Charles Jr., and his two stepsons were off on a fishing trip and that concerned him. His stepdaughter was out at a party, and he worried most about her. Recently, she'd mentioned that she thought some strangers were following her.

Ever since the Lindbergh kidnapping the year before, it seemed like the crime was proliferating daily. The local papers carried constant reports and updates on the William Hamm kidnapping in Minnesota, the John Factor kidnapping in Chicago, the Charles Boettcher kidnapping in Denver, the kidnapping of twenty-four-year-old John

O'Connell, nephew of two of New York's most powerful Democratic Party leaders in Albany and August Luer, an Illinois banker, plucked from his home in Alton.

The New York Times had begun running a regular feature that listed the nation's ongoing kidnapping cases and where they stood in the process of being solved.

On July 14, *The Daily Oklahoman* carried two stories of particular interest to Urschel. The first, datelined out of Chicago, was headlined:

SECRET POLICE FOR KIDNAPPING WAR IS URGED

Warfare on kidnappers through a nationwide secret police body with branches in every city was suggested Thursday by Frank J. Loesch, head of the Illinois Crime Commission.

"Kidnapping has become the greatest menace to the public in modern times," Loesch said, "and the only way we can defeat kidnappers is with their own weapons, secrecy and armed force.

"Kidnappings cannot be solved or kidnappers arrested under the existing police systems," he said, "because they have the advantage of knowing the identity of the police. In some of the epidemic of recent cases it appears that police officers may have been implicated in the actual crime."

In a second story on the very same page, under the headline *Laws being drawn to combat kidnapping,* Attorney General Homer Cummings was mapping out just such a plan, and he hoped that Congress would approve it in its very next session. In the meantime, though, he took the extraordinary step of outlining to the nation how they should behave if indeed they were kidnapped in a three-point program designed to put his agency front and center in the high-profile cases:

1. Communicate immediately the fact of the kidnapping to the nearest official of the Justice Department's Bureau of Investigation so that among other things its vast collection of fingerprints may be put into use at the first opportunity.

2. Take prompt steps to keep out of the picture other than the properly constituted officers so that all available clues will be preserved.

3. Make full disclosure of every fact to the federal officers so that they will not be needlessly handicapped.

Life in Oklahoma and Texas among the

scattered burgs where Urschel and his companies did business had always been rough-and-tumble, but since the market crashed and the Depression spread, people were growing increasingly desperate and violent. He was well aware that a group of gangsters had just shot up the parking lot of Kansas City's Union Station, killing cops and a federal agent, and *The Daily Oklahoman* was making the claim that they'd fled to Oklahoma to hide out and that local killer/kidnapper Pretty Boy Floyd was among the suspects. He worried about the safety of his family.

Today, though, there was news of another sort on the radio, and it was one in which Urschel had a great deal of interest.

Fifty thousand New Yorkers had gathered at Floyd Bennett Field in Brooklyn to watch daredevil aviator Wiley Post land after flying around the world. If he landed successfully, he would become the first pilot to fly it solo. And, unless something went terribly wrong, he was also expected to do it in record time, breaking the previous record he had set flying with a navigator.

The Wiley Post adventure was exactly the kind of feel-good story the weary nation craved, and the press was hyping it at every opportunity. Now, as the conclusion of the flight neared, the story was the province of the newly formed national radio networks, and they had listeners glued to their sets.

Urschel knew all about Post and his exploits. Though he was born in Texas, Post spent most of his life in Oklahoma, and the state was proud to claim him.

Post was a poor farm boy, part Cherokee, who had dropped out of school after the sixth grade. He hated farmwork and was hardly built for it at 5'4" and weighing 130 pounds. He left his parents' farm in Texas to find work in the oil fields of Oklahoma, but he was equally ill-suited to that work. He found it tedious and boring and impossibly hard. He tried to find success as a highway robber, but was arrested on one of his first attempts.

Within months of his incarceration, a sympathetic prison doctor took pity on the despondent prisoner and arranged for his release on parole. Eventually, Post returned to work in the oil fields, but lost his left eye in an accident when a flying chip of steel hit him.

The state compensation board ordered the company to pay him a settlement of $1,698.25. Post would use it to pay for flying lessons and buy a recently crash-landed plane for $240. He rebuilt it, learned to fly it and launched his aviation career without the benefit of a pilot's license, which was denied him because of his disability.

He later went to work for one of Urschel's competitors, oilman F. C. Hall. Hall was looking for ways to gain a competitive edge in the business and needed a pilot to shuttle him to distant fields, where he might lay a claim before others could get there. Post, always the thrill seeker, was willing to brave any kind of weather and take off at a moment's notice. Hall found him to be the perfect fit, and lent him his plane to fly at offtimes in races around the country. From there, he built his legend.

The Daily Oklahoman had been following his exploits since his takeoff on July 15 from New York bound for Berlin, where he landed 25 hours and 45 minutes later. He was greeted on the ground by Chancellor Adolf Hitler's newly appointed Reichsminister Hermann Goring. Two hours later, he took off for Novosibirsk in Siberian Russia, but equipment trouble forced him down in East Prussia. The rest of the flight had been a doozy of a story full of unscheduled stops, equipment failures, crash landings, bad weather and assorted unexpected emergencies. But Post continually pressed on and, with good weather ahead of him, it looked as if he would break his own round-the-globe flying record — but this time flying alone.

The Urschels had invited their good friends and neighbors, the Jarretts, over that evening for a game of bridge on the sun-porch behind the house, where the air stirred and the temperature dipped below that inside the mansion, which had baked in the sun all day. Charles was an excellent player. He had a card-counters memory and, with his wife's mental tenacity, they were daunting competitors. The Jarretts enjoyed the rivalry, but after a long, hot night of losing hands, they were itching to leave.

"It's almost 11:30. Time we were going home, Walter," said Mr. Jarrett's wife.

"I suppose so," he responded.

But Berenice was liking her luck and asked for another game. Walter Jarrett shuffled the cards and dealt.

As they sorted their cards, a car pulled up to the house and killed its lights. Inside the powerful new Chevrolet, George Kelly looked at Al Bates, his agitated partner, and told him to relax. Kelly felt good. Excited. He saw lights on the back porch. The doors were open and the screens were the only barrier.

"OK, Al. Calm down. It is going to be a piece of cake."

Berenice's luck held. Staring at her hand and hoping to run a grand slam, she stoically bid: "Two hearts." Then she froze.

"What is it?" asked Charles.

"I heard something," she said. "Someone moved outside."

Charles turned toward the screen door just as two men rushed inside, both armed. One carried a submachine gun, the other a revolver.

Berenice screamed.

Flipping the machine gun in her direction, Kelly told her to "shut up."

Then, calmly: "Everyone keep your seat, and no one will get hurt."

As he stared at the startled foursome, he realized he had no idea which man was to be his victim. Which man was the richest oilman in the whole damn country and which man was the unlucky chump he was playing cards with?

"Which one of you is Charles Urschel?" he asked politely.

Urschel stared back in stoic silence trying to catalog details of the machine-gun-wielding thug who had no idea who he was trying to kidnap. That the gunman couldn't tell Urschel apart from his pudgy, balding neighbor, who just so happened to be a wealthy oilman as well, was almost laughable.

The trim, muscular machine gunner was awfully well-dressed for a night of marauding. Snap-brimmed Panama hat, pressed short-sleeved shirt, pleated slacks, fancy leather belt, shined shoes. The hat threw heavy shadows over his face, and it was hard to make out any features. His complexion looked dark. Mexican, maybe. But his speech was smooth and unaccented. Probably some thug from up north.

Urschel would kill them both in a heartbeat if he could get to his shotgun. He thought worriedly about his sixteen-year-old stepdaughter upstairs. Would she have it cocked and ready if the intruders had other intentions? He kicked himself mentally for firing his bodyguard, whom he'd caught sleeping on the job.

In any negotiation, time and delay are the weapons of last resort for the side dealing from a weaker position. So Urschel sat, unmoving, as Kelly repeated his demand.

"Once again I'll ask you. Which one is Urschel? If you still refuse to answer, we'll take you both."

Jarrett, playing the hero, began to rise. As he did, Urschel followed.

"All right, if that's the way you want it," said Kelly turning to Bates. "Take 'em both."

As Kelly backed out of the room, machine gun still trained on the frightened women, he instructed them not to call the police or he wouldn't hesitate to kill the two men.

Berenice, who'd grown up with hard-bitten cowboys and ranchers and had raised her children in the gritty oil fields of West Texas and Oklahoma among the roust-abouts and drunks, was no stranger to adversity. And she did not scare easily.

As soon as Kelly was out the door, she ran upstairs, locked herself in a room and called Chief Watts of the Oklahoma City Police Department. Then she grabbed a copy of *Time* magazine and flipped to a page that had caught her interest. She had been discussing it with Charles just that afternoon and had left it on her dressing table. The *Time* article was analyzing the recent spate of kidnappings of wealthy individuals. It included the telephone number the Justice Department had set up to expedite action on any kidnapping that should occur. The department was eager to put the new Lindbergh Law into practice and bring kidnappers to justice as quickly as possible.

She dialed the number immediately.

Nine miles outside of town, Kelly told Bates to stop the car. He turned to Urschel and Jarrett and demanded their wallets. Pulling sixty dollars in cash and a driver's license from Jarrett's wallet, he looked at Urschel and told him he could have saved his buddy all this grief if he'd just spoken up earlier.

A few miles later, they stopped the car again. Kelly tossed ten bucks at Jarrett and kicked him out of the car.

"Have a nice walk home, sucker."

The car sped off into the night.

As it did, there was news of joy and celebration on the radio. Wiley Post, still serving his parole, had landed safely, becoming the first solo pilot to fly around the world, setting a new speed record in the process.

5
WELCOME TO PARADISE

Urschel had not gotten where he was in life by being inattentive or careless. He was, in fact, quite the opposite — a meticulous accountant who was obsessed with details, whether they be numbers on a page, contours of the land, the direction of the wind or the chemical content of the soil. In the cutthroat oil business, he was a shrewd survivor and dogged as a bloodhound.

So with his eyes blindfolded and lying in the back of the car, he began doing what he always did: he started collecting details. Before they'd jettisoned Jarrett, his kidnappers had been driving in an easterly direction. Before they taped his eyes shut, he could see the lights of a power plant near Harrah, Oklahoma, some twenty miles east of Oklahoma City. Now, though, they were driving in what clearly was a circuitous route designed to confuse him. They were heading south over backcountry roads that he knew well from his constant travels back and forth to the oil fields and country farms where he held leases. He knew if ever he were to catch these bastards — and he would catch them — he would need to lead a team back to the place of his hideout. To do that, he would need every clue he could collect.

He was blind, but his other senses were working overtime, and everything was being logged in his memory bank.

About an hour into the journey, Urschel recognized the distinctive smell of an oil field. It was either a small field or they were on the edge of a very large one because the odor was distinctive, but faint. Thirty minutes later, a similar scent returned. Again, either a small field or the edge of a very large one. In the middle of the night, the car stopped. Probably about 3:30 a.m., he calculated. He was pulled out of the car and into the brush, where he was forced to sit out of sight in the weeds. Chiggers attached themselves to his legs and arms and bugs feasted on his sweaty skin. The other abductor grabbed what he guessed was a gasoline can and headed off. He was back in about fifteen minutes, so they must have been just a short three- to five-minute walk to the gas station. They guided him back into the car and were off again.

During the drive, one of his abductors kept referring to the other as "Floyd."

"Hey, Floyd, gimme a smoke." Floyd this, Floyd that. Funny. They were obviously trying to make him believe he was being abducted by Oklahoma's infamous Pretty Boy Floyd, as he was called by the newspapers. But the inferences were so painfully obvious that he concluded the one person who definitely was not in the driver's seat was Pretty Boy Floyd.

An hour later, they stopped to open a gate. Two or three minutes later they stopped and opened another, and then drove into a building that had the sound and smell of what must have been a garage or barn. They transferred the license plates to another car and put him into the backseat, which had been made up into a makeshift bunk where he could mercifully stretch out after being covered up. The car was obviously a lot bigger than the cramped Chevy sedan they'd been driving in. Probably a seven-passenger Caddy or Buick.

After about three hours of driving, they stopped at a filling station and made small talk with the woman who was gassing up the tank.

They asked about the heat, and what it

was doing to the crops.

"The crops around here are burned up," she said. "Although we may make some broomcorn."

Broomcorn? That caught Urschel's attention. Not much of that being grown around here. Most farmers were using what precious little water there was to grow food they could eat to survive. But broomcorn was hardy, and the way the damn dust was billowing through every nook and cranny, a good broom was getting to be as essential as a pickax and hoe.

The abductors got back in the car and again drove off until the sun started rising. At no point, Urschel noted, had the car been driven on pavement. By midmorning, probably 9:00 or 10:00, it started to rain, much to the irritation of Urschel's abductors, who managed to get the car stuck as the rain poured down, turning the parched earth into rivers of mud.

The junior partner was then commanded to get out and push, a situation Urschel might have found almost comical were he not so hungry, tired and disoriented. Having extricated the car, the complaining mud- and rain-soaked assistant jumped back in and the journey resumed.

Hours later, they pulled into a garage and

turned off the engine.

"What time is it?" he asked.

"Two-thirty," was the reply. In Urschel's world it was still pitch dark. He was desperately trying to keep track of time. He was left in the car in the stifling heat for hour after hour. At least, though, he was free to come out from under the covers, get out of the car and try to relax. He sat on a wooden box that sagged into what was unmistakably a couple of bags of golf clubs. What he would give to be strolling the fairways with his golf buddies, hacking balls into the rough and laughing about the sorry nature of their game. But that fantasy was a brief respite from his current state. The sun beat down on the garage and the temperature rose like a baking oven until it finally set in the late evening and the air cooled to a breathable level.

At that point, they led him out of the garage and he felt the cooler air, though still in the upper eighties, on his face. They took him through a narrow gate, down a boardwalk and into a house. As he walked, he counted his steps. In a bedroom, he was told there were two beds. They sat him down on one. It felt more like an iron cot. They stuffed his ears with cotton and covered them with adhesive tape, as well. Unmistakably, this was a farmhouse. He could hear barnyard animals in the distance and began mentally cataloging their number and nature. There were horses, cows and several dogs with barks of different pitches. There were quail — lots of them — chickens, roosters. The usual assortment; nothing special or distinctive. They gave him a ham sandwich and a cup of black coffee in a china cup with no saucer. It was the first thing he'd eaten since they left Oklahoma City.

The man who had been calling the shots on the kidnapping sat on the adjacent bed and delivered a colorful lecture.

"If we thought you would ever see anything here, or ever tell anything when you go back, we would kill you now. That really is the safest way, but if we take your word and release you after the ransom money is paid, and you betray us by giving the federals any information, we will choose our own methods of punishing you," he said.

Urschel was listening intently through his muffled ears, aiming his blinded eyes at the sounds that were filtering through. It was an odd and measured voice. The man had the vocabulary of an educated man, tempered with a slight Southern accent. It was not like the forceful, ineloquent threat one would expect from the kind of lowlife who'd pluck a man from his backyard and haul him off into the night. The man then continued, his voice almost theatrical, and his language as grammatical as a Catholic prepschooler.

"I think the best method of punishment is the Chinese bandit system. They take a victim, strip him of his clothes and place him face downward on a board floor in some old shack where numerous wharf rats are extremely hungry. A hole is bored in the floor immediately under the victim's belly, the hungry rats begin nibbling through the hole in the floor, and slowly but surely eat the lining of the belly and pull out the intestines. The process takes days and the victim has time to repent his error."

A very colorful rant. But a logical listener would conclude that no one fearing capture would go to those lengths, risking both the escape of his prey and relying on the unpredictable behavior of a bunch of smallbrained rodents. Urschel fully understood his life was in danger, but he also realized the most likely way his days would end would be the result of a bullet in the head and a shallow grave in some nearby burnedout wheat field. In the end, what does it matter anyway? Dead is dead. He worried more about the fate of his wife and children, and there would be plenty of threats made to them, as well.

Urschel remained on the cot for the rest of the night, but never slept. One of his captors was always in the second bed. Occasionally, he could hear the muffled voices of another man and a woman in some adjoining room. His world remained black and sounded sunken.

The next day, the two men led him to a car, put him inside and drove slowly over a very rough road for about fifteen minutes to another house.

"All right, let's unload," said one. They took him inside and made him lie on a bunch of blankets in the corner. He could hear the sounds of another man and woman in a different room.

Later, they handcuffed him to a chair and he tried to sleep. In the morning he heard the sound of propellers overhead. A plane passing by, heading west. He remembered hearing one the previous afternoon, as well, heading in the opposite direction. This, too, went into his memory bank. The farm likely was in someone's flight path. When the plane doubled back in the afternoon, the excited aviation buff knew he was on to something. If he could learn the approximate times of the flyovers, he would have an important clue to the location of the farm. But, not wanting to give away his intentions to his captors, he devised a bit of trickery to determine the times. He began counting off seconds and minutes in his head. When he thought sufficient time had passed, he innocently asked what time it was. To further cover his intentions, he would occasionally anticipate the arrival of the flyover and ask the time in advance and then begin counting off. It was a clever dodge that escaped the notice of his captors. Within a few days, he had the flights timed almost exactly. The morning plane crossed over the farm about 9:45. It returned in the afternoon at 5:45. On Sunday, it rained steadily. By late morning, Urschel realized the plane had not passed over. Nor did it come back in the afternoon. Of this he made a special note.

After the first day, Urschel's abductors had turned the guard duties over to an old man referred to as "Boss" and some kid named "Potatoes" (Boss Shannon's son). The two were decidedly less astute and threatening. He found he could chat them up and shrewdly acquire more and more details about his locale. He talked to Boss about their mutual interest in hunting and fishing, innocently picking up details about the local environment and asking questions about the number of hogs and whatnot on the farm.

He'd ask Potatoes to unshackle him for a couple minutes so he could walk around the shack, stretch his legs and get some exercise. After Potatoes would oblige, Urschel would pace off the floor, getting measurements, identifying objects and leaving his fingerprints in strategic places.

Before long, he had enough details that he could draw the shack and the farm in his mind and identify and enumerate every animal that populated it. There were two chicken coops out back, a well with nasty, mineral-tasting water out front with a pulley that squeaked with a distinctive sound. There were four cows, three hogs, two pigs, a bull and a mule. There were cardinals and scarlets chirping.

The rundown farm stretched out for about 500 acres.

He overheard the name of the postman and cataloged it.

He knew just about everything about the farm where he was being held, except that it was in Paradise, Texas, and it belonged to Machine Gun Kelly's father-in-law.

■ ■ ■ ■

Within minutes of receiving Berenice Ur-schel's call, Hoover was on the phone to the special agent in charge of the Bureau's field office in Oklahoma City, Ralph Colvin. Get to the Urschel home. Give her any assistance she needs and wants. But, most importantly, get control of the investigation.

The so-called Lindbergh Law had been passed by Congress less than a month earlier. It gave Hoover's men the authority to chase kidnappers across state lines. The Bureau was the only law enforcement agency empowered to do so. Hoover and Cummings had fought hard to get that authority, and now they would employ it to its fullest. Hoover would not be sidelined as he had been by the New Jersey State Police in the Lindbergh kidnapping, which was still dragging on without any leads. Hoover and his men had been turned into laughing-stocks by the New Jersey State Police, who scoffed at their meticulous, "scientific" investigation and the ridiculous leads they were following. The public, too, was becoming exacerbated with law enforcement's inability to solve the case and stem the kidnapping scourge. If the Bureau could solve this case, Hoover would have a significant leg up on his rivals in his push for power and the creation of the country's national police force. The hotline that Hoover had established was a stroke of genius. When Berenice called it within minutes of her husband's abduction, it gave the Bureau a head start on the investigation and the chance to get in on the ground floor, before local law enforcement could start gathering and hoarding evidence. This would not be a repeat of the Lindbergh kidnapping, during which rivals at the local level neutralized the Bureau's efforts to take over the case. Hoover's men immediately went to work on getting control of the investigation and lining themselves up for the credit when — and if — the case was ultimately solved.

Colvin met Oklahoma Police Chief John Watts and Sheriff Stanley Rogers at the Urschel home and explained the situation to them. The three well-acquainted colleagues resolved the issue without acrimony. Hoover's men would lead the investigation and take charge of the case. Their problem would not be internal cooperation, it would be external. The national press would soon have hold of the latest chapter in America's gangster chronicles, and they would exploit it to the fullest.

Oklahoma City's police department was crawling with reporters even on a Saturday at midnight — especially on a Saturday at midnight. The city had two daily newspapers at the time, and both competed mightily for any nugget of news to sell the street editions that were routinely published throughout the day. The nearby cities of Tulsa and Norman and the neighboring counties had rags of their own all trolling for news, as well. Nothing sold a street edition like crime news, and Saturday night was when crime happened.

Given his druthers, Colvin would have kept news of the kidnapping quiet for as long as possible, at least until the ransom demand arrived and its authenticity could be verified. But when the wife of the city's richest denizen calls in with word her husband has been kidnapped at gunpoint, people snap to attention, orders are barked, cars are dispatched, sirens blare and desperate reporters want to know, "What the hell is going on?"

Watts and Rogers dispatched every car and officer they had. They put cars on U.S. Highway 66 and Highway 81 toward Chickasha, Oklahoma. But Kelly, the old rumrunner, was not on any major highway. He was hauling his victim south along the unpaved dirt roads he knew so well, and where the law rarely ventured. (In fact, the only eyewitness to spot the getaway car was an alert Associated Press reporter, Hugh Wagnon, who saw a Chevy sedan followed by a large green Packard speeding west on Northwest Tenth Street, just minutes after the kidnapping.)

Within minutes, the wires of the Associated Press, United Press and their regional affiliates were humming with the news that yet another wealthy American had been kidnapped by brazen criminals, this time right from the safety of his back porch.

At the Urschel house, Colvin interviewed Berenice. Fully expecting to find a hysterical female, he was relieved and impressed with the cool, somewhat stony woman he found himself deposing. She was calm and relaxed for a woman who'd just witnessed her husband's kidnapping. She recounted the incident with clarity and detail.

She told the lawman that the kidnappers were "swarthy" and "foreign-looking." They were "professional."

"There was nothing amateurish about these men," she said. "They knew just what they were doing. I'm sure they were foreigners, too. Both were very dark complexioned.

I know I could identify them without any trouble.

"They were both nervous, though. When they saw that we just sat there sort of calm about the whole thing, that seemed to disturb them. We thought we had heard something, but none of us thought to get up to look at the car when it first drove in. The men didn't even try to be quiet; they slammed the doors."

Berenice's sixteen-year-old daughter had returned home at about 11.00 p.m. that evening, and when they let her in through the screen door leading to the sunporch, they had neglected to relock it.

"The screen wasn't even locked, and we had let the guard man go several weeks ago. He just slept all night," she added with irritation.

"Lots of threatening letters used to come to the house, but we haven't had any lately. Most of them just came from cranks, and we didn't worry much about it."

She told Colvin that her daughter had thought two men in a blue Chevy had been following her earlier in the week, on Tuesday.

"I'm so thankful that it isn't Betty," she said with relief, before adding what Colvin could not have realized the portent of at the time: "I'm not so afraid for Charley. Charley is a grown man. And he's so resourceful and sensible."

Jarrett got back to the house about ninety minutes after his abduction and hustled his way past the growing crowd of reporters and onlookers, who the police had corralled across the street. Despite the threats from Kelly and Bates, he described his ordeal in the car and confirmed the details of the abduction. Colvin told him not to give any information to the press, family or friends. They would need to hold as many facts as possible close to the vest to help confirm the veracity of the kidnappers when they came forward with a ransom demand.

When he left their custody, Jarrett's statement to the press was terse: "They treated me like gentlemen. There is nothing more I can tell you now."

On Sunday morning, the bare bones of the story ran under inch-deep headlines in papers throughout the South and the Midwest and were blanketing the radio airwaves. *The Daily Oklahoman* screamed:

KIDNAPERS HOLD URSCHEL
JARRETT ALSO SEIZED
BUT IS QUICKLY FREED

Two Machine Gunners Invade
Card Game on Sunporch
Victim Who Is Freed Able to
Tell Police Little

Charles F. Urschel, wealthy trustee of the rich T. B. Slick estate was in the hands of kidnapers early Sunday morning while his companion-victim, W.R. Jarrett, oilman, later released, sealed his lips on ransom demands.

The two were kidnaped at 11:30 p.m. Saturday and were forced by two men, armed with machine guns, from the sun porch of the Urschel home, 327 Northwest Eighteenth St., into a waiting large blue sedan standing with motor running on the Urschel driveway.

Wives of the two men witnessed the kidnaping. Mrs. Berenice Slick Urschel is the widow of the late T.B. Slick, millionaire "king of the wildcatters."

Jarrett, released by the kidnapers, appeared at the Urschel home at 12:45 a.m. Sunday morning.

In Oklahoma City, this news bumped the story of local boy-made-good Wiley Post, who had just become the first man to fly solo around the world while setting the record for the fastest time to do so as well.

Within twenty-four hours of the kidnapping, the press pool across the street from the Urschel's stately manse had grown to a horde of photographers, reporters, radiomen, newsreel cameramen and various assistants and onlookers. The local and state papers were there in force, as were the wire services and the newspaper chains. They came from Texas, Kansas, Missouri and Illinois. Scripps Howard sent their star reporters, Lee Hills and Noel Houston. Hearst sent its top crime reporter, James Kilgallen, from New York. The London *Daily Mail* sent Sir Percival Phillips.

Colvin eyed the assembled mob warily. The mob was going to complicate the kidnappers' efforts to contact the family. They were going to complicate his efforts to investigate the case. They were going to print every shred of evidence they could get about the case, and if they couldn't get any facts about it, they would print speculation, rumors and lies.

He gathered the family and its inner circle and tried to explain the situation: The people assembled outside are hungry. Desperate for news. Anything and everything they print or broadcast will complicate efforts to solve the case and find Mr. Urschel, he told them. Beyond the folks in the room, no information should be shared with anyone, whether they seem trustworthy or not. The men and women across the street will make their reputations by what they can publicize about this case. They are extremely competitive and will stab each other in the back as quickly as they will stab yours if they think it will give them an edge, a story or an exclusive. They will follow you when you leave the house. Right now they are interviewing your friends and neighbors and business associates. They are bribing telephone operators to monitor your calls. Anything they learn or invent will be knowledge the kidnappers will pick up. Secrecy, stealth and obfuscation will be of paramount importance. Trust no one, say nothing, he concluded.

The lawmen couldn't have realized it, but they were speaking a language Berenice knew and understood well. Tom Slick had been a man who hated publicity, shunned the spotlight and spent his whole life trying to avoid those nosy bastards in the press who were constantly poking around about his oil discoveries, his wealth, his taxes, his charitable contributions and everything else that was none of their business. Berenice would be a most composed and intuitive victim.

On Sunday, when news of the kidnapping hit the national press, Hoover was further convinced that he had just been handed the crime that would accelerate his quest for expanded powers. Jarrett had been shown mug shots and he thought one of the abductors looked a lot like the notorious George Kelly — bootlegger, bank robber, expert machine gunner and prime suspect in the Union Station shootout that left four dead. The investigation in Kansas City was going nowhere, and Hoover's best agents had been dispatched there to deal with it. Kansas City was just a short plane ride from Oklahoma City. He called Gus Jones and pulled him out of Kansas City. Get to Oklahoma City immediately and take over. Hoover wanted results, and he wanted Jones to get them fast.

"With what?" Jones asked. "Peashooters?"

Hoover let Jones know there was no need to comply with the agency's prohibition on firearms. Jones, he knew, would never have thought otherwise.

Colvin picked up Jones at the airport Sunday afternoon and drove him to the Urschel home, where he walked in on a meeting Berenice was holding with her brothers-in-law, Arthur and Lamar Seelig-son, and E. E. Kirkpatrick, one of Tom Slick's and Charles Urschel's closest friends. He was also coexecutor of the Slick estate, along with Urschel.

It was the perfect collection of key characters in the case, and Jones wasted little time in charming them with his wizened Texas lawman confidence and reassurance.

"Mrs. Urschel," he said with deference. "This thing you are up against is brand new to you, and you feel licked. I can tell it by looking at you. You haven't heard from the kidnappers yet, and you are concerned about that. No one seems to be doing anything to help you, and you are concerned about that. I know exactly how you feel because I have been through this before. It may be brand new to you, but it is an old story to me.

"First of all, let me tell you that no one is doing anything, and no one is going to do anything, until we hear from the kidnappers — and we are definitely sure it is the kidnappers, not just some gang trying to chisel in — and that is the way we, as police officers, should act at this stage of the case. Right now our prime concern has to be with getting Mr. Urschel back home safely. We have no other concern at this time.

"I have been instructed by my superiors to tell you that every facility of the Department of Justice is at your disposal in this case. I have been told to tell you that the Department will do nothing which will in any way impede the kidnappers from getting in touch with you or prevent Mr. Urschel's release. It is not the policy of the Department to advise whether or not any ransom payments should be made — that is a matter which is strictly up to the family. But we will be available for any other matter for which you may need us. Knowing that we will in no way interfere with any effort to secure Mr. Urschel's safe release, we only ask that you keep us fully informed on any contact you make, or any plans you form. The moment Mr. Urschel is released, we go to work."

Berenice stared across the table at the cocky lawman. "You say you've had experience in other kidnappings. Did they come home alive?"

Jones didn't miss a beat. He smiled and said, "Every one."

There was no way to know if he was lying, but the man sure was convincing. She thanked him warmly, and he headed back downtown with Colvin to set up a command center in the Bureau's office.

On Monday, a flood of tips, offers of help, shakedowns, false leads and phony ransom demands began to flood in. Berenice insisted on taking any call that remotely suggested it might be from the true kidnappers. But it was hard to separate the opportunists from the real thing.

One caller had information about Urschel's whereabouts and was offering to take Berenice or her representative to the location and arrange the settlement. Jones deduced that this was a brazen attempt to set up a second kidnapping, piggybacking on the first, and warned her off.

On Tuesday she took a call from a man who demanded $50,000 for Charley's return. Berenice was to meet him one mile west of the bridge on West Tenth Street. He said he would bring Urschel's watch as proof that he was the abductor. It was the watch, he said, that she had purchased for her husband while they had honeymooned in Europe.

Colvin, who was listening in on another phone, coached her through it.

"I don't drive," she said. "Can I have my brother-in-law drive me?" After a long pause, the caller agreed, but warned her that if he was armed, or anything tricky should occur, she'd never see her husband again.

Colvin didn't like the sound of the call, and he advised Berenice against complying with the demands. To him, the guy sounded like a fraud.

But Berenice was adamant. "If I don't go and anything happens to Charley I'd never forgive myself."

Berenice had to sneak out of the house and into the car lest she be followed by a parade of reporters and photographers in a string of cars behind her. She snuck along the trellis and vines in the backyard garden and lifted herself through the window of the garage. She silently slid into Arthur's car and covered herself up with a dark blanket.

Arthur calmly sauntered toward the car a short time later and backed out into the street, where he explained to the curious reporters that he was heading to the office and would be back soon.

At the appointed time, a car pulled up beside them.

"Do you have the money?" he demanded. Seeligson explained that the timed locks on the bank vault had not yet opened for the day and they couldn't get the funds just yet. "Do you have the watch?" he asked.

The man didn't, but said they should return at 2:00 p.m. with $5,000 of "good faith" money and he would show them the watch.

At 2:00 p.m. they returned. Seeligson had $1,000 in an envelope with fake paper money stashed behind it. Berenice carried another $4,000 in her hat in case the contact actually did have the watch. The man walked up to the car and aimed a revolver at Berenice's head. "Have you got the money?"

"Have you got the watch?" demanded Seeligson. He didn't and Seeligson handed over the envelope with the $1,000 and the fake paper. The man jumped in his car and sped off.

For the first time since the ordeal began, Berenice lowered her face into her hands and cried inconsolably.

That night they received a call from a woman who insisted on speaking with Mrs. Urschel. She picked up the phone in her bedroom. "Hello, this is Mrs. Urschel."

"You'll be sorry you welched and gave us a bundle of cut-up paper. You'll never see your husband again."

The phone rang constantly. Callers made all manner of threats and demands. They threatened to kill or maim Charles. They threatened to kill or capture her children. Through it all, she soldiered on.

Colvin had been keeping Hoover up-to-date by telephone and telegraph since Saturday night, assuring him that the local police were cooperating and the victim's family was working directly with the Bureau.

Hoover, in turn, was peppering Cummings with memos doing the same.

July 26, 1933

Memorandum for the Attorney General

With reference to the case of Charles F. Urschel, who was kidnaped from his home in Oklahoma City, you are advised that two contacts have been made by the alleged kidnapers with the family of Mr. Urschel, but it is believed that both of these contacts were fake. The entire situation is being closely covered by Agents of this Bureau and the family is cooperating with us one hundred per cent, regardless of press stories which have been carried to the effect that Federal and local authorities have withdrawn. We are also receiving excellent cooperation from the local police.

Respectfully,
J. Edgar Hoover
Director

Back at the Shannon farm in Paradise, Urschel was lying on a blanket-covered mattress on the floor of a wooden shack that had been baking in the sun for hours. He lay still, trying unsuccessfully to sleep, but at least trying to conserve whatever energy he had left. His eyes had been taped shut for nearly three straight days and they burned and itched. He was still handcuffed to a chair, so scratching them for relief was nearly impossible, and he tried to distract himself with other thoughts.

He heard the sounds of two men coming toward the shack and of the kid going out to the porch to greet them.

"How is he, kid? Getting restless?"

"No, he don't do nothin'. He just lays there."

"He's a smart man, a very smart man."

"I wish I could say the same thing for that wife of his. She's causing enough trouble for both of them."

One of his abductors, the bigger of the two with the hearty voice and throaty laugh, went into the room and dismissed the moronic kid who'd been guarding him, grabbing his sawed-off shotgun as he did.

"Your wife's been raising a lot of hell back in Oklahoma City. According to this morning's papers she's mixed every kind of law into this except Charlie Chan, and that's going to make it a little rough on you. It's pretty hard to make contact with all of that law around the place."

He asked Urschel if he belonged to a church and if he was friendly with the pastor.

"Yes," said Urschel. "The Presbyterian Church of Oklahoma City." He told them Dr. Gibson was the pastor and that they were good friends.

The man then explained that because the Urschels' house was crawling with cops, they would need a go-between in order to make contact. He suggested using Gibson.

Urschel explained that it wouldn't work because Gibson was away on vacation.

"Your only chance of getting out of this is to give us somebody to write to," he said. "Somebody you trust who can get information to her without going through the cops. Someone not in Oklahoma City."

Urschel suggested a friend of his in Tulsa, a fellow oilman, John Catlett. That was agreeable. They marched him across the room and sat him down on a bench, and when Urschel's captor lifted his blindfold slightly so he could write, Urschel collected more details. He was handed a paper tablet and a black Eversharp pencil. The man's hand was large and covered with dark hair, as was his forearm. On his finger was a gold ring with a red stone, a ruby or an imitation of one, about one-and-a-half carats in size.

"I want you to face straight ahead into that wall, look down at the tablet and write. Try to look left or right to see where you are and that will be the last look you will ever have at anything, so be sure to enjoy it."

When he finished writing the letters as instructed, the man's partner took them and Urschel's wallet and left. The man with the ruby ring stayed behind and guarded Urschel until the evening of the next day, Wednesday, July 26. This was the same man who earlier had tried to intimidate him by threatening to chain him down and let wharf rats devour his bowels. But now the man had turned rather chummy and chatty. To pass the time, and perhaps to impress his captive, the man delivered his opinions on a host of subjects. Urschel was impressed with his knowledge about cars. Cadillac, he said, made the best large vehicles, the '33 Chevy Coupe was the best of the smaller cars. Ford didn't have a decent model in the entire line, but they'd be coming out with a car soon that would be "excellent."

He talked about his twenty-five-year history of crime. The banks he'd robbed, the ones he didn't. He gave his theories on how banks should be designed to prevent people like him and his ilk from robbing them so easily. He talked about gun battles he'd been in. Gun battles his friends had been in. He disparaged the Barrow brothers and their gang, describing them as nothing but a bunch of filling station and car thieves. "My bunch never monkeyed with any of that cheap stuff," he said. Neither, he said, did he steal cars. He seemed to take inordinate pride in the fact that he bought his own damned cars and had them customized to run better and faster by his mechanic buddies, who know a whole lot more about cars than any of those stuffy engineers in Detroit.

Sipping a Coca-Cola, he talked of once living next door to the man who invented "Orange Crush." The man had a younger wife who went bad. He was so heartbroken he killed himself. Tragic story.

He talked about his wild times in the liquor-running business, especially out of the great city of New Orleans. He told a story of how he once delivered a large order to a client in Tulsa that occurred in the middle of that city's notorious race riot, during which, over an eighteen-hour period, white lynch mobs who'd been deputized by the city's police force with orders to "get a gun and get a nigger," killed nearly 300 black Tulsa residents. They then burned down Tulsa's black neighborhood, leaving nearly ten thousand residents homeless for the winter.

Urschel's captor was indeed quite a character, and quite a talker. And Urschel was quite a listener. He banked all the details of the conversation in the hope that they would later prove useful.

On Wednesday morning, July 26, John G. Catlett received a package from Western Union. Inside were three letters. Catlett immediately opened the one addressed to him. A handwritten letter from Urschel was inside. It read:

Dear John,
    You undoubtedly know about my predicament. If Arthur Seeligson has returned, please deliver the enclosed letter to him, otherwise to Kirkpatrick. Deliver in person and do not communicate by telephone. Tell no one else about this letter, not even your wife, and when you deliver it do not go to the residence. Authorities must be kept off the case or release impossible and they cannot af-

fect rescue. For my sake, follow these instructions to the letter and do not discuss with anyone other than those mentioned. This is my final letter to any of my friends or family and if this contact is not successful I fear for my life. When in Oklahoma City, keep out of sight as much as possible because you probably will be used later on in this capacity. I am putting all my dependence in you regarding this matter and feel sure you will take every precaution possible.

Best regards as ever,
Your friend,
C. F. Urschel

Catlett, who'd been shaving at the time the package arrived, quickly cleaned his face and headed to Oklahoma City, where he arranged a secret meeting at a discreet hotel with Kirkpatrick, Seeligson and Berenice.

Kirkpatrick opened his letter.

Sir,
The enclosed letter from Charles F. Urschel to you and the enclosed identification cards will convince you that you are dealing with the abductors.

Immediately upon receipt of this letter you will proceed to obtain the sum of

TWO HUNDRED THOUSAND DOL-
LARS ($200,000) in GENUINE USED
FEDERAL RESERVE CURRENCY in
the denominations of TWENTY DOL-
LAR ($20.00) bills.

It will be useless for you to attempt
taking notes of SERIAL NUMBERS,
MAKING UP DUMMY PACKAGES
OR ANYTHING ELSE IN THE LINE
OF ATTEMPTED DOUBLE CROSS,
BEAR THIS IN MIND, CHARLES F.
URSCHEL, WILL REMAIN IN OUR
CUSTODY UNTIL MONEY HAS
BEEN INSPECTED AND EX-
CHANGED, AND FURTHERMORE
WILL BE AT THE SCENE OF CON-
TACT FOR PAY OFF AND IF THERE
SHOULD BE ANY ATTEMPT AT
DOUBLE XX IT WILL BE HE THAT
SUFFERS THE CONSEQUENCE.

As soon as you have read and RE-
READ this carefully, and wish to com-
mence negotiations, you will proceed to
the Daily Oklahoman and insert the following BLIND AD under the REAL
ESTATE, FARMS FOR SALE, and we
will know that you are ready for BUSI-
NESS, and you will receive further
instructions at THE BOX ASSIGNED
TO YOU BY THE NEWSPAPER, AND

NO WHERE ELSE SO BE CERTAIN THAT THIS ARRANGEMENT IS KEPT SECRET AS THIS IS OUR FINAL ATTEMPT TO COMMUNICATE WITH YOU, on account of our former instructions to JARRETT being DISREGARDED and the LAW being notified, so we have neither the time nor the patience to carry on any further lengthy correspondence. RUN THIS AD FOR ONE WEEK IN DAILY OKLAHOMAN.

FOR SALE — 160 acres land, good five room house, deep well. Also cows, tools, tractors, corn and hay. $3,750.00 for quick sale. TERMS — BOX NO. —.

You will hear from us as soon as convenient after insertion of AD.

At the same time that Catlett was receiving his special delivery, the U.S. Conference of State Executives was meeting in San Francisco and lamenting the spread of racketeering and kidnapping that plagued their cities.

They urged the Roosevelt administration to "pursue the prosecution of racketeers to the end that kidnapping and other kindred crimes be suppressed." Governor Fred Balzar of Nevada urged the President to create a national police force. His resolution declared that "organized crime has become a national menace, kidnaping, blackmail and robberies run wild, gang leaders have usurped the rule of law, racketeering strangles many lines of commerce."

Berenice was relieved that Charley was still alive. She recognized his identification cards, the handwriting on his letter to Catlett and the telegraphic style of its contents. Gazing up from the letter, she looked at the group and said, "I think we should get Gus."

When Jones arrived, Catlett filled him in on the events of the morning as he read the letters and Berenice vouched for the veracity of the identification cards and her husband's handwriting.

It had the look and feel of a professional operation. "There's no question about it. This is the gang that has him."

Berenice turned to Seeligson. "Arthur, please make arrangements for the money. Whatever you have to do to get it, do it."

Then she asked Catlett to place the ad.

Two days later, it had drawn a response. A letter, airmailed from Joplin, Missouri, landed in Box 807, addressed to Kirkpatrick.

Sir,

In view of the fact that you have had the ad inserted as per our instructions, we gather you are prepared to meet our ultimatum. You will pack TWO HUNDRED THOUSAND DOLLARS ($200,000.00) IN USED GENUINE FEDERAL RESERVE NOTES OF TWENTY DOLLARS DENOMINATION in a suitable light-colored leather bag, and have someone purchase transportation for you, including berth, aboard Train No. 28 (the Katy Sooner) which departs at 10:10 P.M., via M.K. &T lines for Kansas City, Missouri.

You will ride on the observation platform where you will be observed by someone at some station along the line between Oklahoma City and Kansas City, Missouri.

If indications are alright, somewhere along the right-of-way you will observe a fire on the right side of the track (facing direction train is bound). That fire will be your cue to be prepared to throw bag to track immediately after passing second fire.

Mr. Urschel will, upon instructions, attend to the fires and secure the bag when you throw it off, he will open it and transfer the contents to a sack that he will be provided with, so if you comply with our demands and do not attempt any subterfuge, as according to the news reports you have pledged, Mr. Urschel should be home in a short while. REMEMBER THIS, IF ANY TRICKERY IS ATTEMPTED YOU WILL FIND THE REMAINS OF UR-SCHEL AND INSTEAD OF JOY THERE WILL BE DOUBLE GRIEF — FOR SOMEONE, VERY NEAR AND DEAR TO THE URSCHELS IS UNDER CONSTANT SURVEIL-LANCE AND WILL LIKEWISE SUF-FER FOR YOUR ERROR.

If there is the slightest hitch in these plans for any reason whatsoever, not your fault, you will proceed on into Kansas City, Missouri, and register at the Muehlbach Hotel under the name of E. E. Kincaid of Little Rock, Arkansas, and await further instructions there, however there should not be, IF YOU COMPLY WITH THESE SIMPLE DI-RECTIONS.

THE MAIN THING IS; DO NOT DIVULGE THE CONTENTS OF THIS LETTER TO ANY LAW AU-THORITIES FOR WE HAVE NO IN-

TENTION OF FURTHER COMMU-
NICATION. YOU ARE TO MAKE
THIS TRIP SATURDAY, JULY 29; BE
SURE YOU RIDE THE PLATFORM
OF THE REAR CAR AND HAVE BAG
WITH MONEY IN IT FROM THE
TIME YOU LEAVE OKLAHOMA
CITY.

The letter did nothing to shake Jones's faith that they were now dealing with the real kidnappers. He noted the additional threat to harm another member of the Urschel family if things didn't come off as dictated. He'd check with Berenice to make sure there was nobody else he should know about that wasn't already under the Bureau's watchful eye. He noted also the grammar and punctuation. Awfully precise. He was not used to words like "subterfuge" and "ultimatum" in the vocabulary of the illiterate psychopaths he was accustomed to dealing with.

The crank calls and phony tips kept coming in, but Jones advised Berenice to keep dealing with each in the same manner she had in the past. So, fighting her instincts to lash out at the con men and criminals who were trying to exploit her situation and further burden her with what she now knew were empty threats and criminal schemes, she kept up a good front.

Jones was still worried about details leaking out. There were now reporters from all over the world poking around the city trying to turn up any lead. The circle of people with details of the kidnapping was tight and small, but it was growing. Arthur Seeligson was racing around to local banks trying to come up with enough used $20 bills to make the ransom. Collecting ten thousand $20 bills? That would certainly arouse suspicion. Kirkpatrick would be buying train tickets and leaving town. If reporters were tailing him, they'd certainly wonder why. One errant phone call on a party line and god knows what kind of headlines might be made.

Jones suggested a ruse to Berenice. Call a press conference. Tell the gentlemen of the press that you fear their presence in the neighborhood is making it difficult for the kidnappers to make contact. Ask them to please leave. They might actually cooperate, but even if they don't it will make a story and send a message to the kidnappers.

Seeligson called a press conference and delivered the request. He told the reporters that the family feared that the kidnappers would make no contact as long as there was so much activity around the house.

"We believe," he said, "that no contact will be attempted through any medium as long as it is known the house is under observation.

"We are not attempting to suppress anything. Our whole desire in asking the removal of the press being to hasten the safe return of Mr. Urschel. Our cooperation with police, the sheriff's office and the government forces has been such that we hope to have the same cooperation with the press."

He told the reporters he believed the kidnappers would lie low for at least a week before attempting to contact them. "We have no basis, as nothing has been received, for believing we will not hear something before then, but everyone now is resigned to waiting several more days."

He said it was his belief that having anyone around the house except members of the family would not "suit the convenience" of the kidnappers. That, he said, "was one of the driving motives in our request that the press as well as representatives of law enforcement agencies be withdrawn."

It worked. The press horde began to disassemble almost immediately. Some, who had been stationed in tents with telephone hookups, established, packed up and moved out. A radio reporter offered the use of his station in the event Mrs. Urschel wanted to send a broadcast message out seeking contact from the kidnappers and asking that her husband not be harmed.

And, as Jones predicted, it gave everybody something to write about that the kidnappers would be certain to read. The press conference was the lead story in the next day's *Daily Oklahoman* under the headline:

WAY CLEARED AS KIDNAPERS STAY IN DARK

Oklahoman Staff Quits Watch over Mansion to Aid Urschels

Next, Jones wanted to know if Kirkpatrick was up for the job of delivering the ransom.

"Put me in any group of eight people," said Kirkpatrick, "and I will give you odds that seven of them will be braver than I. But these ransom notes were addressed to me and that makes it a personal affair between them and me. I've got to be the man who delivers the money. If anybody else did it and got hurt, I'd never forgive myself."

Kirkpatrick was putting on a brave front. In fact, the prospects terrified him. He was well aware that traveling to Kansas City meant that he'd be walking into the gang capital of the Midwest and that whoever he would be giving the money to would have not only Johnny Lazia's permission, but also his protection. If Lazia knew that some unarmed out-of-towner was walking into Kansas City with $200,000 cash, other people would know, as well. Would some rival try to steal the cash before he could make the delivery? Life was cheap in Kansas City. The going price for a murder-for-hire was less than $500. Even if he successfully made the drop, the safest thing for Charley's kidnapper to do would be to hire someone to bump him off later. Eliminating eyewitnesses was a common practice in the underworld.

He resigned himself to the fact that he most likely would never return from Kansas City. He wrote a good-bye letter to his wife with instructions to deliver it to her if he hadn't returned by Tuesday.

6
THE DELIVERY

With the members of the press decamped, the Urschel neighborhood was eerily silent as darkness fell on Saturday night. Kirkpatrick, the Seeligsons and a deputy sheriff armed with shotguns hid in the bushes and shrubs in the mansion's backyard along the driveway. From an upstairs bedroom window, Berenice peered down at the scene below, awaiting delivery of $200,000 ($3.6 million in contemporary value) in used $20 bills from the First National Bank of Oklahoma City. It was a staggering amount of money. More cash than even a woman of her means had ever seen collected in one place. Arthur Seeligson had gone to herculean efforts to raise it and catalog it. It was now being transported secretly across town by bank employees without the benefit of a police escort or any real protection. If the car was hijacked or the money stolen along the way, it was doubtful she'd be able to secure an equal amount in time to save her husband's life. No one had ever agreed to pay so high a ransom, and she knew Charley would be embarrassed that she had.

She nervously scanned the street behind the house, and when the designated car surreptitiously appeared, she flashed a light indicating it was safe to proceed. The car pulled into the drive and a banker from the car stepped out, walked toward the shrubs, handed the bag to Kirkpatrick, turned and left.

Kirk brought it inside and opened it for Berenice. After checking the contents and double counting the amount, Kirkpatrick took it and a second bag with cut-up newspapers in the same shape and weight as the money bag to the Oklahoma City train station. There he was joined by Catlett, and the two walked to their reserved seats in the observation car of the Katy Limited due to depart for Kansas City at 10:10 p.m. But already there was a complication in the plans. Two extra cars had been added to the train to accommodate tourists bound for the World's Fair in Chicago. The Chicago-bound passengers would have to change trains in Kansas City. Because the train was traveling at night and there was nothing to see anyway, the railroad men had added the extra cars behind the observation car, which normally would be the last car.

As an expensive diversion to the wearying Depression, the World's Fair in Chicago was proving to be a remarkable success. Attendees were flocking there from all over the country and the world. With the theme "A Century of Progress," it celebrated the city's astonishing growth and accomplishments from the time it was incorporated as a village in 1833 with a population of fewer than 400 people to its status in 1933 as the fourth-largest city in the world, eclipsed only by New York, London and Tokyo. It was the transportation center of the nation, with the world's largest rail hub and shipping access to the Great Lakes and the Mississippi River. It was the most technologically advanced city in the nation and a gleaming example of the beauty of modern architecture. But it was also famous for its colorful gangsters, wild nightlife and criminality of all degrees. That, too, was attracting throngs to the fair.

Kirkpatrick and Catlett moved anxiously to the end of the train and outside, onto the cramped exposed vestibule of the last car, hoping to use it as a substitute and also hoping that the spotters would see them there and not think something fishy was going on.

"Do you think this will foul up their plan, Kirk?"

"I wish I knew," he replied, explaining that he planned to stay outside, under the signal light, so he could be seen by the kidnappers or their lookouts and try to spot the fire as the train rolled on.

When the train left the station, a porter came back and said no one was allowed to ride outside.

"My friend and I just want to do a bit of quiet, social drinking," Kirkpatrick responded, slipping a few dollar bills into the porter's palm. "Think you can forget we're out here?"

"Sure can," he said, heading back into the car. A short time later he brought two stools for them to sit on. The two sat, talking, chain-smoking and staring off the right side of the train, checking for the signal fire.

When they approached a town or a station, Catlett would slip inside the car to be out of sight and Kirkpatrick would stand under the light, cigarette ablaze, hoping to make himself visible to anyone who might be checking for his presence.

They passed through the little burgs of Arcadia, Luther, Fallis, Carney and Tryon and into the lands where Tom Slick made his first fortune: the Cushing oil fields. Kirkpatrick, a former newspaper reporter and student of history, reflected on his good fortune in joining up with the great Tom Slick, even though it had led him to this dreadful predicament, in which he was convinced he would soon meet his death by assassination.

As they crossed the Cimarron River, Kirk pondered the ironic circumstance he found himself in, entering the territory of the notorious Western outlaws of the recent past.

The Missouri-Kansas-Texas Railroad, the M-K-T (later shortened in the popular vernacular to "Katy," after its stock symbol, *K-T*), was the first to penetrate into Texas after the Civil War and now stretched from Houston to Kansas City and St. Louis. The Katy was a popular target for train-robbing outlaws Jesse James, the Daltons and the Al Spencer gang.

Kirkpatrick considered the legendary train robbers respectable professionals — "gentlemanly miscreants," he called them. Nothing like the loathsome scum in the current-day Snatch Racket.

Under the clear night sky alive with a thousand stars, Kirkpatrick and Catlett passed the time making small talk about hunting and fishing. Catlett was a crack shot with a hunting rifle. He was one of the Urschel team that knew his way around tough situations — and how a quickly drawn sidearm and a well-placed round could get you out of them. Kirkpatrick was glad to have him around; he added immensely to his comfort level. Something of the poet, Kirkpatrick mused about the Indian burial grounds the train was cutting through and how they were once punctuated with tribal signal fires, hoping he'd see his own critical signal fire light up the night. But it never did.

As they headed into the Osage Hills — current-day gangland hideout territory — their hopes were raised. Surely this was the most likely spot for the kidnappers to signal the train. But as they passed through Bartellesville, Dewey and Coffeyville there was nothing.

The sun began to rise and Kirk began to believe they'd been played. The grimy soot from the engine exhaust was caking on his face and the dust clung to his suit. He was well into his third pack of cigarettes and god knows how much coffee. He was tired and panicky. If they'd lied to them here, would they do it again? Would he be snatched along with the ransom and held by the kidnappers as protection against any lawmen who might be in pursuit?

The train was approaching Union Station in Kansas City, where just a month earlier, four lawmen and their prisoner, Frank Nash, had died in a fusillade of machine-gun fire.

Were he and Catlett walking into a similar trap?

They disembarked and headed warily across the platform, through the great hall and waiting room and out onto the plaza, virtually the same path taken by the federal agents as they marched Nash to the car in which he would die.

But today would go without incident. They grabbed a cab to the Muehlebach Hotel, a beautiful, twelve-story luxury spot favored by presidents dating back to Teddy Roosevelt. Babe Ruth had been a recent guest, as had most of the notorious gangsters and playboys of the '20s, who flocked to the city to enjoy the burgeoning jazz and blues clubs, along with the more scandalous delights the city offered. Kirkpatrick registered under the assigned alias of E. E. Kincaid, as instructed. Catlett registered in another room, but joined Kirkpatrick in his suite. The two played cards to pass the time as they awaited further instructions.

Shortly after 10:00 a.m., Kirkpatrick's phone rang and a bellman announced the arrival of a telegram. He would bring it right up.

It was from Tulsa, addressed to E. E. Kincaid. It read:

UNAVOIDABLE INCIDENT KEPT ME FROM SEE YOU LAST NIGHT. WILL COMMUNICATE ABOUT 6:00 O'CLOCK.

E. W. MOORE

The two repaired to the lobby café for breakfast, coffee and more cigarettes. They hadn't slept all night, and when Kirkpatrick returned to his room, he still couldn't. He lay in bed and worried about Charley's fate. He worried about his own fate. He wondered whether it had been a bad idea to bring Catlett along. The man had kept him reasonably sane and calm, but had he spooked the kidnappers? How was Berenice holding up? His mind raced as Sunday morning church bells rang out and the classical strains of Schubert and Mendelssohn wafted through the halls from the Muehlebach's pianist playing in the lobby.

At 5:45 p.m., he picked up the ringing phone.

"Who's talking?" demanded the voice on the other end.

"Kincaid."

"This is Moore. Did you get my wire?"

"Yes."

"Well, are you ready to close the deal?"

"I should be, if I knew that I was dealing with the right parties."

"You ought to know by now," came the reply. "Listen now, follow these instructions. Take a Yellow Cab, drive to the LaSalle Hotel, get out, take the suitcase in your right hand and start walking west."

Catlett was standing across from him, gesturing and silently mouthing a request to ask if he could come along.

"I have a friend who came up here with me. May I bring him along?"

"Hell, no! We know all about your friend, we saw him on the train last night. You come alone and unarmed."

"I'll be there at 6:20."

When Kirkpatrick hung up, Catlett insisted he go with him, but Kirkpatrick wouldn't have it.

"It might be a fatal error."

Similarly, he waved Catlett off when he offered to go in his place. He stuck a .380

Colt automatic in his belt, slipped on his suit coat, grabbed the Gladstone bag with the money and was off.

When he stepped from the cab onto Linwood Boulevard, he tried to look casual and nonchalant. Lighting a cigarette, he tipped his head back to exhale and scan the street. Two large cars were parked across the street with three men in each. From the corner of his eye he saw another with the window down and what looked like a shotgun barrel resting on the doorframe.

Walking toward him was a tall, stylishly dressed man in a fashionable summer suit wearing a turned-down Panama hat. He wore two-tone shoes and a two-toned shirt with a perfectly knotted tie. He approached Kirkpatrick on his right.

"I'll take that grip," he said looking past Kirkpatrick to see if the fool had brought his buddy along or some federal Cub Scout for protection.

Kirkpatrick hesitated.

"Hurry up!"

"How do I know you are the right party?" he asked, trying to stall.

"Hell, you know damned well I am."

"Two hundred thousand dollars is a lot of money. We are carrying out our part of the agreement to the letter. What assurance have we that you'll do what you promise?"

"Don't argue with me."

"Tell me when we can expect Urschel home. I am going back to the hotel to telephone his wife. What shall I tell her? Tell me definitely what I can tell Mrs. Urschel."

"Urschel will be home in twelve hours. Now you turn and walk to the LaSalle Hotel and don't look back."

Kirkpatrick, his mind racing with second thoughts, doubts and worries, did just that. He had just handed over the largest ransom in American history and now he was walking away without Charley or his money. He lacked the nerve to turn and see what scene was unfolding behind him. He'd rather just get shot in the back and not see it coming. When a car door slammed and the cover cars sped away, throwing dust and gravel as they made furious U-turns, he almost collapsed with relief. He had to steady his shaking hand to light a cigarette. At the La-Salle, he grabbed a cab to the Muehlebach. After relating the events to Catlett, he called Berenice.

"I closed the deal for that farm," he said. "I will require about twelve hours for the lawyers to examine the abstracts, then the title will pass."

"Thanks," she said, and hung up.

Catlett and Kirkpatrick checked out and headed back to Union Station. Catlett was bound for Tulsa, and Kirk would get back on the Katy Limited to Oklahoma City for what he prayed would be a jubilant homecoming.

But when he arrived on Monday morning and made his way to Nineteenth Street, his heart sank. The press horde had returned and renewed their vigilant stakeout. Clearly, they had not been reporting about Charley's safe return.

Berenice met him at the door.

"Charley's not here," is all she said. The mood inside the home had turned positively funereal.

Kirkpatrick tried to put a good spin on it. "The kidnappers probably want to wait until after dark, and besides, they may have held Charley a long way away. He'll probably show up after dark."

Gus Jones began grilling Kirkpatrick for details, descriptions, observations — anything he could put into his notes to make the prosecution stick.

After an hour or so, he'd gotten all he could. Kirkpatrick asked him, "What do you think? Will they release him?"

Jones shook his head and lamented that it wasn't very likely, especially if the kidnappers thought Charley could identify the hideout. If so, he said, "he doesn't stand a chance. They told you he'd be home within twelve hours. He isn't. Their letter said they were going to hold him until all the money had been examined and exchanged. That could take weeks. The longer they hold him, the more dangerous it becomes for him. Dozens of things could happen that might make it seem necessary to kill him and get him off their hands."

"Then you don't think he'll make it back?"

"No, I won't say that. But I will say that if he's not back by sunup tomorrow, he won't be back."

Kirkpatrick's heart sank. He headed back to the living room and did his best to keep a game face on as the hours dragged by. It had been raining for most of the day and, as the afternoon slipped into the evening, it continued, adding a pall to the house. The phone had stopped ringing. The occupants could think of nothing else to say, and the gloomy silence began to deafen.

In an attempt to lighten the mood, Kirkpatrick decided to do a little extermination work. There had been a mouse running around on Charley's expensive carpets, and he would have hated that. He decided he'd make a great show of bringing the rodent to justice and grabbed a mousetrap from the kitchen, baited it and brought it to the sunroom to slip under the divan. As he did, it snapped, scaring the bejesus out of the already jangled Kirkpatrick, who screamed an obscenity as he jerked back, flinging the trap skyward. As it flew through the air, the group shrieked and broke into a round of uncontrolled, spontaneous laughter — including Berenice, who hadn't smiled in more than a week. She made a few wicked remarks at Kirkpatrick's expense and decided it was the appropriate moment to head off to bed.

Back in Paradise, Kathryn was also fretting about the return of her husband. He should have collected the ransom and been home by now. She'd stayed behind to make sure Urschel stayed in place and nobody stumbled across him. She didn't trust Mother and Boss with that job, and certainly that nitwit Potatoes could not be left to do any thinking on his own.

She ground out yet another cigarette in the ashtray that contained dozens and looked up angrily at Boss.

"Where the hell are they?" she demanded. "I should have gone up there with them, and I would have, too, if I could have trusted you to take care of things on this end."

"Take it easy, Kat. They'll be here."

Bates and Kelly had been delayed by a persistent rainfall nearly all the way from Kansas City back to Texas. After years with virtually no rain at all, the kidnappers were being confounded by inextricable downpours at the most inopportune moments. With rain slowing their escape, they rerouted further and further off course and onto muddy back roads to avoid detection.

When they finally rolled in at about 2:00 p.m. on Monday, Kelly parked the car, Bates grabbed the Gladstone bag and they sprinted through the rain to the front porch, where Kathryn greeted them.

"Did you get the money?"

"Every nickel, baby. Every nickel," he said, grabbing her around the waist and scooping her up. "We pulled it off, Kit! Two hundred thousand bucks, baby."

"It was the smoothest deal we've ever made," he said. "Kirkpatrick was scared half out of his skin. He only hesitated a second before handing over the money."

In the house, they dumped the loot on the chenille bedspread in Kathryn's room.

Two hundred neatly bound packets of $20 bills, each about four inches thick. They'd done it. Pulled off the most successful kidnapping in modern history. There it was, just lying on the bedspread, a fortune in used $20 bills. A small fortune, sure. But enough money to live like kings down in Juarez. No more small-time bank jobs, no more petty bribes to greedy cops. Kathryn swooned.

"Oh, George!" she sighed. "Think of the fun we're going to have with this!"

She picked up one of the $20 bills and kissed it. "This one is for Kit's new shoes. Mama needs a new pair of shoes, baby." Mimicking her, Bates picked up a twenty and kissed it. "I know a mama who needs a few things too."

Bates began scooping the packs up and started restacking them.

"I don't like them just laying out like this." He wanted to divvy things up and get back on the road, away from the hot farm.

"Suits me, Al," said Kelly. "I have a nut to come off the top. It'll cover that Buick we had to get rid of and the money I laid out for the Kansas City boys to cover us during the ransom delivery. Comes to $11,500."

"Overhead, overhead," Bates replied. "Still leaves $188,500 to cut two ways, right?"

"I'll take care of Boss from my end and Boss can take care of Armon," said Kelly.

"Then I know what Armon will get," quipped Kathryn. "The experience!"

The two men took $94,250 each and flipped a coin to see who got to keep the handsome leather Gladstone bag.

Kathryn brought the levity back down to earth.

"Who is going to take care of Urschel?"

Kelly was incredulous. "What do you mean take care of him?"

"This guy is like a time bomb," she argued. "If he walks out of here he'll squawk his head off!"

"Yeah, I agree," said Bates. "Let's get it over with and hit the road."

"You must be out of your minds. Look, we just went into business. Let's not louse ourselves up with a killing we don't even need." Kelly was adamant. "What can he possibly say? He hasn't seen any more of our faces than those idiots back in Oklahoma City, and look at the miserable descriptions they gave. He could never lead anybody back here. He doesn't even know what state he is in.

"But buy yourself a murder rap against a guy with this sort of loot, and his family can hire the whole U.S. Marine Corps to come looking for us. The law will keep coming and coming and coming. They'll never stop."

"If you haven't got the guts, I'll do it myself," said Bates.

"If this were the only job we had set up, I'd say fine," said Kelly. "But don't let's forget those four sitting ducks we've got lined up on the pond in Oklahoma City. What about them? Now, what happens if we kill Urschel after his family has laid out the loot? How much do you think those families are going to pay off when they know what happened to Urschel? In order to operate, we're going to have to let Urschel go," he declared. "What the hell? It's just good business."

"When the hell did you get so noble?" wondered Kathryn.

Bates acquiesced. No reason to take any unnecessary chances. He wanted his cut and he wanted to get the hell out.

They drove out to Armon's shack and told Urschel it was time to get cleaned up. They were taking him home. They walked him to a bench in the corner and sat him down and told him they wanted him to shave, but to do so without looking around. If they thought he was trying to identify them, or the location, they'd have to kill him. They removed the tape and gauze from his face and red light streamed in through his still-closed eyelids, which he was having trouble opening.

While he struggled, he began depositing fingerprints on everything within reach: the handle of the straightedge razor they wanted him to use, the water basin, the cracked hand mirror.

He squinted through his tearing, cloudy eyes at the dirty mirror and tried to run the blade over his beard. He hadn't shaved in nine days and he couldn't see what he was doing. He'd end up with a face full of nicks and cuts. He asked if he could keep his whiskers. But they wouldn't have it. They wanted him looking as inconspicuous as possible. After retaping his eyes closed, they gave him a clean, short-sleeved sport shirt and a straw hat that didn't fit too well.

Kelly poked him in the stomach with the barrel of a gun and twisted it maliciously. "Feel that?" he said. "That's a sawed-off shotgun. Have you ever seen what one of these can do to a man's face? If you give one bit of information to the cops, neither you, nor your wife, nor any of your kids will ever know when there may not be one of these waiting for you around the next corner or through the next door. And don't imagine the cops can protect you twenty-four hours a day for the rest of your lives. We'll get to you eventually. Each one of you."

They walked Urschel to the car (he silently counted the steps along the way) and loaded him in. Boss Shannon came by, shook his hand and said he hoped he wouldn't have any more trouble.

They put sunglasses over his taped eyes to conceal them and then drove circuitously for about eight hours. Toward the end of the journey, they crossed an old bridge, and the tires thumped along with a distinctive sound. Charley smiled inwardly with amused satisfaction. He knew exactly where they were. They were crossing the Canadian River on the old Purcell-Lexington bridge not far from one of his rural farms, which he used frequently for hunting trips with his buddies.

When they stopped the car a short time later, he knew he could not be far from Norman, a short twenty miles from Oklahoma City. Kelly then explained the situation to him. He asked Charley if he thought he could get home on his own without revealing his identity to anyone along the way. If so, they would turn him loose untethered. If not, they would chain him to a tree and phone in his location to the cops in the morning.

Urschel assured them he could find his way home without assistance.

Kelly gave him back his watch, wallet and ten dollars for cab fare. Then he helped him out of the car, explaining one last time that if he revealed anything about where he'd been held, or what had happened there, or any details of his captivity whatsoever, he and his entire family would be killed.

That, said Kelly, was a promise. "Wait until we leave to take off that blindfold, and don't call anyone but the taxicab."

Once they were gone, Urschel gingerly peeled the adhesive tape off the raw, blistered skin around his eyelids and stood, covering them with his hands as he tried to adjust to the light streaming in.

It was raining and he was exhausted from the ordeal and the eight-hour drive that had ended it, but he began marching off toward Norman in the direction his internal compass dictated on stiff legs and an empty stomach.

When he reached the fringes of the university town, he went into a nearly deserted roadside barbecue, ordered a cup of coffee and asked the guy running the shack to call him a cab. On the way to Oklahoma City, he made small talk with the driver and asked to be dropped off short of his neighborhood. He didn't want the cabbie to realize who his passenger was and go selling his story to the paper and spooking the kidnappers down South.

He walked right through the press pool that had reassembled around the house without being recognized or arousing curiosity, in part because he looked so unlike himself: unkempt, poorly dressed and soaking wet. The guard at the front door didn't even recognize him and shooed him away like some vagrant. He walked around the corner to the back door where, again, he was unrecognizable to the guard. But inside he spotted Arthur Seeligson and called out to him. Arthur let out an exalted yell upon recognizing his friend and business partner, and the house suddenly came alive. Berenice ran into his arms and the two hugged silently as Charley smiled with satisfaction.

Once the Bureau's agents found out Urschel was back, they called Jones, and within a few minutes he was at the house. Jones began priming Urschel for details, but Charley begged off. He was exhausted and near collapse. He wanted some sleep before debriefing Jones. But Jones pressed him.

"Time is the very essence of the successful solution of any kidnapping," he said. Anything he could learn now would give them a head start. Charley complied, but the man who had endured nine days of captivity never losing his control or his determination was beginning to unravel. He paced back and forth in the room, trying to stay awake. He said he hadn't slept more than ten hours since his abduction, and then only fitfully.

"They told me that if I ever told anything they would get me and torture me, would kill and maim members of my family, that they were more powerful than the federal government. But having suffered the torture of the damned, I don't want anyone to have to go through with that to which I have been subjected. I'll tell you all I know, only let me make it brief tonight. I am so tired."

For the next thirty minutes, he filled Jones in on the various threats that had been made about killing him and his family. He lamented that finding the farm where he'd been held would be like finding a needle in a haystack. Berenice was alarmed at Charley's condition and his rambling. She'd never seen him like that, and she carped at Jones, finally calling a halt to the grilling. Jones acquiesced. Charley agreed to start again first thing in the morning.

Arthur Seeligson phoned the city desk of *The Daily Oklahoman.* "Mr. Urschel is home," he reported. The city editor fired back questions. Is he all right? Was he harmed? Was a ransom paid?

"Mr. Urschel is home," he repeated. "That is all we have to say tonight. We will meet the press at 8 o'clock Tuesday morning and give out a statement. I can say nothing more tonight."

The desperate editor was insistent. He had a scoop on the biggest story going, but he needed more details to hang on it. What condition is he in? Was he roughed up? How did he get home? Was he alone when he got there?

Jones wanted no information given out. And he wasn't happy Seeligson had announced an 8 o'clock press conference. Jones had wanted Urschel all to himself the next morning, and now he'd have to deal with this major interruption.

"Mr. Urschel is in good health," said Seeligson into the phone. "Of course, he's been under a great strain and he is very tired. He is going to bed immediately."

"Where was he held?"

"Mr. Urschel does not know where he was held."

"Where was he released?"

"I can't say anything about that now. We will have a statement in the morning."

"How did he get home?"

"He was in a rented car," Seeligson lied.

"How long was the drive?"

"About two hours."

Jones wanted the call to end. Seeligson was beginning to spill too many details for Jones's comfort. He desperately wanted him to hang up.

"Was the ransom paid?"

"I can't answer that question now," replied the exasperated Seeligson. "Please don't ask me for further details. Your newspaper has been very fair and has cooperated with us throughout. We promised to tell you when Mr. Urschel was returned. That's all we can say tonight."

With that, he hung up. Then he removed the handset from its cradle so the son of a bitch couldn't ring him back.

After a good night's sleep in his own bed, Charley was his old self. He sat down with Jones and his men and went over the scenario for the press conference: what he could say, and how he should say it.

Keep it short and sweet, Jones advised. He had a lot of questions of his own and he wanted to get to them as soon as possible. There was no percentage in giving the kidnappers any more time than necessary.

Anything you say to them can blow up on

you like a prairie fire. You've got to talk to them. You've got to give them something. They need to file reports to their demanding editors, who don't really give a damn about you or your family. They need copy and they need it fast. Faster than their competitors, and now their competitors are carrying microphones and whatever you say will be broadcast into the nation's living rooms, just like it was a fireside chat from the President. You've got to talk. You've got to charm them. But most of all you can't give them anything that will give the kidnappers any clue about what you've told us, or even the fact that you have been talking to us.

Charley was an inveterate newspaper reader, but he was not fond of the press. Their incessant reporting on his maneuvers in the oil business had cost him money. After Tom died, their obsession with his estate and how and where it would be probated was a public embarrassment and a legal annoyance. The speculation over his own wealth once it had been combined with Berenice's is what he was convinced had drawn the kidnappers' attention to him in the first place. Tom Slick had hated publicity of any kind, and so did Charley. But now it had come to him and he'd have to deflect it as best he could — lest he bring some new horror down on himself and his family.

Shortly, it would be showtime. The man who had shunned the spotlight his entire career went upstairs to get suited up and to prepare his performance.

When he returned, he could not have appeared more unlike the wasted soul who had wandered up to his own front door, unrecognized, the night before.

He wore a neatly pressed, short-sleeved shirt and tie, casual slacks and black-and-white oxfords. Trim and tall at six feet, he could have been modeling for a fashion magazine except for the fact the skin around his eyes was still a blistered red, making him appear like some oddly colored raccoon.

The family had invited a select pool of reporters and photographers from the local papers and wire services onto the sunporch where the abduction had occurred — the scene of the crime.

It turned out to be a perfectly choreographed press conference, with Charles dancing around the questions: "Where did they take you? How many of them were there? What did they tell you? Did you see their faces?"

He tried to speak in code to the kidnappers.

"I have not a shred of information which would aid officers; I saw the light of day only twice," he announced. "I was handcuffed and my eyes taped from the moment I left until they let me out. I think the house they held me in was probably a backwoods bungalow. It seemed to be of three rooms. The two men who took me seemed to alternate in guarding me. They talked very little, although they were friendly."

He joked and charmed them.

"They didn't like the newspaper pictures," he quipped. "They said I was a better looking man than the pictures."

He and Berenice then posed for some pictures and the whole thing ended as the press corps raced off to file their stories and move their pictures.

Charles went back inside and sat down with Jones and his agents to begin his second interview, the one in which he would reveal details — every one of the thousands he had catalogued in his memory over the past ten days.

"It seems to me like searching for a needle in a haystack," he said at the beginning of the interview.

"You know," said Jones, "we found one of those things one time. You can't tell. We might find another."

He began by recounting the events of the night of the kidnapping that twinned up perfectly with Jarrett's account.

"We drove on dirt roads most of the time. They told me that I was not to see or hear anything on the trip and that if I did I would never come home, for they would kill me. They had some chains in the car and they informed me that if I made any outcry or demonstration, they were prepared to give me a hypodermic injection, which would put me to sleep for twenty-four hours."

After daylight on Sunday morning they drove to a farmhouse to change cars, he said. They continued driving until pulling into another garage. "I asked what time it was, and they said about 2:30 in the afternoon, and that we had driven some 350 miles in a direct line. They kept me in the garage until after dark, then took me into a house. I did not sleep any that night."

On Monday morning they read him the headlines describing his kidnapping. They told him that since his family had called in the feds, negotiations would be hard.

He told of the farm they brought him to; its approximate size, what type and how many animals it contained. He described the distance from the main house to the shack in which he was held. The distance from the driveway to the door. The single step it took to enter.

He described Boss and Potatoes in almost-affectionate detail. One of his kidnappers, the bigger of the two, was dark complexioned, with hairy arms and hands. On his right ring finger was a gold ring with a large red stone.

He told them that the well squeaked and the water had a metallic taste. He gave them the approximate size of the shack and described the furniture and where it was placed. He told them where he stuck his fingerprints.

He said a farm nearby was growing broomcorn. Highly unusual. Perhaps you could spot it from the air. He told them about the local prostitute that he'd heard being discussed and the nickname of the postman who delivered the mail.

The agents were mesmerized by the scope and detail of the facts he was recounting. Never in their careers had they deposed a witness or victim with this type of memory and recall. They wrote furiously in their notebooks, with little time to break in for a question.

Then, like a maestro leading up to his crescendo, he announced the most telling detail of all.

"Every morning at 9:45 a twin engine plane passed over the farm, and every afternoon it returned at 5:45 traveling in the opposite direction."

Then he corrected himself. Sunday, it was raining. The plane did not pass over the farm that day.

They talked for more than six hours. When the interview concluded, Jones looked up at his men and announced that the haystack had just gotten a lot smaller. He began dispatching his agents to follow up on the various leads they had deduced from Urschel's recounting.

He sent agents to the U.S. Weather Bureau to see if they could find a county, region or whatever matched the exacting descriptions that Urschel had recounted. He sent others to check the flight records of anything and everything that was flying in the Oklahoma City/Dallas corridor. He sent others to check into the broomcorn lead. Who was anticipating a crop? Who had put seeds in the ground? Who sold broomcorn seed and who did they sell it to? Urschel was certain he had crossed the Purcell-Lexington Bridge coming over the Canadian River on his roughly two-hour journey home. Jones instructed his agents to look south of there.

Jones sat with Urschel and sketched a map

of the farm as close to scale as possible. It seemed almost laughable at the time. A man who had been blinded, starved and terrified trying to draw an aerial view of a farm he'd never seen. But his recall was incredible. Jones only hoped it was accurate.

(It would turn out that there had been a sympathetic lawman who had visited the farm and knew exactly where it was. Ed Weatherford, the Fort Worth detective who'd been wooed by Kathryn Kelly, had driven down to watch Kelly's father-in-law's farm for a few days to satisfy his suspicions that something untoward was going on there. But, other than a beautiful eighteen-cylinder Cadillac parked there briefly, he had seen nothing to engender a call to the Bureau's agents.)

The agents that had been dispatched to check out the airline schedules and routes quickly turned up a connection. An American Airways flight log showed that a storm on Sunday had forced a pilot to delay takeoff of his Dallas/Fort Worth/Wichita Falls/Amarillo morning passenger flight for twenty minutes. He had made a wide detour to avoid turbulence. The weather, also bad on his return flight, again dictated he use an alternate course.

With that information in hand, Urschel

offered to borrow a plane from one of his friendly competitors. They could retrace the American Airways flight path from a lower altitude and see if they could spot the farm from the air.

It didn't take long until they were focused on Wise County, Texas, and the farms around the oxymoronically named town of Paradise. From the air they spotted a locale that matched Jones's drawing.

Jones sent agent Edward Dowd in under the guise of a banker offering to refinance farm mortgages under more favorable terms. The agent found himself on a farm that matched Urschel's description to the letter and the map in his pocket almost to the inch.

He talked with Boss Shannon as he made mental notes on the farm and its makeup. Boss mentioned that he had a smaller farm just a short piece down the road, run by his son. Dowd said he'd like to see it. Once he got to Armon's place, he chatted up the teenager and feigned thirst. Armon drew water up from the well. The pulley squeaked horribly and the water had a disgusting mineral taste. The agent wondered where a lonely guy might find some female companionship in the area.

Armon said there was a sixteen-year-old

hooker not a stone's throw away and he'd be happy to put him in touch. Bingo. The animals and their various counts also matched Urschel's description.

Dowd took out his handkerchief and mopped his brow, complaining that the sun was killing him. Could he take a look inside and get out of the blistering heat for a minute or two?

Once inside, Dowd cased the room. He saw the iron bed and the high chair to which Urschel had been chained. He saw a long wooden bench and the cracked mirror Urschel had used to shave. He checked the floorboards. They ran east to west, just as Urschel had described. There was no doubt in his mind. This is where the kidnapping victim had been held.

Dowd nonchalantly finished up his conversation with Armon and casually headed back out of the farm. Once out and enough distance away that he would not arouse suspicion, he raced straight to the first pay phone he could find and filled Jones in on what he'd found. Jones immediately called Hoover and gave him the good news.

Hoover told Jones to move in and move fast. Use whatever force necessary, but try to take them alive. Hoover wanted a big, showy trial to put his handiwork on display for the nation to admire, and he couldn't do it if everyone ended up dead. Jones understood and set to planning the assault.

Dowd had not noticed any fortifications at the Shannon farm, and its occupants appeared rather nonthreatening. Boss was wily, but old and rather frail. Armon, the simpleton, seemed harmless. Still, their place had been used to hide the nation's most famous kidnapping victim and was as notorious as a safe house for bootleggers and bank robbers. Who knows what, or who, they would find there on their return. The little digging that they'd had time to do confirmed the fact that there had been a lot of traffic in and out of the farm by big, fancy cars not usually found in rural Texas. Shannon had a somewhat nefarious reputation, but had never been associated with anything felonious or violent. His stepdaughter, however, was married to the man whose name was on the list of suspects wanted in connection with the massacre at Union Station in Kansas City, George Machine Gun Kelly.

Jones needed to assemble a raiding party fast, and he wanted it to be big and well-armed. He brought in two legendary Bureau agents, James "Doc" White and Charles Winstead, both former Texas lawmen who were known for their skills with a variety of weapons. (A year later, it would be Winstead's bullet that would bring down John Dillinger.) He then recruited Deputy Sheriff Bill Eads of Oklahoma City and a cadre of policemen from Fort Worth and Dallas whom he thought he could trust. But Jones was taking no chances. He told them he needed their help making an arrest, but he could not say who they were going after or specifically where they were going. He did not want any information leaking out and giving the farm's residents a chance to bolt. He also called J. T. Faith, the sheriff of Wise County, and asked him to join the force he was assembling to make an arrest in his county.

The group was told to meet in Denton, Texas, and the plans would be made from there.

Urschel insisted on going along, as well, and although Jones went through the formalities of trying to talk him out of it on professional grounds and for matters of his own personal safety, he was happy Urschel refused to back off.

Urschel was the only one who could make a positive identification of whoever they found when they got to the farm. Also, Urschel was an expert marksman, a trained soldier and, most of all, motivated to bring his kidnappers to justice — the very qualities Jones would look for in any assault team member.

When they met up in Denton, they waited and waited for J. T. Faith. That was worrisome. Had Faith double-crossed them? Had the Shannons been alerted that something was up? If so, had they fled the scene, or were they arming up for a fight?

The group loaded into three cars and headed toward Paradise, the final destination being known only to Urschel, Jones and his agents. When they got to Decatur, still short of their destination, Jones pulled over. The sun was getting low, and he worried about running out of sunlight.

"Boys, we've got about twenty-six miles to go over slow roads. We might reach the place to finish the job before dark, but even if we did I doubt if we could finish the job before it got black. I've done enough shootin' in my time not to want to go barging into a strange place where the odds are all on the other side. My judgment is to back off, go down to Fort Worth and get a little sleep, then hit this place at sunrise."

He picked up a stick and started drawing in the dust.

"This is the way that place is laid out:

there is only one road into it, and that is plain as the devil. We can't creep in on the place because it is so flat you can see an ant a mile off. The only way to get in there is to just bang straight in, and for that we need daylight. We'll back off now and hit her in the morning," Jones concluded.

They drove to Fort Worth and checked into a hotel and prepared for the next day's work.

In the morning, Urschel got into the lead car with Jones and cradled his double-barreled shotgun across his legs. A young Fort Worth detective in the backseat wondered out loud about where they were going and who they were going after.

With that, Charles turned around.

"I thought you knew. I'm Charles Urschel, the man Machine Gun Kelly kidnapped. We're going after him."

They stopped about a mile from the farm and waited for the sun to come up, pacing quietly behind their parked cars and smoking cigarettes nervously. The plan was pretty simple. The cars would drive slowly and quietly until they got close to the farmhouse. The lead car would then speed to the farmhouse and the men would jump out and get it surrounded. The second car would race to the barn and be ready to take on whoever might be stationed there. The third car would be stationed in between, ready to react to whatever developed at the other two locations.

Jones told them to expect some "fireworks," and the teams loaded into their assigned cars and drove silently toward the Shannon farm as the Saturday sun began to rise.

When he got within sight of the farm, Jones gunned the engine for the final approach. In the driveway, he stopped quickly in front of the house as his men jumped off the running boards and out of the car to surround the house.

As Jones and Urschel approached the front porch, an angry Boss Shannon came around the corner, hurriedly pulling suspenders up over his shoulders. "Hey, what do you think you are doing here?" he barked.

Urschel leveled his shotgun at Shannon's forehead. "That's the old man who guarded me," he said as Shannon froze in his tracks and went white. As the agents moved in to cuff the protesting old man, Jones warily trotted off toward the backyard, wielding his submachine gun.

There was a man in his underwear lying motionless on a cot. His clothes were folded neatly at the foot of the cot. Beside the cot was a Winchester rifle and a Colt .45. Jones rounded the cot to get a look at the man's face. It was unmistakable: the graying, thick, wavy hair, the handsome jawline. Damn. It was Harvey Bailey. What a prize. The most successful bank robber in modern history. A man so wily and clever he walked in and out of jails and prisons with virtual abandon. It seemed as if Jones and his colleagues had been hunting Bailey and his gang their entire careers. And there he was. Sleeping like a baby under the Texas stars. Jones brushed Bailey's nose with the business end of his submachine gun.

Bailey didn't move a muscle as he blinked his eyes open and looked over the barrel of the machine gun at Jones's expressionless face.

"Go ahead. Reach for it," said Jones.

Bailey didn't move.

"Get up, Harvey," said Jones. "Who's here with you?"

Bailey just kept staring in silence.

"Harvey," said Jones bobbing the machine gun. "If a head pops up anywhere around here, or a shot is fired, I promise, I'll cut you in half with this."

Bailey smiled, sat up and stretched his long frame.

"I'm here alone," he said. "You have me. Hell, a fella's gotta sleep sometime."

Jones had no way of knowing it, but Bailey had stopped by the Shannon ranch frequently in recent days. He had been there before with his compatriots from the Lansing breakout, "Big Bob" Brady and Ed Davis. Bailey had borrowed Kelly's machine gun to use on the bank job he'd recently pulled with Brady and Davis, and was returning it. Plus, Kelly owed him some money, and Bailey wanted to collect while Kelly was still flush from the kidnapping job. The three had joined the Shannons for dinner the night before. Brady and Davis wanted to move on, but Bailey opted to lie low at the farm for a while, as was his usual method after a bank job. Plus his wounded leg was still hurting and he needed to see a doctor. Had Jones not canceled the raid the night before, he would have been walking right into a house full of gangsters on the run and ready for a fight.

Inside the house, the agents found two children and Ora Shannon, who was raising holy hell, protesting and spitting out invectives. "Don't tell 'em nothing!" she screamed at her husband as Jones cuffed him and Bailey to a fence.

Jones left a few men behind to guard

Bailey and the Shannons, and then he, Urschel and the rest of the raiding team headed down to Armon's farm and the shed where Urschel had been held.

With the house surrounded, they went in to find a nervous Armon along with his seventeen-year-old wife and their one-year-old baby. Urschel pointed out all the items he had described in his deposition: the metal bed, the bench, the high chair he'd been chained to, which was now occupied by Armon's screaming infant. There was the cracked mirror he'd used to shave, the places he'd stuck his fingerprints.

After all the outbuildings had been searched and found empty, Jones pulled the trembling Armon into one of them for a little heart-to-heart. By the end of their "fatherly chat" Armon had given up the names of the kidnappers — George Kelly and Al Bates — and also admitted he and Boss had been the ones who guarded Urschel while he was being held in the shack.

Before the agents loaded Bailey and the Shannons into their cars for the ride to Dallas, where they were bringing them for booking, Urschel walked up to Ora. With characteristic sarcasm, he doffed his hat and thanked her for the tasty fried chicken dinner she had prepared and served to him the first night he arrived at the farm. Eyeing Armon, he added that it was the only decent thing he'd had to eat all week.

As the string of cars were driving on the farm road away from the Shannons', Sheriff Faith was speeding in from the opposite direction. He pulled to the side and hopped out, raising his hand to get the caravan to stop.

As Jones, driving the lead car, approached, he floored the accelerator and passed within a foot of the sheriff, spraying him with gravel and leaving him in a cloud of red Texas dust. The trailing cars did likewise.

Al Bates, Kelly's partner, had left town as soon as the ransom was divvied up. He was heading for St. Paul, where he and Kelly were planning to have substantial portions of their loot laundered through the city's robust gambling scene.

He boarded a train in Omaha bound for Denver on Friday night, while Bailey, Brady and Davis were feasting with the Shannons. While walking through the car looking for a seat, he passed a detective from the American Express Company who recognized him instantly. American Express had been looking for Bates for nearly a year. Bates had been passing traveler's checks stolen from a

Tupelo, Mississippi bank, and the company had sent their own operatives out looking for him. The American Express detective stayed on the train with Bates until he disembarked in Denver. There, he alerted the local police, hoping they'd make a move on Bates.

Bates had earlier stolen a late-model Buick Victoria Coupe that he planned to use to duck around the country while trading out his money for some safer bills. He'd picked it up from the safe garage where it had been hidden and drove to the rooming house where he'd rented a room. But his luck was running bad. Another happenstance encounter was about to do him in.

Two Denver patrolmen recognized the stolen car as Bates sat inside listening to the radio. They took him out of the car and told him they were bringing him downtown for questioning. He had thirty-three bills from the Urschel loot in his pocket and he knew that would not look good. Under questioning, Bates admitted to stealing the car, but also confessed to robbing a bank in Texas, where he said he'd be willing to return to stand trial. This was a common ruse. Confess to a lesser crime to avoid detection on a bigger one. Bates also had more police connections in Texas, and if he could get back there his chance to avoid extradition was good, as was his ability to escape.

From his jail cell in Denver, he was able to smuggle a note to a prison trusty. "Get this to my wife. She's got money and will pay you handsomely if you do," Bates's note explained. The trusty was able to get the note to Bates's alleged wife, one Clara Feldman. Clara was guarding a large portion of Bates's take on the Urschel kidnapping. The cryptic note said: "There is nothing you can do for me. Move."

Feldman prepared to flee Denver, but before she did she sent a telegram to Ed Weatherford in Fort Worth, who Kathryn Kelly had claimed was sympathetic and on the Kellys' payroll. Weatherford turned the telegram over to the local Bureau agents, who alerted the Denver office. The agents sped to the Denver jail, where they identified Bates's cash as part of the Urschel ransom and claimed the prisoner as their own, aborting the plans for extradition to Texas. Instead, several days later, they put the shackled Bates in an airplane and flew him to Oklahoma City.

There to greet him were Charles and Berenice Urschel, who immediately identified him as one of the two kidnappers who'd burst onto their sunporch just a few weeks earlier.

"That's him all right," said Berenice. "I'm so glad to see him like that," she said eyeing the heavy chains. "He didn't have on those gold-rimmed spectacles that night, but he is the one."

Charles walked up to Bates, looked him in the eye, and said, "Hello, Albert."

Bates looked at him coolly and said with mock haughtiness, "I don't believe I know you."

Charles stared back and, after a moment, began to chuckle. In response, Bates did too.

7
THE MANHUNT

Jones raced his captured prey from Paradise straight to Dallas, where he put them in jail and immediately got the U.S. Attorney to begin the removal proceedings to get the group extradited to Oklahoma City, where they could be tried in federal court. Boss Shannon was well connected locally, and Jones knew if he stayed in Dallas long enough his friends would work the system to find a friendly judge, or one that could be bought. Jones was not one of Hoover's law-degreed gumshoes, but he'd been around the criminal justice system his entire life and he knew how it worked, especially in Texas.

Harvey Bailey, an escaped federal prisoner with a murder warrant hanging over his head in the Kansas City Massacre case, could not fight his extradition back to Oklahoma City. What Jones worried about with Bailey was that he'd escape, or that a collection of his criminal buddies would bust him out somehow. Dallas boasted an "escape-proof" new jail, and Jones moved Bailey there until the kidnapping trial could get under way in Oklahoma.

Jones had just made the biggest arrests in the new attorney general's War on Crime, but he wasn't doing any victory laps. He knew there would be hell to pay if he allowed his captives to escape or avoid trial on some shady legal maneuver. He still had doubts about Bailey's involvement in the Kansas City Massacre, but tying him to the kidnapping was fortuitous indeed. Plus, the Kellys and Bates were still on the lam. Soon, their names and descriptions would be blaring on every police radio in the nation and carried in newspapers from New York to Los Angeles. Once that happened, he feared they'd disappear into the protection of some criminal mob, or flee the country altogether.

On Hoover's instructions, Jones asked the local press to hold news of the raid for 48 hours to give his men a chance to nab the Kellys and Bates before they went into hiding. It was a big ask, but after some forceful negotiation, they agreed. Hoover also made it clear that Jones should release only the bare facts about the raid and how they found the farm. Specifically, he did not want any of Urschel's statements from his interview about the plane flights over the farm or the hidden fingerprints or the fact that Urschel had been with the agents during the raid released. Hoover was trying to build a case and he wanted to keep as much information under wraps as he could before the trial began. He also wanted to protect his star witness.

The raid on the Shannon farm had turned up a receipt from Kelly's friendly Cleveland Cadillac dealership. Colvin had called Washington immediately after the raid to report that "Kelly, with two other men and a woman, was traveling in a sixteen-cylinder blue-black Cadillac, a 1932 model, motor number 1400263, a nine-passenger, specially constructed, very large car, which was purchased by Mrs. Kelly under the name of Mrs. Ora L. Shannon." He said he had intercepted a letter that indicated the Kellys planned to return there on August 10 or August 11 to purchase a twelve-cylinder convertible coupe on which they'd already made a $500 deposit. He had alerted the Cincinnati office and they had dispatched agents to "cover the Cleveland angle."

Hoover was orchestrating the hunt from his desk in Washington, showering his field offices with telegrams and memos. He sent copies of the massive list of the ten thousand serial numbers on the $20 bills used in the ransom to dozens of Bureau offices, and the staff from those offices got the serial numbers to hundreds of federal and local banks, advising them to be on the lookout for the bills and to notify the Bureau immediately if any were discovered. "Wanted" posters, descriptions and photographs of the Kellys and Bates also went out. Hoover alerted the Bureau offices in New York, Detroit and Portland, instructing them to cover the ports in case Kelly and company attempted to flee to Canada.

When agents got to the Cleveland dealership, they learned they had just missed the Kellys. The dealership's owner told them that Kelly had come in on August 10 to pay off the balance on the sixteen-cylinder Caddy. Kelly was considering the twelve-cylinder coupe, but ultimately decided against it. He also revealed that when the Kellys purchased the car on June 3, they invited the salesman to a party back at their hotel. The salesman returned with wild stories about the party, including the fact that Kelly had $36,000 in cash in his pocket and that his wife had "a large number of Persian gowns designed by Chanel." He said when Kelly left the dealership on August 11 he was wearing "octagonal shaped rimless glasses" and that his wife was sporting a "beautiful Martin diamond dinner ring which was quite noticeable." He said they were planning to drive to Chicago.

The night before, the Kellys had received a telegram from Bates in Minneapolis. It read: "Deal has fell through. Jack and Tom have left. Communicate with me at box 631." It was code for "trouble."

After releasing Urschel, the Kellys had gone to George's old base of operations in St. Paul, where he went to work getting his money laundered at 20 cents on the dollar and Kathryn went on a shopping spree, adding another fur coat to her wardrobe, along with about $2,000 worth of diamond rings and bracelets. Kelly took his cash to the Green Lantern tavern to get Dutch Sawyer's help getting it cleaned. Sawyer sent Kelly to one of his confederates, casino owner Jack Peifer, who took $7,000 of the Kelly loot. He then pedaled it to a group of his minions, who went to work exchanging it through a half-dozen friendly banks.

Bates alerted the Kellys to the fact that several people in Minnesota had been arrested while trying to pass the ransom money. They were being held by police and it was unknown what — if anything — they'd said about the money.

The Kellys then headed to Des Moines, Iowa, to lie low and try to figure out what was going on. They were staying at a motor lodge outside the city when news of the raid on Paradise finally hit the papers on August 14.

The Dallas papers applauded the daring capture and news accounts throughout the region were crowing that Hoover's men had not only nabbed the Urschel kidnappers, but one of the men responsible for the Kansas City Massacre, as well, the infamous Harvey Bailey, who was also being portrayed as the brains behind the kidnapping. The *Dallas Morning News* had the biggest story in the nation breaking in its own backyard and they played it to the fullest. The headlines screamed across their front page:

FIVE HELD FOR URSCHEL CASE AND
KANSAS CITY MASSACRE
GANG CAUGHT AT POINT OF
MACHINE GUN
HARVEY BAILEY AND FOUR MEMBERS
OF SHANNON FAMILY SURPRISED IN
WISE COUNTY

DENVER LANDS ONE

ONE MORE MEMBER OF GANG, GEORGE KELLY, SOUGHT IN BIG CAR

The severe penalties of the new Federal Lindberg [sic] kidnapping law Monday afternoon hung over Harvey Bailey, notorious outlaw and escaped convict, whose capture by Federal Agents here caused them to claim solution to the Urschel kidnapping case and capture of the principals in the outrageous Union Terminal Massacre at Kansas City.

Bailey was lodged in the Dallas County Jail as "Jones, hold for Federal authorities" Saturday along with four others taken in a surprise sunrise raid on the little cottage they occupied in Paradise, Wise County.

The others in jail R. G. Shannon, on whose place the raid was made; Ora L. Shannon, his wife; Armon Shannon, this son and Oleta Shannon, Armon's wife.

Late Monday afternoon, Albert Bates alias George Bates, was reported captured at Denver. He was one of the gang wanted with Bailey in the Urschel kidnapping. Federal agents continued their search of George Kelly, another of the gang who was known to be traveling over the Middle West in a sixteen-cylinder Cadillac sedan, 1932 model with a large black trunk.

All law enforcement agencies in the country were warned to apprehend Kelly on sight and police radios in cities over the Nation Monday afternoon carried descriptions of him and warnings to notify authorities if he is seen.

A second front-page story focused on Bailey.

BAILEY CAPTURE SEEN AS TEN-STRIKE IN WAR ON CRIME ATTORNEY GENERAL SAYS PRISONER IS LEADER OF DANGEROUS GANG

The arrest of Harvey Bailey in Texas was regarded Monday night by Federal officials as a ten-strike in the Government's war against gangsters and racketeers.

Details of Bailey's capture in a before-dawn raid on a remote farmhouse near Paradise, Texas, were announced Monday by Attorney General Cummings who paid highest praise to the Department of Justice agents responsible.

Bailey, in Cumming's *[sic]* opinion, is the leader of one of the most dangerous criminal gangs in the country. The arrest was made only a few days after President Roosevelt had taken personal direction of the Government's anticrime campaign in conference at Hyde Park.

Cummings said Bailey had been identified as the operator of a machine gun which killed five men in Kansas City June 17, and disclosed also that marked ransom money paid in the kidnapping of Charles F. Urschel at Oklahoma City July 22 had been found on the fugitive.

In a paragraph that could have been crafted by Hoover himself, the paper applauded the work of the Bureau:

Incensed over the killing of one of their own Federal agents and three peace officers at the Kansas City Union Station on June 17, all of the energies of the Bureau of Investigation have been centered on solving that crime since then. Officers here early suspected that the Urschel kidnaping tied in with the same group of outlaws, and for the last six weeks Agents Frank J. Blake of Dallas, R. H. Colvin of Oklahoma City and Gus T. Jones of San Antonio have gone without sleep in their efforts to apprehend members of the suspected gang.

From Washington, Attorney General Cummings applauded his team and the Urschel family, noting that the Urschel family did not hesitate to call in the government and local authorities, and that this should be the reaction in all kidnapping cases. Unlike so many in the past, Urschel had stood up to the kidnappers' threats of retribution and had not only called in the feds, but helped them find his captors and build the legal case for prosecution.

Listening to the radio and reading the papers, Kelly learned just how dangerous a criminal he really was. The headlines screamed and the radio waves blasted. The nation's new Public Enemy Number One was a man known as Machine Gun Kelly.

The august *New York Times* claimed, "Kelly and his gang of Southwestern desperados are regarded as the most dangerous ever encountered."

The Bureau released a wanted poster of Kelly describing him as thirty-five years old, 5'9", 177 pounds and "muscular," a ruddy-complected "expert machine gunner." Kathryn's publicity efforts had found a remarkably accepting audience.

A similar poster was issued for Kathryn using stats acquired from her arrest in 1929 — which she must have hated — describing her as twenty-eight (though looking much older), at 5'9" and "weighing 140 (though probably heavier) with a ruddy complexion and a proclivity for expensive jewelry."

Meanwhile, while on the run, George and Kathryn were incredulous that they had been identified as Urschel's kidnappers. Urschel had double-crossed them. He'd gone straight to the authorities. The threats of retribution had been ignored.

Kathryn was especially furious. She ranted at Kelly. If they'd killed Urschel, they wouldn't have any of this trouble. A dead man could not have gone to the authorities. A dead man could not have led the feds back to the farm in Paradise. How had that happened? Somebody had screwed up big time, and it hadn't been her. What had her loudmouthed husband let slip? What about Bates? Had he screwed up? Maybe it was Armon, that dim-witted fool. What had he said to Urschel that made it possible for that ungrateful bastard to lead the feds back to her father-in-law's farm?

Now Kathryn's mother was in jail. She was apoplectic. She had to do something. Her mother must be cleared. What had she done? She wasn't guilty of anything. All she'd done was cook a decent meal for that ungrateful captive and make sure his stay at her farm wasn't life-threatening. She pleaded with Kelly to do something. Her mother was being held on $50,000 bond. They needed a lawyer. Somebody connected. Somebody fast. Kathryn would not let her dear mother sit in some loathsome jail cell.

Despite their threats of retribution, Urschel had not only gone to the feds, he had written a story about his ordeal that moved on the wires and appeared in numerous papers around the country. This incensed the Kellys. They had made it plain what would happen to him if he went to the police, if he helped others pursue them. George was beginning to rethink his decision to let the fool live, and Kathryn was berating him for it.

In his account, Urschel had written that "everything the federal government can do to put an end to kidnappings in the United States is an imperative necessity."

But the most galling account came a day later, on August 15, when the *Oklahoma News* broke the story of Urschel's involvement in leading the agents to the Shannon farm in a front-page, double-deck, bold-faced headline:

The reporters at the *News* had tricked the sheriff into confirming the story by telling him that the Associated Press was moving the details.

With his name in headlines in every paper on the street, and radio newsmen declaring his Public Enemy status nationwide, Kelly could not stay in one place for too long. He'd already been tagged in the Union Station shootout and that was bringing heat, but now he'd pulled off a record-setting snatch job and the feds were crawling all over the usual safe houses and hideouts and making things miserable for anyone with known connections to criminal activity.

So the Kellys packed up their clothes, their liquor and their hot money and took to the road, hoping to disappear in the back-country George knew so well. They hid out in tourist motels in Illinois, Indiana, Iowa and Missouri — all over the Midwest — and fought bitterly. Kelly blamed Kathryn for talking him into the kidnapping and she blamed him for getting her mother thrown in jail. The smoldering Kathryn hatched a plan to save her skin. She told George that if they were to get caught, he should take the blame and say she had nothing to do with it. She hadn't been seen or heard at any time during the job. There were no eyewitnesses to her involvement. Why should the two of them go to prison? She would need to stay on the loose so she could get help for her mother. She couldn't bear to see her locked up.

Kelly could never say no to a lady, especially one as persuasive as Kathryn, who quickly fired off a letter to Joseph B. Keenan, the Department of Justice's Special Agent in Charge of the Criminal Division who was in Oklahoma City to oversee the trial of Bates, Bailey and the Shannons. It was postmarked from Chicago on August 18:

The entire Urschel family and friends, and all of you, will be exterminated soon. There is no way I can prevent it. I will gladly put George Kelly on the spot for you if you will save my mother, who is innocent of any wrongdoing. If you do not comply with this request, there is no way in which I can prevent the most awful tragedy. If you refuse my offer I shall commit some minor offense and be placed in jail so that you will know that I have no connection with the terrible slaughter that will take place in Oklahoma City within the next few days.

Gus Jones had been monitoring the mail going to the Kellys' house in Fort Worth and to the Shannon farm. In addition to Chicago, Kelly had sent letters from St. Paul and from Madison, Wisconsin. He'd also picked up information indicating that Kelly would be traveling to Indianapolis to pick up a package at the general delivery window of the post office.

Hoover dispatched a team of agents, and with the help of Indianapolis police, they laid a trap to nab him when he did. They would grab Kelly if he showed up to get his package. But if Kathryn or another of Kelly's associates appeared, they were to drop back and follow the pickup, who they hoped would lead them to Kelly.

But plans went awry. And, worse, the agents' failure was described to the press. The Bureau's ineptitude went on display in the headlines of the *Indianapolis Star* on August 17.

"DUMMY" SEIZED AS HE ASKS FOR
FUGITIVE'S MAIL
KELLY ESCAPES TRAP SET HERE

George R. Kelly, suspected Kidnaper and one of a gang who is believed to have escaped in a fusillade of bullets from a police dragnet in Chicago Tuesday, yesterday was believed to have eluded Federal agents in Indianapolis.

Anxiety of Department of Justice agents to capture Kelly was said to have resulted in a "tip off" to him and his subsequent flight.

The story later noted that Kelly was wanted for the Urschel kidnapping and for "killing five persons in an attempted delivery of Frank Nash, convict in the Kansas City Union station several weeks ago." Over a picture of handsome Kelly with his slicked-back dark hair ran the headline:

GETS AWAY AGAIN.

Kelly had hired an itinerant kid who'd been hanging out in a nearby park to go in and pick up his mail. Thinking the kid was actually Kelly, the agent on the scene detained him, and Kelly got spooked and fled.

The agents in the field had a hard time determining whether Hoover was angrier that they had missed Kelly or that their failure had appeared in the press. His agents were under a strict admonition to keep all information about the case confidential.

In their memo back to headquarters they noted that the reporter who filed the story, Robert Early, worked out of police headquarters and not the federal building, which indicated to them that the leak had come from the Indianapolis police. They also suspected that someone on the Indianapolis police force might have tipped Kelly about the trap.

The agents on the scene wrote back to Hoover:

In conformity with your instructions on Aug 17, 1933 I conferred with [the] Chief of Detectives and the Chief of Police and advised them of the fact that the publicity emanated from the Police Headquarters and that same had resulted in possibly frightening Kelly away from Indianapolis. I also advised them that we would not use the Indianapolis Police further in this inquiry and they were relieved from the assignment on the afternoon of this date.

But though they were losing ground in their efforts to control the press and manage the information from the investigation, Hoover's efforts were receiving a considerable boost from the editorial writers of the nation's press. Under the headline *U.S. Police Efficiency,* the *Washington Herald* published the following editorial:

This crime-ridden country regards with astonishment and admiration the brilliant exploits of Federal operatives aided by police of three cities in running down and capturing the gang deemed responsible for the $200,000 Urschel kidnaping in Oklahoma and the brutal Kansas City massacre of five men last June.

Climaxing the achievement three hundred Federal State and local officers guided by army airplanes, waylaid and waged a machine gun battle late yesterday afternoon in the outskirts of Chicago against still another group of suspects.

Harvey J. Bailey, ringleader of the Urschel kidnaping outfit *[,]* appears to be as ruthless, daring and resourceful an outlaw as this generation has known. . . . The police characters of the men implicated, the nature of the crimes under scrutiny, and the dramatic completeness of the law officers' coup ought to be the final victorious argument in favor of an American "Scotland Yard," as advocated by the Hearst newspapers and by many eminent penologists.

A grateful Hoover immediately penned the following note to the legendary editor of the *Herald,* Eleanor Patterson:

My dear Mrs. Patterson,

I wanted to write to you to express my sincere appreciation of the commendatory editorial appearing in the Washington Herald of August 17, 1933, entitled "U.S. Police Efficiency."

It is a source of deep gratification to me that the efforts of the Division of Investigation of the Department of Justice in bringing about the apprehension of Harvey J. Bailey, notorious criminal, were such as to merit the approval of the Editor of the Washington Herald. The editorial in question evidences such a keen understanding of the handling of the cases referred to and the organization of the Division of Investigation that I would appreciate it very much if you would express my thanks to the writer of this editorial. I am highly pleased that the work of the Division of Investigation in dealing with the criminal element, and particularly in recent kidnapping cases, has been such as to warrant this editorial consent. I believe that editorials of this kind serve an extremely helpful purpose in acquainting the reading public with the strength of the Federal Government in dealing with the lawless element.

Sincerely yours,
J. Edgar Hoover

The day after the *Herald* editorial, Hoover and Cummings got a similar boost from *The Washington Post,* which reprinted an editorial that had earlier appeared in Louisville's *Courier-Journal.* It ran under the headline:

UNCLE SAM, DETECTIVE.

It must have been a good moment for Attorney General Homer Cummings when he was able to announce the capture of Harvey Bailey one of the king pin criminals of the Nation. Not only is this the man who led the break from the Kansas Penitentiary on Memorial Day, when a warden and two guards were kidnaped; not only is he the man who has been identified as the ring leader in the Kansas City Union Station massacre, when five men were mowed down by machine gun bullets; this Harvey Bailey is the kidnaper of Charles F. Urschel, who was snatched from his home in Oklahoma City and held until his family had paid $200,000 ransom. . . . The most important feature about the Bailey arrest, however, is the credit which it reflects on the Federal machinery for crime detection. Definite steps have been taken by the Roosevelt administration to strangle the kidnaping racket by means of a central agency in Washington. Nothing feasible offers such promise of relief from this national disease as the establishment of confidence among the people in the ability of the United States Government to crush the kidnapers. When such confidence is achieved, the families of kidnap victims may no longer try to hide their dealings from the proper authorities, as they now do most frequently in the hope of negotiating directly with the criminals. The successful handling of the Urschel case should go far to impress the public with Uncle Sam's superior ability to deal with kidnapers.

The Courier-Journal *got a similar note of appreciation from the Bureau's director.*

While Hoover was accepting the praise for his department and ramping up its publicity machine, the hunt for Kelly spread out across the nation. A motorcycle officer in Oklahoma City came forward and revealed that he had formerly had a drinking buddy who was an ex-con. One night, on a drunk, the ex-con told the officer that he had information about "something that may do you some good."

The con said, "I was a cell mate in the penitentiary with a boy named George Kelly. Two days before those officers and Frank Nash were killed in Kansas City, I met George Kelly and another man in Tulsa. They went to a house where they cleaned and oiled two machine guns and said they were then on their way to Kansas City."

It was just about all the Bureau had in trying to tie Kelly to the Kansas massacre, but despite their efforts they could not locate the ex-con and were too stretched to chase down the lead.

On Thursday, August 17, five days after the raid at Paradise, rumors that gangsters were planning to spring Bailey started hitting the papers. The Dallas police boasted that extra patrols were guarding the roads in and out of the city. Even so, Bailey had already bragged to reporters that no cell could hold him.

On August 18, *The Dallas News* answered these threats and boasts with a proud description of just how tough it would be for Bailey to slip free from the new jail. Under the headline *Seven Barred Doors or Grills Face Gangsters if they try to Spring Bailey from Jail,* the story contained a detailed description of what "a gang of gangsters or a mob of mobsters" would encounter in their attempt to even get to Bailey:

On the first floor they would have to fight their way through the lobby of the Criminal Courts Building to reach the heavy door that gives into the outer lobby of the jail. Similar difficulty would be encountered if they approached from the rear through the alley at the entrance of which is a high, barred gate.

If they succeeded in reaching the door they would have to crash it and then fight their way another fifteen feet to reach the ceiling-to-floor heavy steel grill in the main lobby of the jail. Then they would have to crash that door and fight their way to another door in the elevator corridor.

Should they succeed in riding the elevator to the floor where the prisoner is held, then they would face another ceiling-high grill of heavy steel bars. Still between the raiders and the cell block would be a barred door. Passing this door there would yet be between them and their quarry the heavy bars surrounding the corridor, and the inside corridor, the cell door itself.

Jones wanted to leave Bailey in the Dallas jail until he was ready for trial in Oklahoma City rather than risk losing him in transit or putting him in the far less secure jail in Oklahoma.

The U.S. Attorney had told Jones that even if the judge ruled speedily on the extradition of the Shannons, they could appeal. The appeal would be scheduled for a later date, and who knew when he'd be able to get them out of Texas. Hoover and the team in Washington were intent on bringing this case to a successful climax fast and decisively. Jones knew all too well how the law worked in Texas. He hatched his own plan for getting his captives out of the state, and fast. It had its own elements of Texas-style law.

On the morning of the hearing, Jones arranged a chartered flight to fly them directly to Oklahoma City immediately afterward. Before the proceedings began, Jones's men pulled their cars up to the base of the stairs in front of the courthouse, leaving the doors open and the engines running. Timing would be all-important. A speedy departure was critical to the success of his plan.

Jones pulled the court clerk aside for a private conversation. He explained what was about to happen and how the clerk should behave. The Shannons' attorney would almost certainly be filing an appeal. The clerk would be responsible for making certain all of the documents were properly prepared. Jones did not want the clerk to rush the process. In fact, he made it clear the clerk should delay as long as possible. Stall.

When the judge ruled in the government's favor, Jones's men hustled the three Shannons out of the courtroom toward the waiting car.

As they did, the Shannons' attorney leapt to his feet and told the judge he intended to file an immediate appeal.

Go right ahead, said the judge. "There's the clerk right over there."

"But, your honor, those federal agents are rushing my clients out of the courtroom."

The judge explained that the agents were perfectly within their rights and there was nothing he could do about it until the appeal was filed.

The attorney then hustled across the room

with the appeal papers and demanded the clerk hurry up and stamp them for approval.

The clerk, affecting an officious air, explained that he would have to examine them carefully and make sure they were in the proper order. He doddled, while the attorney fumed. When he finally stamped the approval, the attorney grabbed them, raced across the courtroom and handed them to the bemused judge. He leafed through the papers, stalling a little longer then looked down at the lawyer and announced that the appeal was granted.

With that, the attorney grabbed the bailiff and raced from the courtroom to chase down Jones, who was already driving the Shannons to the airport.

Jones drove his captives onto the runway where the plane was waiting, propellers churning. Armon was hustled onto the plane, but Boss and Ora were protesting wildly. They'd never been on a plane and were terrified of the prospect.

Ora clung to the car door and screamed as the agents pried her loose and carried her onto the aircraft. As they closed the doors and taxied down the runway, the bailiff's car was entering the airport with the Shannon's fuming attorney riding helplessly inside.

After Jones had successfully spirited his prey out of Dallas, Hoover fired off a memo to Cummings crowing about the shrewd maneuvers of his agents.

MEMORANDUM FOR THE ATTOREY [sic] GENERAL

I thought you might be interested in a development which arose at Fort Worth, Texas, incident to the removal of the Shannons from Fort Worth to Oklahoma City for trial for the kidnaping of Mr. Urschel. The day when Judge Wilson granted the order of removal for the Shannons to be taken to Oklahoma City, the defense attorneys had a writ of habeas corpus prepared to be filed immediately following Judge Wilson's decision. However, in the interim, the United States Marshal and Agents of this Division executed Judge Wilson's order of removal by taking the Shannons from the Federal Building to the Municipal Airport and placed them in a plane. They were in the air within fifteen minutes after Judge Wilson's order of removal was issued. . . .

As a matter of fact, the officers departed from the Federal Building at Fort

Worth, Texas, at 12:20 p.m., and at 1:50 p.m. the Shannons were safely lodged in the Oklahoma County Jail two hundred miles away. The move of the attorneys for the defense was simply one in which they hoped to get the removal case before the Appellate Court and thereby cause a delay in removing them to the jurisdiction of the Federal Court in Oklahoma.

Respectfully,
J. Edgar Hoover
Director.

Cummings had the high-profile case in hand that stood to be his first big battle in the War on Crime, and he was tasting victory. From Washington, the focus on the case was becoming intense from the highest levels of the government. On Thursday, August 17, President Roosevelt ordered Leslie Salter, special assistant to the attorney general, to Oklahoma City to prepare indictments for the grand jury. Salter was the toughest and most successful prosecutor on Cummings's team. In court, he was considered almost unbeatable, and his demeanor was described as that of a "vengeful, wrathful, terrible god of the Old Testament." In New York he'd won a string of 99 convictions in the 101 cases he prosecuted. Cummings had sent him to Chicago months earlier as he was preparing to launch his War on Crime. Salter was to become a specialist in preparing cases against gangland elements, and Cummings wanted him in crime's capital. But that would have to wait. The kidnapping case was the first in which the newly passed Lindbergh Law would be employed and he wanted it employed with eminent dispatch. If the case could be prosecuted successfully, Cummings planned to use it as an example of the need for expanded federal anticrime laws. It would become the focal point in his argument for the passage of the crime bill he was preparing, and a primary demonstration of the need for the federal police force he hoped to create.

Salter was given explicit instructions to move the case to trial as quickly as possible. Even as reports of Kelly sightings were pouring in from Laredo, Texas, to the Canadian border, the decision was made to proceed with the prosecution of Bailey, Bates and the Shannons immediately and prosecute the Kellys separately when they were apprehended. Hoover and Cummings wanted a quick victory and a showy trial to put their agency's handiwork on display for the nation to behold.

Linked under the same headline that announced Salter's return to Oklahoma City was a second story from the Associated Press out of Springtown, Arkansas, that brought news of the death of another of Bailey's confederates. It also underscored the dangers inherent in working as a lawyer on behalf of your gangster client. It read:

Gene Johnson, alleged confederate of Wilber Underhill's gang of escaped Kansas convicts, was wounded fatally Thursday by a posse of officers from three states in a surprise attack at his farm.

The posse had surrounded Johnson's car and painted it with machine gun fire as Johnson slumped over his wife to protect her. She survived with minor wounds and Johnson's partner Glenn Leroy Wright escaped into the woods.

Another story out of Tulsa dissected the duo's criminal pedigree:

TANGLED UNDERWORLD
CONNECTIONS LINK GENE JOHNSON
AND GLENN LEROY WRIGHT WITH
HARVEY BAILEY AND MORE

267

Wright is more closely connected with Bailey, now held as the brains behind the Charles F. Urschel kidnapping. He and Harry Campbell, also a fugitive *[,]* are wanted here as suspects in the slaying of J. Earl Smith, formerly attorney for Bailey.

Smith was taken for a fatal ride when he failed to appear as counsel for Bailey in the Fort Scott, Kanas, bank robbery case on which Bailey was sentenced to the Kansas state penitentiary at Lansing, and from which he escaped last Memorial Day.

Officers have advanced the theory that Bailey may have obtained the services of Campbell and Wright to dispose of Smith either because he knew too much or because he failed to act as Bailey's lawyer after having conferred with him.

Tulsa officers have expressed the opinion that Wright and Johnson are lesser members of the region's most dangerous criminal ring, of which Bailey and Wilber Underhill are leaders.

As the feds prepared their case in Oklahoma, word came from Denver that two-and-a-half bars of the cell that Bates was being held in had been sawed through. A metal pipe with a weighted end that could be used as a club was found hidden nearby. Consequently, a round-the-clock machine gunner was assigned to guard him, and he was moved to a new cell each day. The Denver police had earlier gotten reports that Kelly was headed back to Denver to free his partner. Kelly's picture had been all over the Denver papers in conjunction with the Bates arrest. None other than Anna Lou Boettcher, whose husband's kidnappers were still at large, reported seeing Kelly sitting in a car outside the Brown Palace Hotel. In addition to his possible escape, Jones was also worried about whether he'd even be able to get Bates out of Denver for trial in Oklahoma City.

Meanwhile, Salter wasted no time cutting through legal technicalities and the mountain of evidence that had been gathered by the Bureau's agents. After conferring with Judge Edgar S. Vaught, who was holding court in New Mexico, Salter announced that a grand jury would be impaneled and indictment papers charging eleven people with complicity in the kidnapping were being prepared.

On August 21, Agent Colvin received a

tip that Kelly and other members of his gang had driven into the Henry Gramm ranch, a notorious criminal hangout in the farm country between Pawhuska and Ponca City, Oklahoma, in a Buick automobile, and were believed to still be there. Colvin immediately organized a raiding posse. He called in the sheriff of Pawhuska, who agreed to round up three or four men and meet Colvin and his agents at the Jens-Marie Hotel in Ponca City, where they would be joined by another posse from Ponca.

Colvin's men left Oklahoma City at 2:30 p.m. When they arrived in Ponca City at 5:00 p.m., they were shocked to find special editions of the local papers on the stands with an Associated Press story announcing that a large concentration of federal officers were heading to Osage County, where the notorious Machine Gun Kelly was believed to be hiding. By then, the Buick had left the ranch and the raid was called off.

In a subsequent letter to Hoover, Colvin noted that the Associated Press story had a Pawhuska dateline and that the only person who knew the details of the raid was the Pawhuska sheriff.

It appears . . . that we can have absolutely no faith in anyone, even officers, to treat in confidence matters which we tell them, and we will in *[the]* future be more discreet than ever with respect to divulging confidential information to them. You will, no doubt, realize that it is dangerous and difficult to conduct a raid or other expedition into a county without taking the county officers more or less into our confidence, especially if we ask their assistance. No one regrets more than this writer the dangerous publicity which has been had in this case.

The Kellys had been working their way south to get back to Texas so Kathryn could find a lawyer with enough clout to get her mother and stepfather released. Along the way, the twosome tried to disguise themselves by donning worn-out clothes and farmer's garb. Kathryn wore a red wig and George dyed his hair blond. The Kellys drove to West Texas, where Kathryn's uncle, Cass Coleman, owned a dried-out, barren ranch. There, they buried their share of the ransom money in a large thermos and a honey jar beneath a tree behind the barn.

The next day, Kathryn bought an old Chevy in the nearby town of Brownwood.

George hid out at Cass Coleman's place in Coleman County. Kathryn dressed in some farm-girl clothing and went off on her own in an old Ford pickup truck. On August 20, Coleman, who was getting nervous about his dangerous houseguest, arranged for him to rent a shack on the farm of his good friend Will Casey, who lived a few miles away.

While the Kellys were hiding out in Texas, Hoover's team was picking up evidence of Kelly's trail from Chicago to Juarez, Mexico, but always a day or two behind his actual movements. Plus, with Kelly's name and face featured so prominently in the national press, it seemed that every third person in the country had seen him and was phoning in a tip. They sent men to the border crossings into Canada in Washington State, Detroit and Buffalo, New York. Even with more than 300 agents around the country, Hoover's men were overwhelmed and working round the clock trying to cover the vast expanse that the Kellys were believed to be passing through.

On August 23, Casey told Kelly that he'd heard some feds were in the area asking questions. With that, Kelly packed his belongings into the Chevy sedan, drove to

Coleman's place and handed him an envelope.

"Give that to Kathryn and tell her, 'Mississippi.'" Then he jumped back in his car and sped away.

A few days later, the police chief of Hattiesburg, Mississippi, called the Special Agent in Charge of the New Orleans bureau and said a man had registered at a Hattiesburg hotel under the name of R. C. Kelly of 221 South Liberty Street in New Orleans, an infamous red-light district.

Kelly had gone to the railway express office in New Orleans and asked to buy $1,400 in traveler's checks. The clerk didn't have enough checks, so Kelly left. He returned at 6:00 p.m. and bought $200 in traveler's checks in $20 denominations and a money order for $71 made out to the Ray Motor Company. The clerk became suspicious when Kelly began signing the checks using the alias W. R. Rawles. Kelly's behavior was peculiar. He would sign one check, then go to the door and look up and down the street and then come back and sign another.

By the time agents from New Orleans got to Hattiesburg, though, Kelly was gone. Employees at the hotel positively identified Kelly from his description and picture. They said he was neatly dressed, wearing a straw hat. He had left at 6:30 p.m. the day before in a new Plymouth Coupe with Texas license plates.

A day later, Kelly checked into the Avilez Hotel in Biloxi, Mississippi. Fearful of being recognized if he stayed in one place too long, he moved to the Tourist Hotel three days later. There, he made the mistake of cashing some American Express traveler's checks. A clerk identified him and alerted the police.

Hoover scrambled his forces and sent in a team from New Orleans. But the press, triple-teaming the biggest story of the summer, got word. Kelly was walking down a Biloxi street when he heard a newsboy hawking the top story of the latest edition: "Machine Gun Kelly in Town!"

Kelly headed straight for the bus station and bought a ticket to Memphis, leaving behind his belongings, including a loaded .45, at the Tourist Hotel.

When Hoover's men got to the Tourist Hotel in Biloxi, they learned that Kelly had registered under the name of J. L. Coleman of Texas. He had been driving a 1928 or 1929 Chevrolet Sedan with Texas plates. Among the items he left behind in the room was the Gladstone bag that Kirkpatrick had given him with the ransom money. The staff described Kelly as extremely affable and friendly and noted that he had an extensive knowledge of the Gulf Coast and was sporting a thin moustache. They said that on Sunday, August 27, he had a date with a woman who they assumed was some kind of "pick-up" or prostitute.

When Kelly got to Memphis, he called his old brother-in-law, George Ramsey Jr. George wasn't around, but the call got through to his younger brother, Langford. In the eight years since his sister and George Barnes had divorced, Langford Ramsey hadn't heard a word from or about his former brother-in-law. In those intervening years, while Barnes was living outside the law and building the Machine Gun Kelly legend, Ramsey was learning the law and became the youngest man in Tennessee history to pass the bar. Whether he knew he was talking to Public Enemy Number One when Kelly called him from the Memphis bus terminal is unknown. But Kelly, no doubt using the more familiar surname, Barnes, told Ramsey he needed a place to stay and a good lawyer, as well.

Ramsey told George that he was entertaining "Geneva, Frank, Hazel and the boys" and there was no room at his house. However, he had a friend whose family was out of town. "He's a little short of cash," said Langford. "I'm sure he will let you stay there for a few bucks."

Langford set Kelly up at Al Tichenor's house on Raynor Street. He also set up a meeting with "the boys," Kelly's two children with Geneva, his first wife, whom he hadn't seen in years. He showed up at their house wearing a handsome gray suit with a 38.-caliber pistol in a shoulder holster under his jacket. He told them he was a federal agent on "a secret mission" and they should not mention his visit to anyone. When George had completed his visit with his sons, he told them to go outside and ride their bikes.

But the boys didn't have bikes. So George pulled an enormous roll of cash out of his pocket, which just awed the kids, who'd never seen so much cash in their lives. He gave them each a $20 bill and said they should go buy some bikes. It would be his treat.

On the morning of September 4, Labor Day, as the day shift jailer brought breakfast to the eighth-floor cellblock where Bailey was being held in isolation, he was surprised from behind by a man with a gun who promptly relieved him of his keys and locked him in a cell. Harvey Bailey, the Bureau's trophy captive, was about to walk out of Dallas' "escape-proof" jail.

Gun in hand, Bailey walked down the stairs to the sixth floor and repeated his performance from the eighth. He grabbed a jailer and made him operate the elevator down to the ground floor. There he grabbed the booking clerk and the keys to the outer doors, then made the clerk walk him to his car. Bailey put him in the passenger seat and drove away.

Gus Jones was in his room at the Baker Hotel in Dallas when the radio blared the story that Harvey Bailey, suspected machine gunner at the Kansas City Massacre and kidnapper of C. F. Urschel, had just escaped from the Dallas County jail, taking one of the prison guards as a hostage.

Jones grabbed his machine gun, jumped in his car and joined the Dallas Police Department, which was already in pursuit. Jones was sure Bailey would head back to the cover of the Cooksen Hills to hide out. Police departments along the route in Oklahoma were alerted and lay in wait.

The jailer's car was hardly the type of driving machine Bailey was accustomed to when he was making his classic escapes over the dusty back roads of the Midwest. In fact, because it was raining, it couldn't handle them at all, slipping and sliding in the mud. Consequently, Bailey had to stay on the paved roads and drove straight into a police stakeout in Ardmore, Oklahoma. The cops chased him for some five miles before he lost control of the car in a high-speed turn, clipped a lamppost and flipped.

Jones and company arrived some twenty minutes later and decided to move their prisoner directly to Oklahoma City. Jones was to make certain the same kind of prison break did not occur in Oklahoma City. He threw cuffs and leg shackles on Bailey, put him in a car, got in and led a heavily armed, five-vehicle caravan north.

On September 5, still wearing his gray prison suit, but now sporting chains and leg irons, Harvey Bailey was put on display. The members of the press were invited to take photographs.

No worse the wear for his escape ordeal and flipped-car incident, the always-confident, wisecracking Bailey smiled into the firing flashbulbs and said, "Get a good one."

Wire service reporter Jack Stinnett was invited along for the ride to Oklahoma City so he could write a firsthand account of the transfer of Bailey out of Texas. When they got to Oklahoma City, Bailey was thrown into the same cell as Boss and Armon Shannon, later to be joined by Bates, who was being flown in from Denver. Jones surrounded the cell with a round-the-clock phalanx of agents armed with machine guns and tear gas.

The county sheriff was embarrassed by Bailey's bold move and immediately tried to throw suspicion on his attorney. He noted that Bailey was placed in the "death cell" and held incommunicado except for visits from his lawyer: "He was supposed to have a special guard watching him at all times. So far as has been reported to us no one not employed in the jail saw Bailey since his lawyer visited him last Friday."

James H. Mathers, Bailey's attorney, was quick to respond.

"When I visited him Friday, the cell looked to me as if it would be impossible to conceal even a hairpin there."

Mathers complained that the sheriff was insinuating that he had had a part in the escape preparations.

"Why, I wouldn't have done such a thing and even if I had wanted to, I couldn't have," said Mathers. "I didn't hand a saw or gun to Bailey nor have I ever done so for any other client."

The lawyer said he thought Bailey was foolish for trying to escape, because from his conversation he judged the outlaw had a meritorious defense to the charge in connection with Urschel's kidnapping.

Bailey had escaped his Dallas confines by bribing a deputy sheriff with the promise of a $10,000 reward at the completion of a successful flight. The deputy had complied by providing Bailey with the handgun and a wrench and hacksaw with which to open his cell's bars.

While Bailey was being transported into Oklahoma, Pretty Boy Floyd, another of the Kansas City Massacre suspects, was desperately trying to get out of it. He had stolen and crashed three cars in the process of fleeing police, who had engaged him and his three companions in a gun battle. Nine miles north of Alva, Oklahoma, Floyd's car got stuck in a ditch. Despite the drought, it had been raining heavily in Oklahoma, making the back-road getaways favored by gangsters increasingly difficult. When a farmer stopped his car to help, Floyd's group took his car, loaded in their weapons and drove away toward the Kansas border.

When police arrived, they searched the car and found a letter on the backseat addressed to Harvey Bailey. Bailey was contemptuous of Floyd and the other gun-happy desperados who were shooting up banks and cops and in general making it hard for professionals like himself to go about their business. Some of his comments had made it into the press, in which he was quoted referring to Floyd as a two-bit hustler and a "small fry."

Floyd apparently took umbrage at that and had fired off a retort that he planned to mail once he figured out what jail Bailey was going to end up in. It read:

Harvey Bailey:
You've talked yourself into the joint. Now you're trying to get heavy by talking about Pretty Boy, and it may be if you talk fast enough, you'll miss the chair. I realize I'm not too tough. As far as kidnappers are concerned it has always been mysterious to me why they didn't design tough guys like you to catch me. Due to the colorful display of machine guns and for your transportation, you have allowed yourself to imagine people think you are tough but it is no object for the law to steal a harmless man.

I don't carry guns around with me to

impress any one. I carry them as a dire necessity. When the time comes I am always positive of my capability to use them. I am not boasting I am too tough to die. I know some day I am going to lose, but when that time comes I will not throw up my hands and rely on brains to get me out.

I may be a 'small-time hister *[sic]*' and you the brains of money, a $200,000 plot. Still, I'm outside enjoying the few dollars I make while you probably are wracking your enormous brain trying to beat the chair.

The editors at *The Daily Oklahoman* just loved that. They ran the letter next to a large picture of Bailey in chains as he was beginning his journey to Oklahoma City for trial.

And although the news media, prompted by the federal investigators, kept referring to Bailey as the "brains" behind the kidnapping, Boss Shannon kept telling them that Bailey had nothing to do with it. Bailey had used the farm various times in July, and once with Bob Brady and James Clark, his partners from the prison break, he said. But Shannon's protestations didn't matter. Based on the circumstantial evidence of the ransom money in his pocket and the fact that he was arrested at the farm where Urschel had been held hostage, the attorney general had decided that Bailey was going down for the kidnapping, and the trial would start in two weeks.

Back in Texas, Kathryn was becoming increasingly distraught over the fate of her mother and stepfather. And without George around with his network of drop sites, safe phones and coded communication, she was having a hard time making legal arrangements on her own. Plus she was steamed that he had left her in the lurch and was probably whoring around with one of his old girlfriends in Mississippi. Her suspicion was heightened when she drove to the Biloxi hotel address he'd left with Coleman and found him gone. She headed back to Texas, still desperate to get in touch with her lawyer, Sam Sayers, and see if he'd made any progress on getting the indictment against her mother dropped. Frustrated, she decided to call him directly from Waco.

"Hello, this is your girlfriend," said Kathryn.

"Which girlfriend?" Sayers responded.

"Your best girl. The one with the Pekinese dogs."

Sayers, who rightly suspected his phone was being tapped, immediately panicked. "I can't talk to you now. You know better than to call me on this phone!" Then he hung up.

Kathryn got back in the pickup truck she was using for cover and continued on the road toward Fort Worth.

She was driving the backcountry roads when she encountered a homeless couple and their twelve-year-old daughter hitchhiking. They were the classic victims of the drought, dust and depression that was afflicting the Oklahoma-Texas farm belt, an itinerant farm family who'd been thrown off their land after the bank had foreclosed on it.

By 1933, 64 percent of Oklahoma's farm production had dwindled away. Nearly 20 percent of the state's population threw their belongings into whatever vehicle they had and just drove west out of the state in search of opportunities as far away as California. They became the despised and derided Okies that were traveling in such swarms that western states began setting up "bum blockades" along Route 66 to keep them out.

Luther Arnold had been working on a farm owned by his uncle in the small town of Tussy, Oklahoma. When the hard times hit, his uncle was forced to sell the farm and Luther had to move out. He took his wife, Flossie Mae, and their twelve-year-old daughter, Geraldine, and started wandering around looking for work. But he didn't find any. They didn't even own a vehicle they could escape in. They had taken all the belongings they could carry and took to the road in search of work and the kindness of strangers. In the town of Graham, Texas, the city marshal took pity on them and bought them breakfast. In Temple, Texas, a Baptist minister gave them money for a room. Then they moved to the Salvation Army.

On Monday, September 4, Luther had just finished shaving in a filling station on the outskirts of Itasca. He and the family had continued their journey and were about ten yards down the road when a woman in a Model A Ford pickup truck pulled up next to them and asked if they wanted a ride.

After the family had climbed aboard, she introduced herself as Kathryn Montgomery and asked Luther what he had been doing.

"Nothing, but I am looking for anything to do to feed three hungry people."

"I live on a ranch near Brownwood, Texas, and might be able to help you," said Kathryn, resplendent in her red wig and overalls.

Kathryn offered to get them a room where they could spend the night and offered to buy them dinner. Over dinner she grilled them with questions about their life and times. Specifically she wanted to know if Luther was wanted by the law. Luther said there was "nothing against" him and he was "not wanted for any offense."

After dinner they drove to a tourist camp with four bungalows. Kathryn sent Luther into the office to rent two of them.

Luther and Flossie Marie Arnold could not have envisioned what Kathryn had in store for them and little Geraldine, but with only six dollars in their pockets and the prospect of sleeping outdoors that night, they readily accepted the stranger's assistance. Kathryn knew the law was looking for her and her husband, and they might have figured that they'd split up. Traveling with a down-and-out couple and their pimply-faced kid would be good cover. But after treating them to dinner, she decided to lay down a bigger gambit.

"I like you people, and would like to fix it so you could make a little money. Can I trust you?"

"Absolutely," said Luther.

"I have driven three thousand miles to see my lawyer and he failed to meet me. I came all the way from Gulfport, Mississippi." Kathryn looked at Luther and asked, "What would you people think if I told you who I am?"

"Go ahead and tell me," said Luther. "You can trust us."

"I am Kathryn Kelly, whom you no doubt have read about in the papers, and I am wanted for questioning," she explained to the astonished Arnolds. "Mr. Arnold, I am going to place a big trust in you. I want you to go to Fort Worth and contact my lawyer, Sam Sayers, of the firm of McClain, Scott and Sayers. I want you to ask Sayers for the details of the situation up to date and to specifically ask him what has happened concerning my offer of compromise by surrendering Kelly for the release of my father and mother."

She told the Arnolds that she and her parents had been wrongly accused. They had nothing to do with the crime. Now, she explained, she desperately needed to get her innocent mother out of jail and cleared of all these ridiculous charges that had been laid against her. She told Luther to try to find out how they were doing and whether they needed anything.

She gave him $50 and a note to Sayers explaining his role and letting Sayers know that Arnold was serving as her go-between. She told him to identify himself as "Ingersoll." In addition, she told him to "find out if he got the diamonds and the $1,000 I sent by messenger from Mineral Wells."

Luther Arnold could not believe his good fortune. In a matter of hours he had transformed himself from a desperate homeless bum to contact man for the most wanted criminal organization in the nation. His wife and daughter were safely ensconced in comfortable accommodations and he had money in his pocket and an important job to do. When Luther got to Fort Worth he called Sayers from a coffee shop and said he was Ingersoll and needed to talk to him right away.

"Come right on up now," said Sayers.

Arnold got to the Sinclair Building at about 10:00 a.m. and went to Sayers's office on the twelfth floor. Sayers wasn't used to doing business with homeless Okies, but as an attorney who specialized in dealing with a gangster clientele, he was ready for anything.

Luther gave him Kathryn's note, which he quickly read.

"I am certainly glad to see you. I know Kathryn is plenty sore because I failed to meet her in Waco. You can tell her that I went to Waco and got a lawyer friend of mine to go to the hotels there, but he could not find her registered there under the name she gave me.

"Kathryn is probably sore because we have not obtained the release of the Shannons on bond. I want you to impress on her that this firm and all other lawyers connected with the case did everything they could, and are still doing all they can, but the judge just wouldn't grant the bond.

"You can tell Kathryn that I put her proposition up to them and talked trade but couldn't get any satisfaction out of the judge or the United States Attorney. I am awful glad that she has got somebody she can trust to make contact and will not have to do it personally herself."

Arnold queried Sayers about the package that had been sent from Mineral Wells.

"Tell Kathryn that I received the diamond ring and the money," Sayers replied.

Luther took a bus back to the tourist camp at Cleburne and delivered the bad news to a frustrated Kathryn. She wondered if her Texas attorney lacked the right connections in Oklahoma City to get the deal done.

"You are an Oklahoma boy, you ought to know some good lawyer in Oklahoma that I could employ," she said.

In fact, Luther said he did know a lawyer.

He lived in Enid.

"Do you think he would be good in this case?"

"I think so," replied Arnold.

Kathryn told him she would take him to Fort Worth and he could go to Oklahoma by "plane, train or automobile" to see if he could get the lawyer to do what Sayers had been unable to.

"I'd rather travel by car," said Luther.

"I have a new Chevy Coupe that Sam Sayers has in Fort Worth," said Kathryn, telling Luther he could use that to get to Enid. After she had driven to the edge of town, she stopped the pickup and wrote a note to Sayers instructing him to give the car to Arnold. She told Arnold she would take good care of Flossie Mae and Geraldine while he was gone and told him to check for further instructions at the General Delivery window at the San Antonio Post Office.

If Arnold had any second thoughts about leaving his wife and daughter in the care of one of the most notorious women in America, he didn't let on. When he got back to Fort Worth, Sayers wasn't available. So with time on his hands and $300 of Kathryn's expense money in his pocket, Arnold decided to blow off some steam. He found a local speakeasy and picked up two women, and partied long into the night.

In the morning he called Sayers and got the car, explaining that he was going to Oklahoma to see if attorney John Roberts could help with the plea deal and the case.

"That's fine," said Sayers. "I believe he can do us some good in Oklahoma." Luther told Sayers that Kathryn wanted him and the rest of the legal team to meet the next Sunday, September 10, at the Skirvin Hotel in Oklahoma City.

Arnold wanted to know if the car was "all right." He didn't want to be driving something that Kathryn's husband had used in a robbery that would draw "the laws."

"Yes, it's all right," said Sayers. "It's paid for and here are the title papers for it."

Arnold then drove his two new lady friends to Enid and hired Roberts to represent the Shannons. He then proceeded to Oklahoma City and checked into the city's premier hotel, the Skirvin, and continued to romance his two new friends in grand style.

Unbeknownst to the clueless Arnold, the Skirvin was also the residence of choice for the Bureau's agents and the prosecutors who would be trying the case against Bailey, Bates and the Shannons.

Agents were watching the defense team

closely and tracking anyone that made contact with them. Word had gotten to Jones about Arnold, whose drunken claims in Fort Worth had been picked up by the local agents there. So Jones put agents in rooms adjacent to Arnold's, but all they picked up from their eavesdropping were the sounds of the drunken orgy inside. Two days later, when Arnold had had enough of his two expensive escorts, he slipped out of the Skirvin, leaving them behind, along with the Bureau's agents who'd been assigned to watch him.

When Jones learned what his rookie agents had allowed to happen he was livid. He'd just blown his best chance to find the Kellys.

Oblivious to the trouble he'd unconsciously managed to elude, Arnold drove off in Kathryn's Chevy to San Antonio, where she'd rented a furnished bungalow and was living with Flossie Mae and Geraldine. When he arrived, Kathryn staked him with another wad of cash and sent him back to Oklahoma to pay the lawyers for her mama's defense. Newly flush, the naïve Arnold headed back to the Skirvin, but not before stopping off in Fort Worth for another night of bacchanalia.

He was still nursing a hangover the next day when he showed up at the hotel, where

Jones's men grabbed him and carted him off to jail.

Kathryn had told Cass Coleman to get in touch with her in San Antonio if her husband showed up looking for her. On September 11, she picked up a telegram from Coleman with the cryptic message: "MOTHER BETTER."

Kathryn grabbed Geraldine and headed off to Coleman's ranch, leaving Flossie Mae at the house, telling her she would be back the next day.

Reunited with George at the Coleman ranch, she greeted him defiantly: "I don't know whether to kiss you or kill you!"

The couple immediately launched into a marital spat that quickly degenerated into mutual accusations and death threats. She accused him of whoring around in Mississippi, he called her a damned liar. She blamed him for getting her mother arrested. He blamed her for dreaming up the vile scheme in the first place.

Kathryn demanded proof of George's repentance. She wanted George to turn himself in to the prosecutors in exchange for their dropping of the charges against her mother. The exasperated George agreed to take the rap for the kidnapping, but told her she'd have to make the deal first, because once he turned himself in, they'd have no leverage.

While the Kellys were bickering at the Coleman ranch, Gus Jones's agents were busy beating information out of the hapless Arnold in Oklahoma. After about six hours of forceful conversation, he'd given up just about everything he knew about the Kellys and their hideouts.

At the end of his statement, Luther wrote, "I realize that I have been very foolish in engaging in this proposition of being a contact man for Kathryn Kelly and I am willing to tell the Government representatives anything else that I can think of concerning this matter and it is my desire to wash my hands of the entire proposition, and I hope any leniency possible will be shown me in connections with my actions."

The agents in Oklahoma dispatched a team in San Antonio to raid the Kellys' rented house. They descended in force, but all they found was the distraught Flossie Mae, who told them the Kellys had taken her daughter and left for Cass Coleman's ranch.

Once again, Hoover's men had missed their prey by a matter of hours.

Cass Coleman's neighbor, Clarence Durham, had been getting nervous about his proximity to the hot Coleman farm. He also didn't like the fact that Kelly seemed to think he could use his house to stay out of the glare that was focused on Coleman. Durham wanted to stay out of trouble, and he wanted Kelly to stay away from him. The day that the agents had crashed the Kelly pad in San Antonio and found the tearful Flossie Mae, Durham had pulled up to his place to find the Kellys lounging on a mattress he kept on the front porch for sleeping in summer heat. In a rage, he booted them out and immediately after they left he headed for the county sheriff's office and unloaded everything he knew about Machine Gun Kelly and his comings and goings around his house and the Coleman farm. As he was giving up all that he could, the Kellys had loaded their car and headed off to Chicago with Geraldine in tow.

The sheriff put out an all-points bulletin, dispatched his men and set roadblocks. Soon, reports were pouring in from all over the county and beyond. From the reports, it appeared as if they were headed back to Oklahoma City and right into the trap laid by the combined law enforcement teams. But, once again, the Kellys had slipped right through it. They sped past Oklahoma City, with their twelve-year-old hostage, and were heading straight for Chicago. George had finally gotten his way with his headstrong wife. They arrived there on Sunday, September 17, and rented an apartment on the city's near North Side. They told the landlord they'd come to the city to visit the World's Fair.

George knew a mechanic and garage operator named Joe Bergl in the southwest suburb of Cicero, in the heart of Capone's turf. Bergl did much of his underworld business through the Michigan Tavern at 1150 South Michigan Avenue. The tavern was run by Abe and Morris Caplan, and Kelly had used the bar as a meeting place when he was in Chicago, and also as a mailing address and a friendly phone. This time he asked Caplan to flip his car for something newer and faster. Caplan explained that Bergl was up to his neck in work (he was outfitting an armor-plated car for Alvin Karpis and the Barkers for a raid on the Federal Reserve Bank), but that he would arrange something if Kelly could wait a few days.

The Kellys tried to blend into their new neighborhood, living as a happy couple with their charming preteen daughter, but Kelly was wound too tight to relax. Everywhere they went, he thought he saw suspicious people watching him. He'd get up and leave dinners prematurely, throwing money on the table as he left. He continued to berate Kathryn for her harebrained kidnapping venture. All of this in front of the absorptive Geraldine.

8
CATCHING KELLY

On September 16, John Roberts appeared in Oklahoma City and made his offer to the prosecution. Acting on behalf of his clients, George and Kathryn Kelly, Roberts announced that George Kelly, the man whom federal agents had chased over fully one-third of the nation, was willing to turn himself in if the government would drop charges against R. G. Shannon, his wife, Ora, and their son, Armon.

The Shannons, he claimed, were mere victims of circumstance, unwilling hosts who were forced under threat of death by Machine Gun Kelly to guard and house his kidnapped victim.

"The Kellys," he said, "were willing to go to any expense, to go to any extreme, to see that the Shannons, their relatives, do not suffer."

Keenan thought this deal sounded good. The Kellys were proving to be extremely elusive, and getting them in custody and bringing all the ringleaders down in one quick, dramatic trial would prove how serious and how effective the new administration would be in prosecuting its War on Crime. The Shannons were really small timers. Even Bates with his pages-long rap sheet was a relatively unknown thug. The now infamous Machine Gun Kelly was the marquee character they needed to convict in a most decisive fashion. Kelly and his colorful moniker had been blaring from the national news radio reports. His menacing nature, enhanced in no small part by the Bureau's descriptions and publicity, was on display in the press as his story unfolded in serial fashion as the weeks dragged on. Keenan felt the time was right to bring him in, and if no one got killed in the process, so much the better.

He wrote to U.S. Attorney Herbert Hyde in favor of the deal: "If we could obtain the return of Kelly and the ransom money without any commitment as to what shall happen to Kelly, I am hoping that Judge Vaught could see his way clear to being very lenient to Mrs. Shannon and Mrs. Kelly, even to the point of absolute release if Kelly and the money could be obtained and if we had a free hand to deal with Kelly, Bates and Bailey as the facts justify."

But Keenan had failed to check the strategy with Hoover, who was orchestrating the manhunt and the prosecution from Washington. He wanted a string of convictions. He would pursue them all, no quarter given. When he heard the mere suggestion that Kathryn Kelly should be dealt with leniently, it made him apoplectic. He believed Kathryn was the criminal mastermind behind the kidnapping who manipulated her husband into carrying it out. He described her as a "cunning, cruel, criminal actress . . . who could conceive a kidnapping, and force it through to a conclusion largely through her domination of her husband . . . who could only bow before her tirades and do as she bade him."

Hyde was quick to dismiss the offer:

"As attorney for the government, I am interested in only three things as far as the Shannons and Kellys are concerned. First, the arrest and conviction of George and Kathryn Kelly; second, the conviction of the Shannons; and third, the return of every cent of the $200,000 ransom money lost by one of Oklahoma's leading citizens.

"If they expect any recommendation of leniency from the government as to the Shannons, we will expect the Kellys' unconditional surrender and return of the ransom."

Roberts, who actually had no idea where his clients could be found, scoffed at the government's demands.

Bailey's attorney, James Mathers, whose client was absolutely innocent of any charges associated with the kidnapping — but in fact guilty of so much more — had very little he could do on behalf of his unlucky client, who just happened to be sleeping at the hostage holding pen with $700 of ransom money in his pocket when the feds arrived looking for Kelly.

He petitioned the court for a change of venue. "The newspapers have published inflammatory, untrue, false, highly colored, and exaggerated articles, making it impossible for Mr. Bailey to get a fair trial in the western federal district of Oklahoma."

Judge Vaught was unmoved and not willing to entertain any motion that might delay his proceedings, noting that the national press had made the story front-page news in nearly every state in the country. "I was in another state (New Mexico) in August. There was just about as much in the newspapers there as anywhere else. It is a matter of such great public interest and importance that the press of the United States has carried a great deal on the case. Newspapers have speculated on the case and the witnesses. I can see no advantage to the defendant in a change of venue."

The press with its wire services and the radio with its instant national voice had made the case something that the entire nation was aware of. There were few places in the country with a federal court where you could go to find an uninformed, unprejudiced jury. The nation had shrunk. On matters of national import, everyone knew everyone else's business. Harvey Bailey had achieved the level of national fame and recognition he had spent his life trying to avoid. There were few, if any, places in the country where he could get a fair trial — certainly not Oklahoma City. But that mattered little. The Bureau's agents assigned to guard the affable Bailey admitted to him that there were few who believed he was involved in the kidnapping. But that didn't matter. He had gotten away with so much in his lifetime that no one could build a case on. If, ironically, a good case could be made for something he didn't do, so what? Tables turned. Guilty or not, they told him, you are going down for this one.

The grand jury would convene in two days.

While Keenan was rejecting the plea deal, Urschel received a death threat in the form of a letter from Kelly:

Ignorant Charles:
   Just a few lines to let you know that I am getting my plans made to destroy your so-called mansion, and you and your family immediately after this trial. And young fellow, I guess you've begun to realize your serious mistake. Are you ignorant enough to think the Government can guard you forever? I gave you credit for more sense than that, and figured you thought too much of your family to jeopardize them as you have, but if you don't look out for them, why should we? I dislike hurting the innocent, but I told you exactly what would happen and you can bet $200,000 more everything I said will be true. You are living on borrowed time now. You know that the Shannon family are victims of circumstances the same as you was. You don't seem to mind prosecuting the innocent; neither will I have any conscious qualms over brutally murdering your family. The Shannons have put the heat on, but I don't desire to see them prosecuted as they are innocent

and I have a much better method of settling with them. As far as the guilty being punished, you would probably have lived the rest of your life in peace had you tried only the guilty, but if the Shannons are convicted, look out, and God help you for he is the only one that will be able to do you any good. In the event of my arrest, I've already formed an outfit to take care of and destroy you and yours the same as if I was there. I am spending your money to have you and your family killed — nice, eh? You are bucking people who have cash, planes, bombs and unlimited connection both here and abroad. I have friends in Oklahoma City that know every move and every plan you make, and you are still too dumb to figure out the finger man there.

If my brain was no larger than yours, the Government would have had me long ago, as it is I am drinking good beer and will yet see you and your family like I should have left you in the first place — stone dead.

I don't worry about Bates and Bailey. They will be out for the ceremonies — your slaughter.

Now say — it is up to you; if the Shannons are convicted, you can get another rich wife in hell, because that will be the only place you can use one.

Adious, smart one.

Your worst enemy,
GEO. R. KELLY

I will put my fingerprints below so you can't say some crank wrote this.

Give Keenan my regards and tell him maybe he would like to meet the owner of the above.

See you in hell.

Kelly's letter landed in Oklahoma City as jury selection for the trial of Bailey, Bates and the Shannons was about to start. In response, security precautions were ratcheted up even higher.

Hoover had sent his number-two agent, Assistant Director Harold "Pop" Nathan to Oklahoma, to oversee the operations on the ground. Nathan called a meeting with Keenan, the Urschels and Kirkpatrick. Nathan wanted the contents of the letters withheld until after the trial. But Urschel wanted them published immediately. He believed if they were not published, the gangsters would feel that law enforcement officials, as well as the Urschels, were intimidated. Urschel wanted there to be no doubt that he had thrown his lot in with the feds. He responded with a statement to the press:

> We are eager for this letter to be published so the people of the United States will know it is no fabrication from the air and will know the sort of people we have defied and are opposed to. We still have faith in the ultimate success of the federal government in its struggle with crime, and are gambling the safety of every member of our group on that success. We have thrown our lot with Law and the Government and are in this fight to the finish. The Urschel family does not waste one moment in giving gangland its answer.

The next day, Urschel carried Kelly's threatening letter folded in his suit coat pocket and calmly watched the jury proceedings from his front-row seat in the courtroom. Unbeknownst to Kelly, his loving wife, Kathryn, had penned her own communication to Urschel proclaiming her innocence and that of the Shannons, noting that the "blame for this entire mess is squarely on the shoulders of Machine Gun Kelly."

George had followed up his letter to Urschel with one to *The Daily Oklahoman* coauthored by Kathryn. He prefaced it with a perfectly genteel request couched in nonthreatening, respectful language, as if he were writing a letter to the editor with a counterpoint to one of their editorials:

Dear Sirs —
You will please publish the enclosed in your paper as I want the Shannons to be sure to read it. Yours truly, G. Kelly
Gentleman:
I desire the public to know that the Shannon family are innocent victims in the Charles F. Urschel case the same as Urschel was.

I understand that they are now government witnesses also defendants, and I don't want them convicted, for I desire to settle with them in my own way and with no assistance from the government.

Mr. Urschel and the government prosecution know that the Shannons had no part or no intentions of aiding in the matter and were forced to do so the same as Urschel was forced to leave his home.

Why didn't Urschel call the law to Norman when he was released, instead of riding a cab peacefully into the city and waiting a given time to call them? Fear, gentleman, fear, the same fear that dominated the Shannons.

I hate and despise the government for their crooked dealings and do not wish them to convict people as innocent of that crime and guilty of one thing — talking to me. I can take care of my end and will the way I want to. You might state for Mr. Keenan's benefit that he has never come anywhere near catching me, although I have been in Oklahoma City four nights and up town each day.

We will see how the trial progresses and can adjust our end accordingly. I am putting my prints on this so you will know it is genuine.

Yours truly,
Geo. R. Kelly

Nathan had reunited the Arnolds, bringing Flossie Mae into Oklahoma City, where he waited for the Kellys to make contact. On Thursday, September 21, they did. Kathryn penned a letter to Flossie Mae writing in coded language about what a good job Luther had done arranging the legal team to defend her in court.

Dear Midge,

How are you? I am just fine, so is the baby. She has a lot of new clothes. Shoes, and etc. She is having a nice time. Tell the "boy friend" I want him to drop me a letter to the below address and tell me what is needed when he wants to meet me, etc. Tell him his friend has been swell in my estimation, and I believe I will have my part here fixed within the next week anyway as I am waiting on some New York people. If he wants me at any time write that address, below, and tell him anything he can do for those people, to do it. . . . I am taking care of the baby honey. She's never out of my sight, and be careful to take care of my clothes for they are all I have so don't lose them . . . Communicate with — Burt Edwards, 1150 S. Michigan Ave. Chicago, Ill.

After weeks of near-misses, the Bureau finally had a solid lead on the Kellys. Nathan called Purvis in Chicago. He gave him the address of the Michigan Tavern and told him the Kellys were using it as a communications center. Stake it out. When they show up, grab them.

By then, Caplan had obtained a car from

Joe Bergl for the Kellys and dropped it off at a tire store so that it could be equipped with four new tires and two spares. He told the Kellys to meet him at the tavern at 9:30 a.m.

On September 21, George, Kathryn and Geraldine went into the Michigan Tavern and told the bartender they were there to see Caplan. They then took a seat in a booth and ordered two beers, some pretzels and a soda for Geraldine. Caplan joined them a few minutes later and plopped a whiskey bottle down on the table, giving Geraldine a quizzical look.

"She's all right," said George. "She's a nice little girl."

Caplan told Kelly the car was ready and could be picked up at the General Tire Company at Twenty-third and Cottage Grove. Kelly handed over $265, shook hands, grabbed Kathryn and Geraldine, got in a taxi and drove off to get their new ride.

That very morning, Purvis finally got around to following up on his instructions to stake out the Michigan Tavern. He put two agents on it, but before heading to Michigan Avenue, they went to the post office to interview the tavern's mail carrier and see if they could intercept any interesting deliveries. They were too late. The car-

310

rier was already on his route.

When they managed to catch up to him outside the tavern, they quizzed him about suspicious special deliveries going in and out. Of course, no postal clerk servicing the Michigan Tavern would last very long giving information to the cops, so not surprisingly, the postman gave up nothing the agents found useful. They got back in their car and returned to the Bureau downtown.

Had they gone inside the Tavern to look around, they would have found the Kellys sitting in the booth with Geraldine.

When Hoover discovered what had happened he went ballistic. His favorite agent had blown the best tip they'd had for nabbing Kelly. Why had he waited? What reason was there for the delay? Time was of the essence and he let a notorious kidnapper slip through his grasp. This was unconscionable. "This," lamented Hoover in a note he put in Purvis's file, "was a miserable piece of work."

Purvis and his men were about to let a second prized capture slip through their fingers. Purvis had received a tip that a close friend of Verne Miller's girl, Vi Mathias, was living at the Sherone Apartments on Sheridan Road. They put the apartment under surveillance and discovered that Mathias herself had moved in. One of Purvis's junior agents, Johnny Madala, moved into the apartment building to keep her under surveillance. When a man answering to Miller's description showed up, Madala phoned in the information and agent Ed Guinane arrived with a team of agents and Chicago policemen. They surrounded the apartment and waited.

The next morning, Miller emerged and disappeared down a hallway as the lawmen in Madala's apartment delayed while trying to make a positive identification as their frustrated junior agent kept insisting in a stage whisper, "It's Miller! It's Miller!"

By the time Miller was jumping in his car, agent Lew Nichols caught up to him and ran after the fleeing car shouting, "Stop!"

Miller turned and fired two shots at Nichols, uncharacteristically missing with both. Nichols returned fire as panicked pedestrians screamed and ran for cover. A state trooper sprayed the car with a burst of machine-gun fire, but it sped away. Despite a citywide police alert, Miller disappeared.

(While the agents had earlier been chasing Miller in cities like Chicago, Detroit and New York, he'd been on a cross-country road trip visiting the nation's top resorts and playing golf on some of its finest courses.)

On Monday, August 31, signed confessions from Ora, Oleta and Armon Shannon were handed over to the prosecutor. Salter said they would be included in the evidence presented on Wednesday by U.S. Attorney Herbert Hyde. In Washington, DC, Joseph Keenan boarded a plane headed for Oklahoma City.

(The kidnapping scourge continued unabated even as Keenan was headed toward the airport. Dr. E. L. Beck, a noted Texarkana surgeon, had just started up his car and was leaving the hospital when a masked man jumped on his running board, stuck a gun in through the window and ordered him to stop. Another man jumped in the passenger seat and the gunman got in back and ordered him to drive away.)

In Dallas, reporters pressed the Bureau's agents for details about the confessions, but they stayed mum.

"No person outside the government service knows what is in those statements and no one can know until the proper time. It is our policy when a statement is given to us to protect it. We must on account of prospective witnesses and the like and we do, even if it tears the hide off," said agent

Frank Blake.

"We have to do one thing above all else: to stop this kidnapping business. We have to make victims realize they can tell us whatever they want to and that their confidence will be respected. We have got to treat the statements of witnesses — codefendants or otherwise — in the same way. We have to protect them to that extent. It might be bad indeed for certain persons on the outside to find out who made this or that confession and what they said."

Blake was well aware that witness intimidation and witness elimination were part and parcel of the gang business. The Bureau had a cooperative witness and victim in Charles Urschel. With everything that was going on, they did not want him getting cold feet. He, his wife and their associates were ready and eager to testify in the most important case in the Bureau's history. Nothing was being left to chance.

On Monday, the county sheriff's department ordered in twenty machine guns for the guards who would surround the courthouse when the grand jury convened on Wednesday. Six deputies had spent two weeks being trained to operate the weapons expertly. Each witness would be guarded by federal agents armed with submachine guns and automatics. U.S. Attorney Hyde announced that the grand jury would deliberate behind an armed wall, which "will result in an impregnable barrage of gunfire should any desperate effort be made to approach witnesses or principals in the Urschel case."

Hyde also announced that if indictments were handed up by the grand jury, he would seek an immediate trial.

"While this is a matter completely discretionary with the court," Hyde said, "I will ask that it be given precedence over all pending criminal matters. I hope to see it go to trial not later than the first week in September. We will not wait for the arrest of George Kelly. Evidence on hand is sufficient to convict nearly all of those now held, even if we do not ask Urschel or others who contacted the kidnappers to testify."

Meanwhile, Keenan had arrived in Kansas City to assess the case the county prosecutors there had against Bailey. They wanted to tag him for murder in the Kansas City Massacre. If they could, they would send him to the chair. Keenan wanted Bailey taken down by the federal prosecutors in the Urschel case and he was virtually certain of success. Conversely, the county prosecutor in Kansas City had very little evidence to go on. His case was weak. Nevertheless, he wanted to take a crack at it on the basis of just two eyewitnesses that could identify Bailey as one of the shooters.

Keenan knew how things worked in Kansas City, the biggest organized crime empire west of Chicago. Bailey's connections could buy an acquittal if they didn't simply decide to spring him from jail. In Oklahoma City, the shoe was on the other foot. It was the victim who had the courts on his side. It was the victim whom the police wanted to protect. No, it would be in Oklahoma City where Bailey would go on trial with Charles Urschel's longtime friend and hunting partner, Edgar Vaught, sitting on the bench. Keenan, with the force of the federal government behind him, made it clear Bailey would not be moved to Kansas City. He'd stand trial in Oklahoma, where the kidnapping occurred. And the federal government would get the credit for bringing down the nation's most notorious bank robber.

The next day, he made the announcement that Bailey and ten others would be tried in Oklahoma City. He would seek life sentences for every one. On the morning the grand jury convened, three county sheriffs in suits and ties appeared on the front page of the newspapers showing off their new weaponry. The caption gave the details:

"George Kerr is shown demonstrating a Thompson submachine gun similar to those used by Charles F. Urschel's kidnappers. [Tom] Miler in the center, is holding a heavy Browning automatic rifle of a type especially developed by the army to pierce armor plates. Bullets from this gun will rip through the armored cars used by many eastern gangsters. [Earl] Gordon is demonstrating a new gas gun, with its seven-inch cartridge. One shot would start tears in the eyes of every person within fifty yards. These are the types of guns that will be used by officers during the federal grand jury quiz of the Urschel kidnap suspects which opens Wednesday."

The grand jury's decision didn't take long. Twenty-one witnesses, including the Urschels and the Jarretts, testified. The jury deliberated and handed up indictments for fourteen people, including Kelly, Bates, Bailey, the Shannons and five underworld figures from St. Paul who'd been caught passing or laundering Urschel ransom money.

Keenan took to the stage immediately to announce the government's "new deal" in the War on Crime, which he said would soon lead to the "hanging and electrocution" of the nation's racketeers. The case would go to trial in two weeks.

The measured Ivy Leaguer said the federal government intended to stamp out organized crime even if it had to use the United States Army to do it. With a hint of a smirk, he added that that would not be necessary.

"We are ready to meet the challenge of these gangsters fearlessly and with our own weapons. We are in deadly earnest and this statement is made with no desire to be melodramatic," he said.

"Representatives of the federal government in Washington are very much pleased with the cooperation received locally in this case. They are pleased with the dispatch with which the matter was handled, with the earnest attention given it by Judge Edgar S. Vaught, Herbert K. Hyde, the U.S. Attorney and the grand jury.

"We appreciate fully the patriotic response of Mr. Urschel in casting aside personal considerations. It is encouraging to the government in its drive to wipe out gangster depredation in which he offered his services as a witness. The federal government will respond by giving Mr. Urschel and his family full protection. Neither Mr. Urschel nor anyone else will be left to further fear attacks of the underworld," Keenan concluded.

Effects of dust storms
on Oklahoma farms.

Union Station, scene of the Kansas City Massacre.

The Urschel home, in Oklahoma City, where the kidnapping took place.

Berenice and Charles Urschel
(COURTESY OF *THE OKLAHOMAN*)

J. Edgar Hoover
(LIBRARY OF
CONGRESS, PRINTS
AND PHOTOGRAPHS
DIVISION)

Hoover and Melvin
Purvis, Special
Agent in Charge of
the Bureau's
Chicago office.
(LIBRARY OF
CONGRESS, PRINTS
AND PHOTOGRAPHS
DIVISION)

Joseph Keenan,
head of the
Department of
Justice Criminal
Division.
(LIBRARY OF
CONGRESS, PRINTS
AND PHOTOGRAPHS
DIVISION)

Attorney General Homer Cummings leaves the White House after conferring with President Franklin Roosevelt.
(LIBRARY OF CONGRESS, PRINTS AND PHOTOGRAPHS DIVISION)

George "Machine Gun" Kelly under the guard of heavily armed law enforcement officers.
(COURTESY OF *THE OKLAHOMAN*)

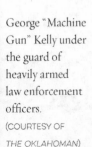

George and Kathryn
Kelly during the trial.
(COURTESY OF
THE OKLAHOMAN)

Charles Urschel
in court.
(COURTESY OF
THE OKLAHOMAN)

President Franklin Roosevelt addresses a conference on crime
with Attorney General Homer Cummings in 1934.

Alcatraz

■ ■ ■

As he was speaking, William F. Wood, a cousin of President William Howard Taft, was being held captive by kidnappers in California. Howard Meek had kidnapped Wood, and tortured him relentlessly while trying to determine the extent of his wealth. After learning Wood had large amounts of cash and securities in his safe-deposit box, Meek took him to the bank and forced him to withdraw it.

With more than $10,000 in his pockets, Meek decided to indulge himself as he and his captive walked through San Francisco's crowded Market Street. He bought a bag of walnuts and, as he struggled to crack one open, Wood shouted to a nearby policeman, "Get that man! He's got a gun!" and started running away.

Patrolman Michael McDonald looked over at the gesticulating Wood, but before he could respond, Meek drew his gun and fired, hitting McDonald three times as pedestrians on the crowded street scrambled for cover. The wounded McDonald chased Meek, who was firing wildly over his shoulder, wounding an elderly woman in the process. McDonald continued his pursuit, chasing Meek as he unknowingly ran toward two other officers, who shot him dead. Mc-Donald, a forty-year-old father of six, died a short time later.

Kidnapping out West had been so rare prior to the '30s that states rarely saw the need to address it with stiff penalties. Armed robbery, however, was quite another matter. On the roads that traversed the wide-open prairies and high deserts, holding up travelers at gunpoint was a practice that had a long tradition dating back to the early settlers. As automobile travel exploded in the '20s and '30s, hijackings and holdups proliferated, and the sparsely staffed, underfinanced sheriff's departments could do little to stop it.

In Oklahoma, the state legislature tried to solve the problem by passing a draconian law designed to instill fear in any criminal who would contemplate holding up some innocent traveler on the road. They made highway robbery a crime punishable by death in the electric chair. The irony of the fact that Kelly and Bates could fry for stealing $50 from Jarrett, but not for kidnapping Urschel, holding him against his will for nine days and ransoming him for $200,000, was not lost on Joseph Keenan. But there was no way he was going to allow two notorious outlaws to be convicted for a $50 highway robbery and be sentenced to death before he got the chance to put the power of the federal government on display on the national stage. Keenan, Cummings and Hoover needed a big victory in their first prosecution to fuel their drive for federal laws and federal law enforcement. They were not about to let some county prosecutor take that opportunity away from them.

Nevertheless, Keenan would not let the gross incongruity go to waste. On Monday, September 11, he announced that following the federal kidnapping trial, he would assist County Attorney Lewis R. Morris in seeking the death penalty for Bates and Kelly for the armed robbery of Walter Jarrett during his abduction from the home of Charles Urschel the night of the kidnapping.

"This offense carries the death penalty in Oklahoma and we feel that the good citizens of Oklahoma would not be averse to bringing the desperate criminals to the bar of justice in that court," he stated.

George had learned from his brief stay in Chicago that his usual contacts could not, or would not, be of much help to him. In fact, they wanted him gone. Capone's lieutenant, Frank Nitti, had put the word out that Kelly was "too hot." So with their plans to lie low in Chicago thwarted, the Kellys, with their adopted daughter in the backseat, got back on the road and headed to the city where Kelly had launched his criminal career: Memphis, Tennessee.

While Kelly was driving south, Alvin Karpis was putting to work the armor-plated car that Joe Bergl had customized for him. With the Barkers, George Ziegler and Bryan Bolton, he handily stole a cartload of sacks thought to contain cash and securities from two bank employees under armed guards who were wheeling them out of the Federal Reserve Bank. They pulled the heist off flawlessly, but in his haste to get away quickly, Karpis slammed into an oncoming car. The accident happened right in front of two Chicago cops walking their beat. As they approached the cars, Bolton began firing his submachine-gun, killing one of the patrolmen.

Within hours, news of the machine-gun murder and bank robbery was blanketing the Chicago papers and blaring from the radio. Purvis and the Bureau announced that the prime suspects were Machine Gun Kelly, Verne Miller and Pretty Boy Floyd.

The investigation led them straight to Joe

Bergl and turned up a pair of octagonal glasses, the very type known to be worn by Kelly.

Based on the very slim evidence he had, Purvis called a press conference and announced that the machine gun that had killed Chicago police officer Miles Cunningham was the same one that had been used in the Kansas City Massacre. The nationwide hunt for Kelly and his fashionable wife had just intensified tenfold.

The Kellys made it to Memphis a few days later and moved back into Tichenor's house on East Raynor Street. Once there, they no longer needed the kid for cover. What they were going to need was a lot more money. Once again, Kelly turned to his brother-in-law, Langford Ramsey, for help.

Kelly persuaded Ramsey to drive back to Texas with Geraldine as his guide to retrieve the rest of the ransom money, which was buried at the Coleman farm. After that, Kelly wanted him to reunite Geraldine with her parents at the boardinghouse in Oklahoma City and bring back the rest of Kit's wardrobe, which Flossie Mae was holding there.

So Geraldine, who had just endured a six-hundred-mile journey in the backseat of the

Kellys' car bouncing along back roads, got back into the car with a perfect stranger for the final leg of her summer road trip, heading back to the desolate prairies of wasted West Texas. After two days on the road, they arrived at the Coleman farm at 5:00 a.m.

Ramsey tried to introduce himself to Coleman and explain what he was after. But Coleman, realizing he was being watched round the clock, was not about to tell some clean-cut "lawyer" whom he'd never met where the Urschel ransom was buried, especially one that was traveling with an exasperated twelve-year-old kid.

"I'm the contact man for George and Kathryn Kelly," Ramsey explained.

"I don't care anything about your name," Coleman replied. "Or the Kellys."

Ramsey then asked if he could at least take some of Kathryn's fur coats back with him.

"No," said Coleman.

"I'm not hot," said Ramsey.

"You will be before you get far. They'll tail you out of here."

He sent Ramsey away empty-handed.

Ramsey then drove back to Fort Worth, put Geraldine on a train to Oklahoma and sent a telegram to the Arnolds telling them when the kid would arrive.

He then sent a second telegram to Kathryn:

Had several tough breaks. Ran into several rain storms. Caused brake trouble. Deal fell through. Tried to get later appointment. But prospect was afraid. Impossible to change his mind. Didn't want to bring home a sad tale. Can go on if advisable. Wire instructions here.

Both wire transmissions ended up in the hands of the federal agents guarding the Arnolds. After intercepting the first one about Geraldine's return, they contacted Western Union asking if the person who sent it had sent any others while he was there.

The wire operator told them another telegram had been sent to one J. C. Tichenor, c/o Central Garage, Memphis, Tennessee. They phoned the Memphis police, who looked up the name in the telephone directory and found a J. C. Tichenor at East Raynor Street. They immediately put the house under surveillance.

After Ramsey gave Geraldine her ticket back to Oklahoma City and left her at the train station, the precocious kid fired off her own telegram to her parents after he'd left:

Meet me Rock Island station ten fifteen
tonight. Gerry.

Her parents were there to meet her when
she arrived, but so were Pop Nathan and
his agents. Geraldine was not at all reticent
to speak. She rambled on chapter and verse
about all the places she'd been dragged, all
the odd manners she had been expected to
affect. She told everybody about the Kellys
and their marital battles, their professional
battles, their battles about everything.

She'd been dragged off here, she'd been
dragged off there. Kelly had taken her to
places she'd never been. Places she didn't
like. Introduced her to creepy people. Sent
her off with some stranger named Ramsey,
who put her on this train with a ticket and
a couple bucks and that was that.

The agents asked if she knew where the
Kellys were staying in Memphis.

Her answer was decisive. They were in a
house on East Raynor Street. Staying with
"some guy named, Tich."

Might the name be "Tichenor?"

Yes, that was it, she said.

Nathan wasted no time. He immediately
got word to the Special Agent in Charge of
the Birmingham, Alabama, office, William A. Rorer, a young World War I vet. Get

to Memphis and raid this home before daylight. The Bureau had only one agent in Memphis and it did not want that limited kind of involvement. The Bureau had chased Kelly over about one-third of the country and they didn't want some local police force to get credit for his capture. Shortly after Nathan's call, Rorer got another from the director himself in Washington. Hoover reiterated how important it was to get to Memphis immediately. He should arrange air travel using any means necessary. Nathan also called the St. Louis office, the next closest to Memphis, and told them to dispatch agents, as well. The race was on. Who would get to Memphis first to capture the Kellys.

It was after midnight when Rorer got the call from Nathan. He knew he had almost no time to get to Tennessee to complete his assignment. It was too long a drive and there was no train service. He'd need to fly. But there were no night flights. He appealed to a local air charter service, but they weren't allowed to fly at night. The charter service told him the only planes that could fly out of Birmingham at night were at Roberts Field under the command of the National Guard. In desperation, he tried the National Guard, finally getting through to the wife of Commander Sumpter Smith, who told him her husband was out of town in Montgomery. When the desperate Rorer finally located Smith at his hotel, Smith told him he lacked the authority to release the planes. Well, who has it, demanded Rorer. Smith told him he'd have to get in touch with General Edward King at Fort McPherson, Georgia. When he did, King ordered two planes to carry Rorer and anyone else he could round up to Memphis.

At about 3:00 a.m. Rorer boarded a flight from Birmingham to Memphis. When it landed at 5:30 a.m., he was met at the airport by the Bureau's local agent and a squad of local police he had rounded up. They immediately headed off to East Raynor Street.

It was a smaller force than Rorer would have wanted to be going after the crazed machine gunner who'd been identified as the shooter in the Kansas City Massacre and had been accused of gunning down a Chicago cop during a botched bank robbery. There was nothing to suggest that Kelly would allow himself to be taken alive. For the last six weeks, Hoover's men had chased the Kellys over twenty-thousand miles as they crisscrossed the nation's midsection. More than sixty agents and hundreds of police officers had been involved. Phones had been tapped, telegrams had been intercepted, yet every time the Bureau had them in their sights, they managed to slip away. Was it about to happen again? Did Kelly have an inside informant at the Memphis cop shop? Rorer did not know what to expect. Would he be walking into an empty house or a murderous trap set by "an expert machine gunner"?

At the house, George, after a day and night of heavy drinking, was having a hard time sleeping. He awoke early and wandered out to the front yard to pick up the newspaper to catch up on the latest mythology that was being created about him by the feds and their willing accomplices in the press. On his way back in the house, he neglected to relock the doors.

The street of small, neat homes was quiet when Rorer and his men arrived. Rorer, in completely unfamiliar territory and with a squad of personnel he didn't really know, sent the Memphis cops around the back to get the place surrounded. He and Memphis detective William Raney drew their guns and gingerly opened the screen door at the front of the house. Once inside, they quietly navigated the cluttered living room, which was strewn with empty liquor bottles and cigarette butts.

To one side of the living room was a bedroom with two men passed out on the bed in their underwear. It was Tichenor and his brother-in-law, T. A. Travis. Rorer motioned for one of his fellow agents to cover the room.

Rorer and Raney hustled into the hallway and opened a second door into another bedroom, where the comely Kathryn was asleep on the bed in some green silk pajamas.

Still, no Kelly. No machine guns.

As they turned to make their way back to the front of the house, they encountered the groggy Kelly in only his underwear, a .45 limply dangling at his side as he rubbed his dyed yellow hair with his free hand.

Raney raised his sawed-off shotgun and aimed it at Kelly's belly.

"Drop the gun!"

Kelly smiled. "I've been waiting all night for you."

"Here we are," said Raney, gun trained.

As the other officers of the law poured in, Kathryn emerged. Before they could cuff her, though, she threw a fit, insisting she needed to put on something decent and get herself ready for the trip downtown. Raney gave her fifteen minutes.

With a half-dozen guns trained on her and

her husband, she walked over to him and draped her arms around his neck. "Honey, I guess it's all up for us. The G-men won't ever give us a break."

While the lawmen milled around like a collection of aggravated husbands waiting for their primping wives, Kathryn finally emerged, resplendent in a skinny black dress with bright buttons and furry epaulets. She complained that her best clothing was still on its way from Texas, along with her beloved Pekinese pups. She looked at one of the lawmen as if he were a personal servant and asked him to please make sure these things were taken care of in case she was not back on the premises when they arrived.

9
THE KELLYS' TRIAL

After the Kellys were hauled off to the jail downtown, the International News Service sent the following alert to the nation:

George "Machine Gun" Kelly, America's no. 1 desperado, sought for a series of abductions, bank holdups and massacres that have terrorized the nation, fell into the clutches of the law today.

The man who sent the organized forces of law of the 48 states and the federal government on the greatest manhunt in history, taunting his pursuers with scornful, threatening letters, surrendered meekly to Department of Justice agents who trapped him in a Memphis hideout.

While locked up in Memphis, George was reacquainted with the cops who'd arrested him in high school and throughout his early bootlegging career. They all came by to say hello to their new celebrity prisoner and to reminisce about old times, astonished that George Barnes, the high school bootlegger, had grown up to become the notorious Machine Gun Kelly.

Before long, throngs of Memphis denizens were swinging by the county jail to get a glimpse of the famous local outlaw who'd just been arrested by the hometown cops.

As the crowds swelled outside the jail by the hundreds, police officers had to leave the jail to direct traffic. Kelly quipped to his jailers that they ought to set up a barbecue stand outside and make some side money.

While Kelly was busy yukking it up with his jailers, Kathryn was busily trying to save her own skin, repeating her claim that she had nothing to do with the kidnapping and that Kelly had forced her and her family to help him under threat of death.

"I was going back [to Oklahoma City] tomorrow to give myself up. Kelly told me he would kill me if I did, but I was going anyway," she claimed.

"I feel responsible, not for the kidnapping, because I'm absolutely innocent of any part in that, but it's all my fault that my parents are in this because I married him in the first place. I'm glad of one thing though — that we're both arrested, for I'm not guilty and can prove it. Afterward I'll be rid of him and that bunch. I don't want to say anything about that guy Kelly, but he got me into this terrible mess and I don't want to have anything more to do with him."

She also offered a bribe of $15,000 to one of her jailers to arrange her escape. He wisely declined.

The chatty Geraldine Arnold had told the Bureau's agents where Kelly had hidden his loot. On September 27, the day after Kelly's arrest, Gus Jones, Ralph Colvin, Frank Blake, Charles Winstead and a posse of county deputies drove down to Cass Coleman's farm to collect it.

They arrived around midnight, and Jones did not like the looks of what he found. The farmhouse was lit up and appeared to be a hubbub of activity. A large number of cars were parked outside.

Jones had the group surround the farmhouse as he grabbed his machine gun and approached the house. Meeting up with Coleman, Jones asked what the hell was going on. Coleman explained that his daughter was inside about to deliver a baby. *Well isn't that swell,* thought Jones. But he had a different assignment for the new grandfather.

"Cass, we have come for that money. Lead

us to it." When Coleman started to protest, Jones cut him off.

"No explanations, no excuses. Take us directly to that money. And bring something to dig with."

Coleman walked the group through the cotton field to a small mesquite tree, stopped and looked back at Jones, who lowered his machine gun, pointing it at Coleman's midsection.

"Where is the money?" he demanded. Coleman walked off five paces and pointed down.

"Right here," he said.

"Dig," said Jones.

After ten minutes of chopping through the hardened earth, the sweating Coleman hit the thermos and molasses jar that contained the loot.

The agents spent the next hour counting and labeling it. When they were finished, it totaled $72,240 in marked bills from the ransom, and another ten that had been inexplicably thrown in, bringing the sum to a neat $72,250.00.

They packed up the money and walked Coleman back to the house, where the arrival of his grandchild was being celebrated. They led him to the car and Winstead hauled him off to the county jail. Jones,

Blake and Colvin drove off to Dallas where they had a quick breakfast before proceeding on to Oklahoma City. By the time they got there, they had driven nearly one thousand miles in twenty-four hours in the service of the Bureau and its mission to bring Urschel's kidnappers to justice.

Later that day, the Associated Press moved a story that sent Hoover through the roof.

Memphis, Tenn., Sept. 27 (A.P.) George Kelly, reputed machine gunner for the underworld of the Western bad lands, tonight confessed, officers said, to a part in the kidnapping of Charles F. Urschel, Oklahoma oil millionaire, and named Albert Bates as the actual accomplice.

"You got me right on the Urschel kidnapping," Kelly was quoted by W. A. Rorer, Department of Justice agent as saying tonight.

Kelly admitted the kidnapping, Rorer said, "but not the Chicago robbery or the Kansas City union station job."

"Kelly made no formal confession but he told the Department of Justice agents that he and Bates were the ones who did the actual kidnapping and that they took Urschel to Paradise, Texas and returned to Oklahoma City to collect the ransom," a source close to the Department of Justice agents said. . . .

Kelly's alleged statement on the Chicago robbery referred to the holdup of Federal Reserve bank messengers and the slaying of a policeman on the night of September 21. His reference to the "Kansas City Union Station job" was to the machine-gun slaying of four officers and Frank Nash, notorious criminal whom the officers had in custody.

Police forces linked Kelly's name with both slayings.

John M. Keith, federal agent from Chicago, confirmed the confession as reported by Rorer and by implication connected Kelly with the Chicago holdup.

The story went on in great detail about Ramsey's confession as to what he had done and where he had gone, whom he had talked to and what was said. He told of how he had transported young Geraldine to the Coleman farm and that he had sent her back to her parents on a train to Oklahoma City. It was later, the story said, that "the little girl tipped officers as to the where-abouts of the Kellys."

Hoover was shocked, first of all, because

he was reading news of the most important case of his career in the press before he was hearing it from his agents themselves. Agents were under strict orders to call in daily with their whereabouts and information about how the case was proceeding. Secondly, they were not to share information with the press without clearing it through Washington first. Now he was reading about his agents' work in wire reports and seeing his agents quoted by name giving critical information that needed to be kept secret for use at trial and to protect the identity of government witnesses. But the information was leaking out at flood-stage levels. Now one of his agents had publicly identified a twelve-year-old government witness. What was her life now worth? And would she stay alive long enough to even make it to trial to testify? And how willing would any witness be to help government investigators if their identities would be revealed so carelessly by the very agents who had sworn to protect them?

Hoover assigned one of his minions to call Chicago agent Keith to express the director's displeasure and read him verbatim the lines from the Washington papers that Hoover found most upsetting.

The chastised Keith could only say that

he'd been misquoted. He said the court-house was "absolutely surrounded by news-papermen from all over the country" and that every time he went near the jail or the courthouse he was "mobbed by dozens of newspapermen." He said they asked if Kelly had confessed, and he said no. He told them Kathryn had made no statement. They told him that the Associated Press moved a story that Ramsey had gone to Texas, and he did not mention the money, but stated he had gone for some furs. Keith said the story in the papers sounded suspiciously like a telegram he had sent to the division. Obvi-ously, somebody in the press had gotten hold of it.

Why hadn't he sent the telegram using the Bureau's code as instructed? Keith confessed that the Memphis office did not have a codebook and he hadn't brought his with him.

Hoover had a codebook rushed to Mem-phis. The Kellys would soon have to be transported to Oklahoma City, and any information about those plans would need to be kept secret lest the nation be subjected to a repeat of the Kansas City debacle, when loose-lipped agents boasted to the press about their high-profile prisoner and their travel details had been revealed.

Rorer told Hoover that it would be impossible to get their prisoners out of the jail without the reporters finding it out, since there were scores of them around the jail day and night. Rorer wanted to meet with the editors of the local papers and wire services and give them some kind of ultimatum that all information about the removal of the prisoners be withheld until they got them to Oklahoma. Hoover was now convinced he'd get no more cooperation from the press, that there was no way they could effectively keep a lid on this story any longer. He told the agents in Memphis to have planes ready to go at a moment's notice and to keep throwing up smoke screens in front of the press.

Meanwhile, the President himself was leaning on the Secretary of War to see if military planes could be used to get the Kellys out of Memphis.

As their exit plans were being arranged, the Kellys started talking. Kathryn pressed her case that she was not involved in the kidnapping and that she and her family had only helped George, to the extent that they did, because he threatened to kill them if they didn't. She told the agents that her husband had arranged the escape of Holden and Keating from the Federal Penitentiary at Leavenworth, and that while they were hiding out in Chicago, George had met with Verne Miller and made arrangements for the assassination of Charles Urschel. The Bureau's failure to capture Miller was looming large. He could be organizing a military-style assault to free Kelly, as he'd tried to do with Frank Nash in Kansas City, or he could be laying plans to take out Urschel, using the skills he'd so frequently put on display against so many other members of the underworld.

George Kelly told the agents that Jarrett was the "finger man" on the kidnapping. He'd been their inside man, who'd shared the Urschels' schedule and habits and tipped them off about the infamous bridge game. He said he'd met with Jarrett on the Fourth of July at the Hopkins Hotel in Oklahoma City and then later again at the Blackstone. He said he had worked out a code with Jarrett about where his Pierce Arrow automobile should be parked to indicate that the time was right to pull the job. Though Nathan had his doubts, he put Jarrett under surveillance, but found no evidence to back up Kelly's claim. Kelly was probably attempting to get some measure of revenge on Jarrett for cooperating with the Bureau's agents and testifying against

Bates and the Shannons. Also, if Kelly could tie Jarrett to the kidnapping, the highway robbery charge with its death penalty would no longer be a viable option for the state authorities in Oklahoma. (After his conviction, Kelly would back off this claim and admit that Jarrett had nothing to do with the kidnapping.)

On Sunday, October 1, agent Rorer and four others loaded the Kellys in an army plane and flew them to Oklahoma City. When they landed, a phalanx of machine gunners lined the runway and the path into the terminal. Several hundred curious onlookers crowded behind chain-linked fences, gawking and yelling at the celebrity gangsters as they deboarded the plane.

Agents, fearing another Kansas City–style rescue attempt, scanned the crowd over machine-gun barrels while Kelly made his way down the staircase to the runway with his wrists and ankles shackled and his trademark Lucky Strike dangling from the corner of his mouth.

Seeing the crowd, he brightened.

"Hello gang. Nice trip," he yelled as the unshackled Kathryn walked down the runway in a fashionable black silk coat and black hat.

With two machine guns trained on Kelly, the agents marched him over to Charles Urschel, who was standing next to his car on the runway.

"That's the man," said the laconic oilman. Berenice looked out the window of the car and said, "That face will haunt me as long as I live."

With that, the agents yanked Kelly away toward the motorcade of ten heavily armed cars that would race him back to the Oklahoma City jail to await trial. As they did, Kelly complained that he couldn't keep up with his legs shackled together. "I can't walk fast in these things!"

After locking Kelly up, Deputy Marshal Elman Jester asked Kelly about the threatening letter he had sent earlier to Urschel.

Kelly said he intended to make good on everything he said. "I wouldn't sell Urschel any insurance," he added. "He hasn't got long to live."

While the Bureau's agents caught and shuttled Kelly back to Oklahoma, the proceedings against Bailey, Bates, the Shannons and seven others, who were charged with a variety of offenses — from laundering the ransom money to conspiring to aid the kidnappers — continued.

The kidnapping and subsequent manhunt had captured the imagination of the nation in ways that even the far more brutal massacre in Kansas City had not. In part, that was because the investigation there was going nowhere, and Hoover was deflecting attention away from it and toward Kelly. The President's attention had been drawn to the case in part because of his association with Urschel during his efforts to promote regulation of the oil industry to help stabilize pricing and drilling, but also because the children of his son-in-law, Curtis B. Dall, had been threatened with kidnapping.

Kirkpatrick had talked with Dall about the experience on August 15, after which he fired off a telegram to Roosevelt.

As the man who personally contacted and paid off in their appointed place, the kidnappers of Charles F. Urschel, I implore you to exert immediately the entire energy and powers of the Federal Government to the stamping out of kidnapping, racketeering and gangsterism. I am convinced that the city, county and state police, limited by territorial boundaries and lack of finances are helpless in the warfare against this appalling menace, which unchecked, will threaten even the White House. In my opinion there is one force, and only one, which can wipe out this insidious threat. My intimate contact for three weeks with this force, convinces me that it is seriously handicapped by lack of personnel and finances. Give to [the Bureau of Investigation] unlimited power and money and it will hang or imprison every gangster.

Hoover himself couldn't have put it any better and, in fact, some of the language was suggested to him by Jones and his agents. In any case, the War on Crime had some powerful new proponents, and FDR was too good of a politician to let a crisis go to waste, especially when he had the eyes and ears of the nation focused on it.

In a few months, Hoover, Cummings and Raymond Moley, a member of FDR's Brain Trust, would go before Congress and ask for sweeping new powers. They wanted new federal statutes to help prosecute the War on Crime.

The federal government's efforts against crime were strictly limited to violations of customs, internal revenue laws, postal laws and counterfeiting. Prior to the Lindbergh Law, the Justice Department Bureau of Investigation was only empowered to go after stolen cars that had been taken across state lines and women transported across state lines for prostitution, termed "white slavery" at the time. Treasury enforced the tax laws and had its corruption-laden Prohibition Squad, and the Secret Service protected the President, to a degree.

Cummings was looking to expand the Justice Department, and he needed legislation to do it. He wanted it to be a federal offense to kill a federal officer. Similarly, he wanted it to be a federal crime to flee to another state to avoid arrest. He wanted it to be a federal crime to rob a federal bank, or to take stolen property across state lines. He wanted tough federal regulation of the sale of firearms, especially machine guns.

Most of all, he wanted to strengthen the Lindbergh Law to make kidnapping a federal offense punishable by death. In short, he wanted the federal government to take over the policing of serious crime throughout the country.

When the trial of Bates, Bailey and the Shannons began on Monday, September 18, the security measures around the courthouse gave the city the look of an armed camp. Streets around the courthouse were either blocked off or lined with machine gunners and law enforcement officers with sawed-off shotguns and rifles. All those entering the courtroom were searched, patted down and their packages emptied. The elevator was taken out of service so that anyone headed to the courtroom had to climb two flights of stairs lined with armed guards.

The city's leading citizens stood in line in the Oklahoma heat to get a seat in the courtroom, wearing suits and ties and fine dresses, as the etiquette of the time dictated. They carried food in sacks so they would not lose their seats at lunchtime. As the 90-degree heat wafted up to the second-floor courtroom, they sweated out the proceeding in rapt attention as they smoked cigarettes and fanned themselves incessantly.

In his opening statement, Oklahoma District Attorney Herbert Hyde laid out the allegations that the government was about to prove over the coming days as the trial sped on. It gave just a small preview of the massive amounts of evidence the Bureau had gathered in the previous months as they had tracked the Kellys across the country. The sheer volume of the allegations Hyde outlined swamped the defense attorneys, who had had little or no time to prepare for the case.

"The evidence will show that two men

went into the home of Mr. Urschel under the cover of darkness, that they kidnapped him and sped into the night, out of Oklahoma County and into Pottawatomie County, to the home of a relative of George Kelly, one of the defendants, and then to Texas.

"The proof will show that the defendant Kelly was, on or about July 15th, or 16th in Dallas, Texas, that he sent a wire to his friend Bates, who was in Denver, and that wire said, 'When and where will I meet you in Oklahoma City?'

"It will show that Bates wired back to Kelly under the name of R. G. Shannon, and that he said, 'I'll meet you on July 19th at the Biltmore Hotel,' which was just three days before the kidnapping.

"The proof will show that they met in Oklahoma City, and that Bates at that time had the car they hauled Urschel away in. It was a Chevrolet, 1933, with an Indiana tag.

"We will show that Bates owned that car in Denver.

"We will show by the apartment house owners in Denver, where he stayed under the name of Davis . . . that he had a Buick car and that they changed to his car after hauling Urschel away."

Hyde spoke on and on to the rapt jurors

and spectators, referencing the enormous amount of detail and data that the agents had gathered from the hundreds of interviews they had conducted, from the telegrams they'd obtained and the mail they'd intercepted. He seemed to know exactly where the defendants had been and when they'd been there. He knew what had been said, and to whom.

"The proof will disclose," Hyde continued, "that while Urschel was held prisoner down on the farm, Kelly was present until Friday, the day of the second note, and that Kelly warmed up and got kind of chummy. We'll show that Kelly said: 'This place is as safe as it can be. We used it in the old days as a hang-out when we were running liquor from Mexico to Chicago. All the boys use it. After they pull a bank job or something, they come down here to "cool off." '

"We'll show that Harvey Bailey, Bob Brady and Jim Clark had been at the farm — that he told all about the Kansas City Massacre. We'll show that Bates said they gave Shannon $200 or $300 to use the place as a hang-out."

Then he turned his attention to the Green Lantern gang that had laundered the ransom money.

"We'll show that the day these defendants

were arrested at St. Paul, a wire was sent from Minneapolis to Cleveland, Ohio, to George Kelly. We'll show that the telegram said, 'The deal is off. Wire me box 631, Denver.'

"We'll show that was the box of Albert Bates or George Davis [his alias]. We'll show that Bates was in Minneapolis at the time of the arrests there after the ransom money showed up. And we'll show that the Kellys lived there. Further, that these defendants from St. Paul took $5,500 from Bates or Kelly or Mrs. Kelly.

"Now when these St. Paul defendants were arrested, Bates wired Kelly at Cleveland, where Kelly was paying $1,500 he owed on a Cadillac. We'll show that wire was sent in care of the Cadillac Motor Company, and we'll have the dealer here.

"We'll show that at the time Bates left Minneapolis by train . . . going through Omaha, and that at Omaha he sent a wire to Denver to the woman he was living with at 1275 Pearl Avenue, and that wire said, 'Be home soon.'

"The evidence will show that this woman was not Bates's wife, but had lived with him under the name of Feldman, and of Davis in Denver. We'll show that she had the kidnap car. We'll show that she had a

Pekinese dog, and we'll trace that dog from January to the day Bates was arrested."

He then described the day of the raid on the Shannon farm, the myriad details Urschel had collected there and how he had strategically left his fingerprints all over the house.

"He turned all this information over to the federal officers who met at the Shannon farm at dawn, August 12th.

"Shannon walked out and was met with an order to hold up his hands. In a building — the same building where Urschel was kept — we found Harvey Bailey sleeping. And, lo, at the same time we find a machine gun that Kathryn Kelly had bought in a pawn shop in Fort Worth for $250. And, lo, gentlemen, we find it was the same gun that was used in the kidnapping of Mr. Urschel. We find it, gentlemen, on the Shannon farm.

"We will show that the officers found $700 on Bailey's person, ransom money paid by the Urschel family. Now we go a step further in the story . . ."

He then went after Bailey, detailing how he had paid the Shannons for his lodging, how Bailey had been coming to the Shannon farm since 1930 and how he had been using it as a "post office, a stopover, as a place where he might cool off."

The criminal case that Hyde and Keenan had prepared was unprecedented. The mountain of evidence, gathered by dozens of agents across one-third of the nation, was almost too much for the defense team to absorb, let alone refute.

It had been gathered expertly, using the very latest in the technology of criminal science. The defendants had been tracked over a path twenty thousand miles long. The investigators had gathered receipts, photographs, bills of sale, license plates, fingerprints; they had eyewitnesses, they had confessions and they had cooperation from dozens of participants in the case.

They had little Geraldine Arnold, whose desperate parents had dragged her into the crime and made her a most unwilling participant. She was now enthusiastically spilling her guts to any lawman who would listen.

But on top of all of that, they had Charles Urschel, a victim like no other. Not only did he cooperate fully and immediately with law enforcement to track down and capture his kidnappers, he'd led them to the criminal lair where he'd been held. He led the assault team into the fray. While blindfolded, deafened, half-starved and sleep-deprived, he had collected — and planted — a mountain of evidence that the federal prosecutors would use to crush the Kellys and everyone else involved in the case — and some who weren't.

It was Hoover's dream being played out on a stage as if he'd scripted every scene.

Unfazed by the proliferating threats against him and his family, Charles Urschel took the stand and, in his stoic, unemotional style, delivered a data dump of all the information he'd collected during his ordeal. He walked over to the equally icy Bates and identified him as one of his kidnappers. He identified Kelly as the other from a picture shown to him by the prosecution.

He identified young Armon, "the man with the light blue tie and purple suit," as one of those who had guarded him. Then he identified Boss Shannon as the other.

He was asked if Shannon had said anything about Bates and Kelly.

Urschel told him Shannon had said "that they were both very bad men, that they were desperate, and they were very hot and would never be taken alive. He said they would shoot it out if they met any officers."

When he was asked if Kelly had said anything about Urschel's family, he said Kelly "told me that he knew all about our family; knew all about the children; knew about the cars they drove; that he had been by the house and had seen a trailer set up in our backyard which the boys used in going on a camping trip the week before.

"I made the statement or asked him whether he didn't consider they were lucky that they found that door unlocked, and he said they probably were, that it would not have made any difference; they were coming for me that night and would have taken me even if I had been in bed. He also said he knew what room in the house I slept in. He talked a good deal about automobiles. He seemed to know a lot about cars, especially the mechanics of cars. He preferred Chevrolets and Cadillacs."

The federal agents let Bailey know that despite the flimsy evidence holding him to the kidnapping, he would indeed be going down for the crime and it would be unwise to fight it too vigorously, since he was wanted in Kansas for kidnapping the warden in the Memorial Day prison escape that had gotten him shot in the knee. He could fry for that.

He was also wanted in Kansas in connection with the massacre at Union Station. Bailey knew well the benefits of a conviction for a lesser crime, and his lawyer did not dissuade him from that view.

So he sat bemusedly in the courtroom, chewing tobacco and preening for the society ladies who were photographing him constantly. "Be sure you get a good one, ma'am," he would quip politely.

Hyde put Geraldine Arnold on the stand and she recounted her enslavement with the Kellys in expert detail.

"We left San Antonio to go to Cass Coleman's but did not go there. A man told us that the law had been to Cass Coleman's place. George said we would go to Chicago and see Joe Bergl."

Bergl ran a garage in Chicago on Twenty-second Street, next to the Chicago branch of the Cotton Club, which was run by Al Capone's older brother, Ralph. (Although he was the lesser brother, Ralph, aka "Bottles," was quite successful in his own right. He ran a large bottling company that not only made the containers for his younger brother's illegal liquor operation, but also for his legitimate business selling soda water, ginger ale and other mixers that would dilute the rotgut gin sold during Prohibition. During the Chicago World's Fair in 1933, he had cornered so much of the concession business that his company was second only to Coca-Cola.)

Bergl's garage specialized in obtaining and customizing cars for gangsters and bootleggers. Bergl had figured out ways to alter the suspension on cars and trucks so they could carry heavy loads of liquor and still maneuver nimbly without looking suspiciously loaded down. He could soup them up so they would run faster than their Detroit designers could imagine. For Capone and his lieutenants, he would add bulletproof windows and armor plating. He also experimented with police-evading features, such as oil-dumping tanks in the undercarriage that could be released to create slicks behind the vehicle to cause pursuers to spin out of control and smoke-producing exhaust pipes that would create a noxious screen to frustrate shooters chasing those vehicles.

For liquor and gun runners, he would add larger gas tanks so they could speed through the back hills and roads without having to stop for gas.

"We went to Chicago," Geraldine continued. "Kathryn wrote a letter to Mother on the way. Before we left Texas we changed cars and had to have our battery changed too."

"Where did you stay in Chicago and what was done there?" asked Hyde.

"We stayed in an apartment and they tried

to phone Joe Bergl, but they could not get him for two or three days."

At that point, Bergl didn't want anything to do with Kelly. He knew Kelly was being tracked by the feds, and he didn't want to become collateral damage. Eventually, though, Bergl provided Kelly with a new car, a Chevy coupe, $200 and a quart of whiskey and told him to get out of town. The Kellys then headed to Memphis.

In Memphis, Geraldine told the prosecutors, the Kellys started plotting to get the ransom money from Cass Coleman's farm.

"Langford Ramsey and I were to take a car and go to Texas and get the money and some furs that Kathryn had left . . . get Kathryn's clothes and necklace. Then they wanted me to come back . . . They said I was a good shield.

"When I got to Oklahoma City, I did not want to go back [to Memphis] and Mother did not want me to go back either."

Hyde asked if Geraldine had seen the Kellys writing any letters.

"Lots of them," she answered. "George and Kathryn both wrote letters and George put his fingerprints on them. I seen him put his fingerprints on them. I bought the stamps for the letters at the post office substation."

Geraldine told Hyde that when they weren't writing letters they were drinking and talking about killing people.

"George said he was going to kill Judge Vaught, Keenan, Urschel and [you]."

"What did he say about Urschel?" Hyde asked.

"George said they should have taken Urschel to Arizona and buried him. Kathryn said, 'That's what we ought to have done.'"

During cross-examination, Kathryn's attorney, James Mathers, who looked every bit the legal scholar with his shock of tussled white hair, round owlish wire rims, three-piece suit and fine cigar wedged in his fingers, asked Geraldine if Kathryn had treated her well. She smiled, and answered, "Yes."

"She bought me this dress and a coat in Chicago," she said, brightening.

"Are you sure it was not in Cicero?" asked Mathers.

"No, we went to Cicero but it was in one of Bergl's saloons in Chicago where we saw him," she said definitively.

"Kathryn thanked him for what he had done for us and said something about the car and the money," she added, to Mathers's chagrin.

Once he got on the stand, the nervous Armon broke down and confessed to everything. When the prosecutor asked why he agreed to guard Urschel, he replied, "Kelly said if I didn't, he would shoot me with a machine gun."

After Armon caved, Ora and Boss did so, as well. They told the jury that they feared for their lives if they didn't cooperate with Kelly and Bates. Ora wept on the stand, saying she was "forced into this thing with machine guns, the same as Mr. Urschel . . . I was afraid of George Kelly."

Boss expressed similar fears, saying that if he didn't help out Bates and Kelly they would have come back and killed him and his family. Boss claimed that if he hadn't cooperated, "I would not be alive, my boy would not be alive, and maybe Mr. Urschel would not be alive today.

"The reason I didn't phone no officers or the sheriff was for the simple reason I had a boy over there at this place, and if I phoned the officers, or if they had come over there, there would have been a battle and perhaps my boy would have been killed or perhaps Mr. Urschel would have been killed."

Later, in his comments at the trial's conclusion, Judge Vaught would scoff at this reasoning. "The threat of future injury is not enough. The evidence shows that the Shannons knew there was a kidnapped man at their home. If they knew he was kidnapped and they guarded him, then they would be just as guilty as if they had kidnapped him, transported him, and collected the ransom. Fear of individual punishment is no excuse for a violation of the law."

Vaught wanted to put teeth in the new Lindbergh Law, and if he could do it with the gang that had abducted and ransomed his good friend Urschel, so much the better. He'd earlier let his feelings be known, when he described the new law as "absolutely revolutionary."

"Congress passed it for one reason only — to try to stop kidnapping," he said. "A kidnapper is more than a murderer and is so recognized over the country. No more vicious character in this country exists than one who kidnaps a man and holds him for ransom."

In his concluding argument, prosecutor Keenan took a similar tack. "If this government cannot protect its citizens, then we had better, frankly, turn it over to the Kellys and the Bateses, the Baileys and the others of the underworld and pay tribute to them through taxes.

"Kidnapping has become a modern art.

The plotters lay their vicious plans, bold strong-armed men carry out the abduction, hirelings stand guard and later when the ransom has been paid, the money changers arrange for its dissemination through underworld channels. In this case, the government has shown you the whole picture of how this heinous scheme was conceived and carried out."

In their closing arguments, Keenan and Hyde lowered the hammer, Keenan telling the jury they would decide whether "we are to have a government of law and order, or abdicate in favor of machine-gun gangsters."

Neatly through his statements, he detailed the need for a strong national government and a federal police force to protect its citizens when the states, and their local forces, could not:

"Through four states of the Union these criminals plied their trade and defied the government. A single state could not control such swift operations. The federal government was forced to step in and take a hand. Now that government has been defied by these gangsters and we have caught them red-handed. We are convinced that they are all guilty of this conspiracy and demand that a verdict of guilty be returned."

Hyde reminded the jury that the kidnappers had put Urschel through "the tortures of hell."

"I beg of you, in the name of my government, to return a verdict of guilty against these defendants. This is one of the most important cases ever tried. Precedents are being set that will guide the courts and the bar in all future trials that grow out of this determined effort of your government to stamp out this most damnable of crimes — kidnapping!"

Even Bates was impressed with Hyde's summation. When Hyde, dripping with sweat, walked by to return to his seat, Bates congratulated him. "That's the best I've heard," said the veteran bank robber mockingly.

Hyde grinned and shook Bates's hand.

The trial ended and the jurors, who had been sequestered for the trial, broke for dinner and began their deliberations. Within an hour, and with just one round of voting, they had reached their verdict. But it would have to wait until the morning.

George and Kathryn Kelly were taken to the courthouse the next morning. Judge Vaught was expecting pleas of guilty from both, which would have buttoned things up nicely with the conclusion of the trial of the other defendants and the sentencing ready to be handed down.

However, the Kellys ruined everybody's morning when they both pleaded not guilty. The headstrong Kathryn remained convinced she could use her charms and acting skills to persuade the jury that she had been dragged against her will into the kidnapping by her threatening husband. George had no such illusions, and he knew if he took the stand that Hyde and Keenan would grill him about Bates, Bailey and others, and there was no way he would testify against or about his compatriots. So he told Mathers he would sit it out and watch the proceedings from his box seat. He would not take the stand and be bullied and insulted by the federal stooges who were running this three-ring circus, he said.

Vaught was not happy. Now there would need to be another trial for the Kellys, the marquee players in this courtroom battle. He shunted them aside and made them wait as he read the verdicts and sentences for the other defendants.

With Bailey, Bates and the Shannons standing shoulder to shoulder in the courtroom (the statuesque Bailey towering above the rest in his handsome double-breasted suit, slicked-back, wavy hair and chiseled features), Vaught read the verdict.

"The jury has returned a verdict of guilty. The court is of the opinion that this verdict is fully sustained by the evidence."

But before launching into the sentencing, he teased the audience with an assessment of the enormity of the case.

"Something more is at stake than the mere punishment for the crime that has been committed in this case. The question before the American people today is whether or not crime will be recognized as an occupation or a profession. Or whether the people will enforce the laws of the nation as they are written. So far as this court is concerned, it is its purpose to try to enforce the laws as they are written."

He then sentenced Bates, Bailey and Boss and Ora Shannon to life in prison. Armon got a ten-year sentence.

The hammer had fallen, and Kathryn was crestfallen and shocked. Her mother had just been sentenced to life in prison for a crime she had no part in. Bailey also had taken the fall for something he didn't do.

Hyde and Keenan gloated to the press that the government now had the upper hand in the fight against kidnapping and was ready to "shoot the works."

So now they would have to have another

trial with another jury for the two principals in the case, George and Kathryn Kelly. But this was going to be a pummeling. The same evidence that had just been presented to incarcerate the hangers-on in the case was simply going to be resurrected to convict the principals. It was the ultimate anticlimax, and the only one who thought the outcome might be different was the delusional Kathryn.

At this point, Kelly knew he was cooked and didn't care. He could have a trial and a conviction, or he could plead guilty. If Kathryn thought she had a shot, there was no loss in playing along. He was going to prison either way, and he'd been there before. He knew the prison system and how it worked. He could live comfortably on the inside, and when the time was right, he could get out.

On October 9, the second trial began. Two days earlier, Judge Vaught had received another threat in a letter that read, "If you do not dismiss these people, you and your family will be killed and your house will be blown up."

From his jail cell in Oklahoma City, Kelly tried to get a message out to the rest of his gang, pleading with them to kidnap Hyde's four-year-old son. "Snatch the child of this prosecutor to calm him down," wrote Kelly.

The message, of course, was intercepted, and Hyde's wife and son were placed under protective custody for the duration of the trial.

George fully intended to take the rap for everything and let Kathryn try to plead and lie her way out of it by sticking to her story alleging that he had forced her to cooperate.

But Hoover was convinced that Kathryn was not only a willing participant, but the actual brains behind the operation. He wanted her brought down with equal force.

The press, however, was smitten with the comely gangster moll. Kathryn gave a jailhouse interview to Jack Stinnett of *The Daily Oklahoman* that the paper bannered across their front page with a tight glamor shot of the gangster couple dressed to the nines and looking more amused than concerned about their impending trial.

Kathryn made for great copy, and Stinnett didn't let his exclusive go to waste.

Quick-witted as a lynx, sharp-tongued as a vixen when aroused, Kathryn Thorne Kelly, wife of the notorious gunman George "Machine Gun" Kelly [,] hides behind the most disarming smile imaginable and literally talks with her light blue eyes. Sitting on a bunk in the heavily guarded county jail, coarse blankets wrapped around her, Kathryn Sunday night good-naturedly discussed her plight, talked with some heat about the "injustice done her mother," and dismissed questions she did not wish to answer with "That'll all come out at the trial."

"I'm not worried about myself, I never have been. It is only mother. She had nothing whatever to do with this. A wife certainly has a right to stay around her home and tend to her own business and that is all she did.

"It is Kelly's fault that mother and dad got mixed up in this. They are the best people you ever saw. I don't know how that little community down in Wise County is going to get along without them."

He described her eyes, which:

. . . fairly snap. Little wrinkles run away from the corners of them and her mouth, which, under the pressure of anger presses into a cold hard line, curves upward at the corners. Anger flashed across her face when she mentioned that her daughter had been called to testify

367

against her in the kidnapping case.

"They just think I'll break down if they put her on the stand. I'd plead guilty in a minute if I could keep her out of the courtroom," she said.

Kathryn complained to Stinnett about the lousy food she was getting and said she'd prefer that it be sent in from the outside. Twice during the interview she bummed a cigarette from Stinnett, which he said she "smoked slowly, deliberately, belying any hint of nervousness . . . in contrast to her action upon her arrival here from Memphis, when she lighted one cigarette off another."

On the opening day of the trial, Kelly walked into the courtroom and glared at Urschel, who was sitting behind the prosecutors, legs crossed and relaxed.

Kelly ran his fingers across his throat and said, "This is for you. You'll get yours!"

The guards snapped to attention and the crowd gasped, but Urschel didn't flinch, returning Kelly's glare without any display of emotion.

Jones and his team looked on in anger, wondering what else they could do to rein in the recalcitrant Kelly. The bloated alcoholic had been living on a diet of bread and water since his arrest and there wasn't much else they could do to make his prison conditions less accommodating.

On her way into the courtroom, the heavily guarded Kathryn paused and walked toward her father, who'd come to the trial. She was intending to give him a kiss.

An agent roughly shoved her back and she stumbled. After regaining her balance, the indignant Kathryn slapped the agent. George, though shackled and cuffed, rushed forward to go to Kathryn's aid. As he did, an agent clubbed him on the back of the head with the butt of his gun and proceeded to pistol-whip him vigorously.

Kathryn defiantly explained to the courtroom that she had "stopped to kiss my father and the agent hit me in the back. When George told him not to hit me again, he began beating George with his pistol. Sure I slapped him, and I'd like to do it again."

For the rest of the morning, Kelly sat wordlessly in court dabbing the blood from his swollen face and head with a handkerchief as Kathryn and her attorneys tried to lay the blame for the kidnapping squarely on his shoulders.

The Urschels and the Jarretts positively identified Kelly as one of the men that had kidnapped them. Then the prosecutors went to work tying Kathryn to it.

First, they put the loquacious Geraldine Arnold on the stand, and she explained again how Kathryn and George were constantly writing letters and threatening to kill people.

"Whom did he say they were going to kill? What did Kathryn say about it?"

"Well, she said that — I don't remember what she said about it."

"Whom did he say he was going to kill?"

"Judge Vaught, Keenan, Urschel and Hyde."

"Was Kathryn there when he said that?"

"Yes, sir."

Then the prosecutors put Luther Arnold, who had agreed to testify in return for leniency, on the stand.

"Did you hear any conversations between George and his wife about the Urschel kidnapping matter?"

"No, I never heard any details of it at all, any more than I heard George remark that 'If I had that to do over again, I would stick his head in a barrel of lime,' or something like that. He said they should have took him out in Arizona and buried him — killed him and buried him," Arnold replied.

"Who said that?"

"George."

"What did Kathryn say when he said that?"

"She said, 'That is what we ought to have done.'"

Then it was Flossie Mae Arnold's turn. She claimed that Kathryn said she ought to "kill the son of a bitch, is what she said she ought to do to him."

"When this statement was made, that she ought to kill him, did she mention anybody's name?"

"Only one . . . Mr. Urschel," said Flossie Mae.

"What did she say?"

"She said she would like to kill the son of a bitch herself, referring to Mr. Urschel."

"Did she use Mr. Urschel's name?"

"Yes, sir."

"Who was present at the time?"

"Her husband, Mr. Kelly."

Flossie Mae told Hyde that she began co-operating with the Bureau's agents because she wanted to get her "baby" back from the Kellys.

On cross-examination, Mathers asked, "When you were in Oklahoma City and talked to Mr. Roberts [John V.], after he was employed as attorney for Mrs. Kelly by your husband, did you say that you would trust your baby anywhere with Mrs. Kelly?"

"No."

"Did Roberts suggest you ought to get your baby back?"

"No."

"Did you ever hear the Kellys talk about surrendering?"

"No."

Then agent Rorer, the Bureau's agent from Birmingham who led the raid that captured the Kellys in Memphis, took the stand.

He recounted a string of important details he had gleaned from George Kelly after his arrest.

"Kelly told me that while he was living in Fort Worth, he and Bates and two other men who were wanted for robbing a Colfax, Washington, bank, discussed kidnapping 'Frank P. Johnson of the First National Bank and Trust in Oklahoma City.'"

Somehow, the authorities had gotten wind of it and a warrant for the two was received. Rorer said a Fort Worth officer "tipped off" Kelly about it, and they backed off. Kelly paid him $500 for the information."

Rorer said Kelly told him of other men they considered snatching: John A. Brown, department store owner and M. K. Goetz, a St. Joseph, Missouri, brewer.

"He said the reason they did not pick any

of these men was because they felt they would have trouble raising a considerable amount of money immediately," Rorer testified.

"Kelly said he and Bates came to Oklahoma City July 1 and registered at the Huckins hotel. On July 6 they moved to the Biltmore and cruised the vicinity of the Urschel residence.

"He said on July 14 they went to the home of an 'old thief' about 150 miles from Oklahoma City and made arrangements for the kidnapped man to be taken there. At the time it was said Wilbur Underhill, Ed Davis, Jim Clark, Harvey Bailey and Bob Brady, all notorious desperadoes, were at the home of the thief. He refused to give the name of the man harboring them," Rorer said.

Keenan asked if he had said the name of the man was Boss Shannon, but Rorer said he never mentioned the name.

"Returning to Oklahoma City, Kelly said he and Bates cruised around the Urschel residence the nights of July 18, 19, 20 and 21," Rorer stated.

"The night of July 22 they saw him playing bridge but were prevented from entering the home earlier than 11:15 p.m. because there were so many cars passing and because a couple of cars had come to and left the house.

"Kelly said the screen door was unlocked. After getting Urschel and Walter R. Jarrett — later letting Jarrett out — they went to the home of the old thief, but relatives were there and they couldn't stay.

"They then went to Coleman, where Mrs. Coleman cussed them out and they left for Paradise, Texas, for the Shannon farm.

"The elder Shannon made them go to Armon's house, where Kelly and Armon guarded Urschel while Bates went north to make arrangements about the ransom money.

"After they collected the ransom money from Kirkpatrick in Kansas City, divided it equally and released Urschel near Norman, Bates and Kelly agreed to meet up later in Minneapolis–St. Paul," stated Rorer.

Kelly then went back to Paradise to get Kathryn.

"He told Kathryn to leave with him immediately, but she argued she ought to have some new clothes and wanted to go into Fort Worth to buy them," Rorer said.

"Kelly said he went to Minneapolis, Minnesota, where he saw Bates, then to St. Paul and on to Memphis.

"He said he passed $2,000 of the money

in the north and gave $7,000 ransom money to a man to pass for them in a liquor deal, with his payment to be 20 percent for passing the money.

"Going to Cleveland, Kelly made a $1,000 deposit in good money on a Cadillac automobile for his wife. He said he read in the newspapers about some of the ransom money being traced to Minneapolis, and tried to call his friend there to determine what had happened, but was unable to get him," he said.

According to Rorer, the Kellys were in Des Moines, Iowa, when they read newspaper accounts of the raid in Paradise and the arrests of the Shannons and Bailey. Kathryn insisted they return to Oklahoma to help her mother.

"Kelly returned to Oklahoma City and later went to south Texas where he bought an automobile in which he later went to New Orleans and then Biloxi, Mississippi," Rorer testified.

"He said he returned to the Cass Coleman farm at Coleman, Texas, to pick up his wife . . . and took her and the Arnold girl from San Antonio with him. He said Kathryn was wearing a red wig.

"Kelly left an automobile in St. Louis, Missouri, and proceeded in another car to

Chicago. He said he telephoned Gus Winkler [one of Capone's lieutenants] and also saw Verne Miller, another desperado.

"Winkler told Kelly not to come near him . . . wouldn't be seen with him for $10,000. Kelly said they returned to St. Louis where he borrowed money to employ lawyers to defend the Shannons," said Rorer.

Then one of the Bureau's agents who had questioned Kelly in Memphis after his arrest testified that Kelly had told him that he had contracted with his friend, Verne Miller, to kill Urschel if he was unable to do it himself.

On the stand, Ralph Colvin, of the Bureau's Oklahoma City office, testified that Kathryn told him that Urschel had filed suit to seize her jewelry, which had been found in a Fort Worth safe-deposit box.

"She wanted me to ask Mr. Urschel to come and see her. She said she couldn't afford to lose that jewelry because it was all she had left to provide for her daughter, Pauline, and she thought Mr. Urschel was a heartless man to try to do that," Colvin testified. "And she went on to remark that if he won the suit, it would not do him much good because he wouldn't have long to live anyway and that was about the extent of the conversation . . . She said this jewelry was not bought with the ransom money, that she had bought that long before."

"But did she say that Mr. Urschel did not have long to live?"

"Yes," Colvin said.

"How did she say she knew that to be the fact?"

"She said she knew some of George's associates would get him."

Next, the prosecutors put on the stand a series of Kathryn's relatives, who would prove not only how unpopular she was with her own family, but provide damning testimony, as well.

Her eighteen-year-old cousin, Gay Coleman, grandson of Mary Coleman, whose house Kelly and Bates had stopped at en route with Urschel to Paradise, testified that Kelly had told him in July that there would soon be a kidnapping in Oklahoma City. To that, according to Coleman, Kathryn had quickly added, "We're going to be in the big money before long."

Then Kathryn's stepsister, Ruth Shannon, recounted how Kathryn had dragged her, Armon's wife and Kathryn's daughter, Pauline, who was being raised by the Shannons, off to her house in Fort Worth, where they were required to reside for a ten-day "vacation." These, of course, were the very same ten days that Urschel was being held at their farm.

Then Mary Coleman, Kathryn's grandmother, entered the courtroom in a wheelchair. She corroborated her grandson's testimony and added that Kelly and Bates had stopped at her farm the night of Urschel's abduction and transferred him from one car to another.

Even Kathryn recognized the damning nature of the testimony. As her grandmother condemned her from the witness stand, she sat next to George at the defense table and wiped tears from her eyes. During the morning's recess she ordered her lawyer to tell the judge she'd be willing to change her plea to guilty in exchange for her mother's freedom.

But Judge Vaught scoffed at the offer and lambasted the attorney for even bringing it to him.

Chastened but unbowed, Kathryn collected herself and prepared to take the stand and testify in her own defense. It was the moment the court, the cameras and the press were waiting for, and Kathryn did not disappoint.

She approached the stand with the grace and poise of a Broadway star entering the stage. She sat down, crossed her legs, smiled at the jurors, recognized the judge with a demure glance and played to the exploding flashbulbs from the press pool and the newsreel cameras that were fixated on her every move.

The reporters took special note of her attire. One wrote that she wore a "smart black dress and hat." Another was more detailed: "She was smartly attired in a black skirt and a black satin waist, with a black bow at the neck. She wore a small black hat, black pumps and sheer stockings. A murmur of comment went up from the many women in the crowded courtroom."

Alternately wiping tears from her eyes with her dainty handkerchief and twisting it as she spoke, she told the jury about her domineering husband, who had forced her into the kidnapping, and how she knew nothing about it or any of the other crimes George had participated in.

"He always told me not to mess in his business in any way, and I didn't."

The prosecutors pressed her.

"What did you ask Kelly about the kidnapping?"

"He told me it was none of my business, that they had a man at Armon's house. I told them if they did I'd tell the officers, even if he killed me. I begged him to release him. I said he would get my folks into trouble . . . He threatened me. He said it was none of my business," she testified.

"Did he say anything about what he intended to do with the kidnapped man?"

"He said he was going to kill him."

"What did you do then?"

"I begged him not to. Asked him to please release him."

Keenan continued to tear into her story on cross-examination. As he did, her act began to come apart. Her demure countenance, according to E. E. Kirkpatrick, who was sitting next to Urschel during the trial, "changed to one of a cornered tigress . . . The sweet girlish smile changed to a fiendish snarl. If she had held any hope in her heart when she took the witness stand, it had completely vanished when she left it."

Kathryn claimed that her removal of the children from Paradise was only coincidental. She said her taking ice to Armon's house, where Urschel was held, was not part of a plot to make the kidnappers comfortable, but a ruse on her part to talk to Kelly.

Keenan had a field day with this.

"You say your husband likes ice? . . . And when you wanted to talk to him about something you would go to him with a chunk of ice in your hand?"

He asked Kathryn if she still loved her husband.

"Yes."

"Do you still trust him?"

"No."

Kathryn's attorney jumped from his seat with objections like a spring-loaded jack-in-the-box, only to be overruled constantly by a simmering Judge Vaught.

Keenan asked how much money the Kellys had in a lockbox in the Fort Worth bank when she first went there from Stratford, Oklahoma. He tried to elicit from her the information that she knew the money was stolen from a bank, but she denied it.

"How were you going to get any more money?" Keenan asked.

"From my husband who was going to get in touch with me," she replied.

"Where did you get the diamond wristwatch for which you expect to file suit to recover?"

"From my husband, I don't know where he got it."

"You were on good terms with your mother and stepfather at this time?"

"Yes," Kathryn asserted.

"Then why didn't you tell them you thought George Kelly had a kidnapped man with him?"

"He asked me not to tell anybody."

"You loved your husband at this time?"

"Yes."

Mathers was apoplectic. He was continually jumping in and objecting in an effort to get Keenan to stop badgering the witness. But Vaught did not intervene.

"Were you at the Shannon farm Tuesday night?"

"No."

"Then if your mother said you were — in the previous trial — she was mistaken."

"I believe so," Kathryn said.

"When you left Stratford, where did you go?"

"Straight to Paradise."

"Did you ask Mr. Shannon's advice about the kidnapping?"

"No."

"Why not?"

"George said he would kill me if I mentioned it."

"How long were you at Paradise before you went on in to Fort Worth with the girls?"

"About thirty minutes," Kathryn replied.

"Did you read about the Urschel kidnapping?"

"Yes, and I was worried to death."

"After you got back to Fort Worth you

were so worried about it you went to the cabaret?"

"No! To the lake."

"At this time you say you were unaware Urschel was at Paradise."

"That's right."

"When you went back to the farm did Mrs. Shannon say George Kelly and [Albert] Bates had a drunk man there?"

"No."

"Did you read her testimony about this case?"

"I don't care what she said, I am telling the truth," asserted Kathryn.

"When did you first talk to your folks about the Urschel kidnapping?"

"When I went back to the farm, Mr. Shannon said George Kelly had a drunk man there."

"Why did he skip telling you an important fact like Kelly's having a machine gun on the man and that he was blindfolded?"

Kathryn claimed he didn't tell her about that.

"If Mr. Shannon said at the previous trial that he didn't know there was a kidnapped man at Armon's house until you told him Wednesday, would you say he was telling an untruth?"

"Yes."

"And if your mother, whom you dearly love, said the same thing, she also was telling an untruth."

"Yes," replied Kathryn.

Keenan then began peppering Kathryn with questions he hoped would prove she'd been to Armon's shack and had discussed the kidnapping with Kelly while he was there.

"And didn't you take newspapers to him so he could find out how the case was proceeding?"

"No."

Roberts raised an objection to Keenan's asking questions so rapidly that the witness did not have time to answer but, again, he was overruled by Judge Vaught.

"What did you ask Kelly about the kidnapping?" Keenan asked.

"He told me it was none of my business that they had a man at Armon's house. I told him if they did, I'd tell the officers even if he killed me." She said she was in tears during the conversation.

"Was there any crying when you learned Urschel had paid $200,000 for his release, or when you sent $1,500 to your parents or when you paid some money on a new Cadillac automobile?"

"No," Kathryn responded.

"Now, when you were at the Shannon farm during the absence of Bates and Kelly you had a fast car and could have left at any time, couldn't you?" asked Keenan.

"Yes."

"Did you talk to Harvey Bailey much?"

"No."

"Did you talk to him about machine guns, or anything like that?"

"Oh, no sir," Kathryn stressed.

"Didn't you know your mother was harboring a desperate criminal and why didn't you tell her?"

"George had told me not to mix in his business."

Kathryn testified that she drove to Norman, Oklahoma, to pick up Kelly, who had been driven there. She described the trip they made north and said they stopped overnight in Omaha, Nebraska, and Mason City, Iowa.

"Surely you knew you were wanted by the officers," Keenan interrupted.

"I didn't know it then," she replied.

Kathryn said she and Kelly registered as Mr. and Mrs. R. G. Shannon in Cleveland, but insisted they were not fleeing.

"But Mrs. Kelly, you could have surrendered at any time, couldn't you?"

"But I didn't know I was wanted," she

kept insisting.

"When you took Geraldine to Chicago, you knew that you were wanted by police, didn't you?"

"Yes, I knew it then."

"Now, Geraldine is a sweet little girl, isn't she?"

"Awfully sweet," Kathryn said, smiling.

"Yet you were herding this girl around with a dangerous murdering scoundrel?"

Roberts objected to Keenan's language.

Keenan said it was hard to use dignified language with a man like Kelly and withdrew the question.

Keenan then turned his attention to the Michigan Tavern in Chicago.

"Did you not know this was a gathering place for some of the worst criminals in the country? A place where they would gather to plan their illegal activities. Drink their illegal liquor. If you were so fond of Geraldine, why would you drag her to one of the most notorious saloons in the city?" he asked.

"It was not a saloon. It was just a place where they served sandwiches and beer. George introduced me to the man as Mr. Edwards. I did not know anyone named Bergl," said Kathryn.

Pointing his finger at George Kelly,

Keenan asked, "Would you turn your daughter, Pauline Frye, over to that man Kelly?"

"I love George very much, he has been good to me," Kathryn said. Keenan ignored this answer and asked his question again.

"Would you turn your daughter over to that man?"

"No, I —"

Keenan jumped in and interrupted her.

"You would take this little Geraldine Arnold, of tenderer years than your own daughter, along with this rascal?"

"He made us go. We did not know we were going to Chicago," Kathryn cried.

Roberts then cross-examined Kathryn, and then called her elderly father, J. E. Brooks, to the stand. He had been living in Kathryn's Fort Worth home at the time of the kidnapping.

"Did you ever tell Mrs. Arnold this kidnapping was planned three months before it was done?"

"I certainly did not," he replied.

"How much of that week Mr. Urschel was kidnapped was Kathryn at her home in Fort Worth?" Roberts asked.

"Well, practically all week. She was home every night." With that, Roberts rested.

The coverage in the press was as prejudicial as the courtroom theatrics.

In the midst of the trial, *The Daily Oklahoman* reported:

Keenan, who acquitted himself so brilliantly in the other trial with his subtle and mockingly sympathetic cross-examination of the Shannons, methodically frayed Kathryn's nerves and destroyed her poise as he carried her through her early life.

He wanted to leave her stumbling and frightened, stripped of her smiling calm when he reached the vital testimony of the actual kidnapping. He succeeded.

When she stumbled thankfully from the witness chair at a brief court recess, the last vestige of her flashing smile was gone and her eyes had a haunted look. But the respite was brief and when the recess ended the special prosecutor soon placed her again on a worried defensive.

A lurid and sordid past life that wouldn't stand close examination ruined the confidence she possessed when she seated herself in the witness chair and turned her appealing half-smile on the jury. Her past life came out, stark and unlovely under the skillful questioning of Keenan.

It was the story of a girl, married first at 15 years old and a mother within a few months who was carried by a passionate yearning for luxury and a lawless nature to husband after husband . . . until she ended as the wife of a "big shot" George Kelly, who matched her criminal temperament and gratified her desire for clothes and jewelry with a free hand.

Her confident voice replaced by a plaintive whisper, Kathryn told of her first marriage while a country schoolgirl to J. C. Frye, and the baby who would come within a few months. The baby, now Pauline Frye, sat in a front row seat watching her mother with *[an]* uncomprehending face.

Frye was divorced. Then came Allie Brewer, of whom she remembered little. He too soon passed out of the picture, followed by Charles. F. Thorne, a Texas man with a small fortune.

"He died a violent death, didn't he?" demanded the merciless Keenan.

"He committed suicide," she answered in a defiant, almost inaudible voice.

That was seven years ago. That was when longed-for luxuries came — from the estate of Thorne. She bought a house in Fort Worth, paid $12,000 for it. She bought an eight-cylinder Cadillac and she bought jewelry worth $3,500. And she started living the way she wanted to.

There had been slim days before, though. She worked as a manicurist in Oklahoma City, was tried for robbery and convicted. It was reversed. The story was dragged from her piecemeal and when she finally spoke the admission, she snarled at Keenan as only a mad woman, "Is that all?"

"Answer the questions that are asked you and eliminate any comments," Judge Vaught told her sternly. She looked at Vaught, the light of battle still in her eyes, then dropped her head.

Keenan hammered on. He made her the "girl friend" of bootleggers and small-time hijackers, always leaving them for bigger criminals. Always moving toward the "big time."

She met Kelly seven years ago in San Antonio. Three years ago, after a six-month correspondence during which Kelly asked her to marry him, they were married in Minneapolis.

"He deceived me," she cried. "I didn't know he made his money dishonestly."

Cleverly Keenan led her into a trap until, startled, she found herself admitting that she knew Kelly was in Leavenworth penitentiary during the six months that they wrote letters to each other.

"So long as you got pretty clothes and a nice place to live in and good food, you weren't particular how your man made his money, were you?" Keenan asked.

"I thought he would sell whisky but I didn't know he would kidnap anybody," she answered.

Then Roberts turned her testimony to the backwoods Coleman farm owned by Kathryn's grandfather, near Stratford, Oklahoma.

"Just what happened; you were there?" Roberts asked.

"Yes. Well, about 4:30 o'clock on that morning [Sunday, July 23, a day following the Urschel kidnapping] someone flashed a flashlight in my face and told me to get up. I noticed a car in the backyard.

"My grandma then was getting up and she asked me what was going on. I said I didn't know but I'd find out. I met George on the porch . . . We had quite a little argument."

As she told of their "fuss," she smiled coyly at the jurors and the crowd.

"My grandmother said if they didn't leave, she would scream. They left only a few moments later. I didn't see anyone else there . . . I think someone else was there, though."

"Did you see the kidnapped man?" Roberts asked.

"Oh, no sir."

"After they left with the kidnapped man what did you do?"

"I went to Fort Worth."

"Why did you go there?"

"Well, I had wanted to go for some time, but my husband wouldn't let me. He told me I could go," Kathryn replied.

"Where did you go first?"

"I went to my mother's, Mrs. R. G. Shannon."

"When did you get there?"

"About 11:30 or 11 o'clock in the morning. I went down to get the kiddies and take them to Fort Worth with me. I took them and Oleta and her baby." (It was then, the government charges, that she was "clearing the scene" for the arrival of Urschel later in the day.)

She continued to Fort Worth, arriving early in the afternoon, and went to her house, where her father was staying, she said.

"Now Thursday. What did you do Thursday?"

"Well it was either Thursday or Friday. I think it was Thursday. I drove up to my mother's [in the afternoon]."

"What did you do? Whom did you see?"

"Well, I went into the house and said hello to my mother like I always do. Mother looked very worried and so did my stepfather, Mr. Shannon. There was another man there, Mr. Bailey. I knew him as Mr. Brennan.

"I talked with Mr. Bailey — about trivial things — and then I got my mother away from him and talked to her. She was almost crying and told me about what had been happening. I talked to my stepfather and he told me the same thing. I told them I'd stay over and find out what was going on . . . at dark I went over to Armon's place and then I found out.

"I talked to Kelly there by the house. I had taken him some ice water and he told me what was going on. He came down to the barn and talked to me. He said they had a kidnapped man there," Kathryn said. "I begged him to please release him. I said he would get my folks into trouble."

"What did he say?"

"He said for me to go back in the house. He threatened me. He said it was none of my business."

"Did he say what he intended to do with the kidnapped man?"

"He said he was going to kill him."

"What did you do then?"

"I begged him not to. Asked him to please release him. Then went back in the house."

Roberts questioned her about the days and dates of her flight, but she feigned confusion.

"I had just so much on my mind, I don't remember those exact things," she admitted. "I left with George for Minneapolis, then."

They went first to St. Paul and Minneapolis, she testified, and from there to Des Moines, Chicago and to other cities before their return to the Coleman farm.

"Did you see any money there?" Roberts asked.

"No sir. I did see some money in Minneapolis, though. I had been out shopping. I had to shop because I didn't have much when I went up there and when I came in George had some money, a lot of money out on the bed. He asked me if I'd ever seen $100,000 before. I don't know what money it was," Kathryn testified.

"Did you see George and your uncle bury the money?" asked Roberts.

"They were gone a long time but I didn't know where they went."

"How long did you stay at your uncle's?"

"Overnight. Then I went to Dallas. I stayed there two days and talked to some attorneys."

Kathryn's smile flashed continually as she talked, swinging in the chair to address first the judge and then the jury. The jurors watched her attentively.

"I didn't see George until two weeks later. I met him at my uncle's after I had been to San Antonio."

In the interval, she said, she had picked up the Arnolds near Waco and had arranged for Luther to act as her contact man.

Finding her husband at Coleman's, she went with him back to San Antonio, where she had an apartment rented.

"George said he was going to Chicago. He asked me to drive him to Coleman's. I took Geraldine with me and told her mother we would be back later in the day."

"Did you come back?"

"No. When we got near the Colemans' we found there was some laws there so George made me and Geraldine go on to Chicago with him."

"Did the Arnolds consent for the little girl to go with you?"

"Oh, yes," Kathryn said emphatically. "We rented an apartment and stayed there five or six days."

"Were you in contact with anyone in Oklahoma City?"

"Yes, I wrote twice to Geraldine's mother."

Then she said they continued with Geraldine to Memphis, where they were arrested.

"When you were in Chicago, I'll ask you if you ever wrote any letter to anyone besides Geraldine's mother."

"Yes . . . Mr. Keenan."

At this point Roberts stopped.

"The defense at this time asks that Mr. Keenan produce the letter in order that the handwriting may be compared to the other letters," he said.

Hyde objected, and Judge Vaught sustained the objection, saying there were other samples of handwriting in evidence.

Roberts handed Kathryn a letter and asked her if she'd written it.

"Yes, I wrote this to Geraldine's mother," she said.

Roberts handed her Government Exhibit No. 8, a letter written threatening the life of Urschel.

"Did you write that?"

"I did not!" she snapped.

"Have you ever threatened anyone since this case or those cases have opened?"

"I have not!"

"Have the officials ever done anything to you to make you want to deprive them of their lives?"

"No!"

"Take the witness," said Roberts.

In a mocking, sarcastic voice, Keenan then dragged Kathryn through the history of her short life, starting with her shotgun wedding while still in high school, her two divorces and the mysterious death of her third husband, Charles Thorne, the criminal partner of George Kelly, her fourth husband.

"Have you ever been arrested and convicted of any offense?" he asked.

"Objection!" yelled Mathers.

"Answer the question," ordered Vaught.

Kathryn hung her head meekly. "I have never been to the penitentiary."

"That is not what I asked you. You have not been to the penitentiary *yet*. Will you answer the question. Have you been arrested and convicted of robbery?"

"Yes."

"And how much was your sentence?"

"Five years. But I appealed and the case was reversed and thrown out."

Keenan squawked, and the judge cautioned her not to elaborate on her answers.

"Where was that?"

"Here in Oklahoma City," answered Kathryn.

"And how long ago was that?"

"About seven or eight years," she answered.

"Under what name?"

"Cleo, Mrs. Drewer, and Mrs. J. E. Barnett and Berniel."

The government then called a handwriting expert, who testified that, without doubt, it was Kathryn's handwriting on the threatening letters that had been sent to Urschel.

Then, perhaps the most exquisite evidence of her involvement was established — the fact that it was she who purchased Kelly's infamous machine gun.

Keenan showed records tracing it from Birmingham, Alabama, to New Orleans and from New Orleans to Fort Worth. He then produced the pawnbroker, J. Klar, who testified he sold it to Kathryn in late February 1933.

Hyde knew that Hoover was convinced Kathryn was the brains behind the kidnapping and emphatically wanted her to go down with the full sentence of life in prison, and that Cummings felt likewise. Hyde knew how to please the boss, and in his final argument he twisted the knife just a little more:

"How can you believe that this was the demure, loving and fearful wife she pretends to be after hearing that she roamed the country like a millionaire's daughter or wife, buying machine guns? This sweet-smelling geranium. Do you think she schemed with George and others under threats? I tell you she was the arch-conspirator," he said, addressing the jury.

Young Pauline squirmed in her seat as her mother was demonized by the prosecution.

Hyde would sarcastically refer to "sweet little Kathryn" and "little George" as he painted Kathryn as a woman who drove her husband to commit crimes so that he could supply her with the luxuries she demanded.

He painted a picture, based on scant evidence, that when Kelly drove Urschel to Norman, Oklahoma, where he was released, Kathryn was right behind him in their treasured Cadillac to pick up her husband and flee the scene.

He pointed out how they had changed license plates in Stratford, Oklahoma, at the Colemans', as they fled to Texas.

"Oh, they didn't intend to stay at the Colemans'," Hyde declared.

As the fifteen-year-old Pauline looked on

in dismay, her mother was depicted as an evil seductress and acquisitive manipulator who would stop at nothing to get what she wanted.

"This woman's whole life has been one of deceit. Do you think she would hesitate for a moment to try to deceive this jury? Her liberty is at stake," Hyde said.

Keenan asked the jury to consider the type of woman Kathryn had been.

"She knew her husband was an outlaw, a human wolf who slept by day and prowled by night. This woman masqueraded under her own mother's name. She deserted her daughter and all other members of her family. Did she do all this because she was afraid of her husband?" asked Keenan.

"Kathryn did her part in the Urschel kidnapping when she cleared all the children away from the Shannon farm. The testimony shows that afterward she and Kelly were hundreds of miles apart . . . that he was down in Mississippi. Was she afraid of him then? No, instead she was going after him as fast as she could," he said.

After three days of withering testimony and evidence, there was little that James H. Mathers could do or say in his closing statement.

He argued that Kathryn had nothing to

do with the planning of the kidnapping, implying that Bates and Kelly originally wanted to stay at the farm of the mysterious "old thief" or the Coleman farm in Stratford.

"Kathryn had nothing to do with the kidnapping up to that time," he argued. "And force and coercion was used upon her when the kidnappers made the fatal mistake of crossing the state line."

If they hadn't done that, he pointed out, the federal government wouldn't even have jurisdiction in the case.

"There is no legal and competent evidence to show this little lady is guilty and you should acquit her," he concluded.

As he closed the proceedings, Judge Vaught's instructions to the jury contained incredible statements of partiality and assertions that she lied on the stand.

He began by saying, "The court would feel cowardly and derelict in its duty if it did not point out its conviction that the defendant, Kathryn Kelly, was not wholly truthful.

"This court will not hesitate to tell you that Kathryn Kelly's testimony concerning the removal of the little girls from the Shannon farm near Paradise, Texas, the day Mr. Urschel was brought there, did not sound convincing.

"Her conduct at the Coleman farm near Stratford, Oklahoma, not only is a strong circumstantial point but is convincing to this court that Kathryn knew about the kidnapping and knowingly participated," the judge concluded.

The defense attorneys howled in protest, saying that the judge's statement "virtually amounted to an instructed verdict of guilty."

Their protests fell on deaf ears.

The jury returned with a verdict an hour later. Legendary wire service reporter James Kilgallen described the scene:

A hushed silence, broken only by the faint whir of motion picture cameras, fell over the crowded courtroom as the verdict was read.

Kelly, the man who boasted he can write his name on a wall with machine gun bullets, and his 29-year-old wife, who had stuck with him throughout during their hectic married life and criminal career, stood up, side by side.

She was pale, her lips tightly compressed and her long slim fingers closing and unclosing. She wore a black silk dress, with red buttons down the front of her waist, and a smart black hat of the latest mode.

Kelly, a heavy-set ex-convict, wanted for murder and robbery in several cities, tried to appear nonchalant, but his face was serious as the judge leaned forward. Kelly's dyed hair stood out like a beacon, its yellowish-red hue giving him a grotesque appearance.

"Have you anything to say?" asked Judge Vaught in a quiet voice.

"No, sir," said Kathryn in a low, tremulous voice. Kelly said nothing.

Judge Vaught gave them both the maximum sentence: life in prison. Kathryn trembled and began to weep softly.

The Kellys were then removed from the court by a heavy guard of men armed with machine guns, rifles and shotguns.

The judge turned his attention to the assembled scrum of newspapermen, photographers and newsreel cameramen. (The Kelly trial was the first federal trial to allow cameras in the courtroom. Weekly excerpts were shown in movie theaters around the country as the investigation and the trial progressed. But, in part because of the national hysteria created by the reports, cameras were subsequently banned from federal courts. They would return on an experimental basis in the late '90s.) He asked for silence and, except for the whirring sounds of the motion picture cameras, he got it.

"Of its own volition and without apologies to anyone, this court has permitted various facilities in the courtroom for the purpose of giving publicity to this case," said Judge Vaught.

"Our attitude toward kidnapping is such that we should like the world to know what the United States Court of the Western District of Oklahoma does in such cases. Further, the Attorney General of the United States suggested that this be done for the reason that giving of wide publicity to it would have a tendency to deter crime," he explained.

When they asked Urschel for his reaction to the verdicts, the man who literally had led the investigators to his captors, and whose cooperation had resulted in the string of convictions, responded in his characteristic modest and taciturn manner: "The government deserves all the credit in the world in this case. I have no feeling of revenge or triumph, but only the highest regard for the officers who worked on the case and the juries which rendered the verdicts. Now, back to work."

(On the day the Kellys were convicted in Oklahoma, the state legislature in Texas passed a law making kidnapping punishable by death. The bill was sponsored by Grady Woodruff, who had been one of the attorneys for the Shannons in their trial with Bates and Bailey. Woodruff said his experience there convinced him that gangsters thought no more of kidnapping and holding someone for ransom than they would "going to the coast for a vacation.")

10
THE G-MEN TAKE THE SPOTLIGHT

In the remarkable ninety days since Berenice Urschel woke J. Edgar Hoover from his sleep with her urgent call about her husband's kidnapping, Hoover had achieved what three months earlier would have been thought of as impossible: he captured and convicted the perpetrators of the most notorious kidnapping since the Lindbergh baby abduction. He incontrovertibly demonstrated the need for a national law enforcement agency whose authority was not limited by locale or boundary. The national melodrama that had played out over the nation's radio networks and on the pages of its newspapers gave the Roosevelt administration not just proof positive of the need to expand the powers of the federal government, but the first real victory of his administration — a demonstrable triumph in his offensive against the forces that were dragging down the country.

Although the War on Crime was merely a bit player in FDR's ambitious first hundred days of legislative and policy initiatives, it was now made a first priority. Hoover's Bureau of Investigation, previously viewed as a dumping ground for incompetents and the hopelessly corrupt, was now, in the public's mind, the model of efficiency and relentless pursuit — dragon slayers in business suits. Hoover, under Cummings's tutelage, had become a skilled practitioner of managing the message and building an image. Questions about his age, competence and fastidious fashion all but disappeared. Cummings would reappoint him as director, and he would continue in that position for the next forty years.

While the other members of FDR's Brain Trust were fighting a battle against an abstract enemy — the economic calamities of the Great Depression — Cummings and Hoover were fighting a real war against a definable enemy armed with real bullets and the actual accoutrements of modern warfare. Their success was measured by arrests and convictions, and they had just run the score up in an impressive display of crime-fighting capability, bringing to justice a notorious criminal gang without firing a shot.

They had won their case in the court of public opinion, as well. Their accomplishments were celebrated episodically by virtually every newspaper chain, radio network and movie theater. America would get its version of Scotland Yard, with crafty investigators using the latest in scientific criminal-detection methods, and it would be headed up by the most unlikely of candidates: J. Edgar Hoover.

Later, when arguing for expanded federal laws and increased power for the Justice Department, Attorney General Cummings would cite the Urschel case as a prime example of the need for federal forces to fight crime "between the federal and state jurisdictions," where there existed "a kind of twilight zone, a sort of neutral corridor, unpoliced and unprotected in which criminals of the most desperate character found an area of relative safety . . . the unholy sanctuary of predatory vice."

In the Urschel kidnapping case, Cummings told the Continental Congress of the Daughters of the American Revolution on April 19, 1934, "the operations of the criminals took place in seven states; and it was necessary for the agents of the Department of Justice to go into nine additional states before their efforts to solve the crime and bring its perpetrators to justice proved successful. The seven states referred to have an area of about 683,000 square miles, which exceeds in extent the combined areas of Austria, Denmark, France, Germany, Italy, Holland, Switzerland, England, Scotland, and Wales. . . . This accentuates the need of a nationwide approach to the problem. . . . Crime today is organized on a nationwide basis . . . in many localities there exists an unholy alliance between venal politicians and organized bands of racketeers . . . Undoubtedly crime costs our country several billion dollars each year; and it is conservative to say that there are more people in the underworld carrying deadly weapons than there are in the Army and the Navy of the United States."

Immediately after the Urschel trial, Keenan went straight to the microphones to crow about his department's victory. FDR's War on Crime had won its first battle.

"This is just a skirmish," he declared. "We are going right on down the line until every predatory criminal and gangster in the United States is exterminated. The new law has proven a powerful weapon and we are eager to use it to the finish."

Keenan's choice of the word "exterminated," rather than "incarcerated," was an odd choice for a man of the law, but it would prove to be prophetic, as the Bureau's men would soon prove as adept at killing gangsters as arresting and prosecuting them. (The following year, during the nationwide hunt for John Dillinger, Cummings would remove any ambiguity from his policy directives, telling his agents to "Shoot to kill — then count to ten.")

With the Urschel trial behind it, the Bureau would begin to arm up heavily. Hoover began buying his agents automatic weapons and submachine guns and hiring new crack-shot agents. He would bring in instructors who could teach them how to use the latest weaponry effectively — and with deadly accuracy.

Hoover, realizing his vision of creating an elite force of investigators armed only with law degrees and accounting skills was unrealistic, added marksmanship to his list of requirements. He built a gym in the Bureau's office building so his men could get fit and train in the martial arts. He installed a firing range and brought his old-line field agents into Washington to teach his college boys how to shoot. His "Briefcase Army" would now be packing heat. And lots of it.

Hyde announced that the Urschel case convictions would "serve as a notice to those who would violate and set aside our federal laws that no individual or group of individuals is more powerful than the federal government."

The government's decision to allow cameras in the courtroom proved a brilliant stroke in their campaign to burnish the image of their agents into the public's mind as invincible detectives who would stop at nothing until they brought the bad guys to justice.

Before the Kellys were even on their way to prison, movie theater audiences were standing and cheering the newsreel accounts of the trial and its sensational verdict as the narrator announced: "Uncle Sam Wars on Kidnappers! . . . Abductors of Charles Urschel, oil millionaire, are sentenced for life under the new so-called Lindbergh federal law . . . Machine Gun Kelly, mastermind of a snatch gang and desperado extraordinary, gets life too . . . a telling blow to gangdom's rule!"

The clip featured actual courtroom scenes, re-creations of the crime and the Shannon farm, with an actor playing Urschel being chained to the high chair at Armon's place. It concluded with a shot of the Kellys being taken from the courtroom to the armored car that would take them away as the narrator claimed: "Thus, Uncle Sam rolled up his sleeves and dealt gangland a swift, decisive blow. They are going for a ride, and with the federal government at the wheel." Over a shot of Leavenworth prison, he concluded, "And here's the end of the road — and oblivion — the inevitable destruction of the lure of easy money."

Reporters and headline writers had a field day with the colorful quotes and descriptions they were being fed by Hoover and his publicity machine. They described Kelly as "one of the most vicious and dangerous criminals in America," a "known killer," the "machine gunner for the underworld of the Western badlands." And, taking the Hoover line, they convicted him in printed innuendo for the Kansas City Massacre.

The G-man image was hatched, but the actual story of Kelly's arrest lacked the drama Hoover was looking for, and six months later, when it was fed into the Bureau's publicity machine, it was quickly enhanced. Hoover's friendly inside man at *The Washington Star,* Rex Collier, who'd formerly worked as "Buffalo Bill" Cody's public relations man, embellished Kathryn's quote and attributed it to Kelly in a colorful story he crafted at Hoover's bidding and published in July 1934. In all subsequent official accounts of the capture, the Bureau would claim that when their agents surprised Kelly in Tichenor's Memphis home, he dropped his gun, cowered in a corner and pleaded, "Don't shoot, G-men! Don't shoot!"

Hoover latched on to the G-man moniker that would define his brand for the next forty years. It would soon be on movie marquees, books and comic books that would portray his agents as smart, handsome detectives equipped with the most modern contrivances and scientific technology to bring criminals to their knees. From then on, Hoover would go to extraordinary lengths to make sure his agents were portrayed as the heroes, and the outlaws as scum.

Six of the nine defendants in the Urschel kidnapping were sentenced to life. Cass Coleman and his neighbor, Will Casey, would be tried later in San Angelo, Texas, for harboring known criminals. Langford Ramsey, Tichenor and two others were under arrest in Memphis and awaiting trial. Clifford Skelly and Edward Berman of Minneapolis were sentenced to five years each for laundering the Urschel ransom money.

It was quite a takedown, and it not only saved Hoover's foundering career, but burnished the image of the nation's top lawman that he was creating for himself.

It was the first victory in the nation's fight against gangland forces and Western outlaws, and it was described in the press as "the finest piece of detective work in modern times."

But, other than desk-jockeying the case from his perch in Washington, DC, Hoover had very little involvement in catching the Kellys or prosecuting their case. However, he had no hesitancy taking credit for it or allowing his name and image to become the trademark for the Bureau. The public would come to regard him as Public Hero No. 1, the perfect antidote to the Public Enemies that were prowling the country and making it unsafe for good, law-abiding citizens.

The agents who had worked the case in the field were a bit taken aback that no credit at all was being given to the victim in the case, who had stood up to the kidnappers and led the agents to his place of captivity, participated in the arrest of Bailey and the Shannons, gathered a wealth of evidence for the prosecution and testified in court — all under threats to his life and his family's. When Colvin, who described

Urschel as "brilliant" and "cool-headed," suggested to Hoover that Urschel at least ought to be thanked or celebrated for his participation, Hoover did nothing publicly, but instead fired off a terse letter of appreciation to Urschel privately.

Perhaps I should have at an earlier date advised you of my gratification because of your wholehearted cooperation with this Division in its conduct of the investigation of the kidnapping of which you were the victim. The convictions on Saturday, I am sure, bear ample testimony to the wisdom of the advice given by this department to the families and friends of persons who have been kidnapped and I am quite sure that if the government enjoyed the same measure of cooperation which you have afforded it from all others who are visited by this despicable crime, kidnapping would no longer be popular in the underworld.

I thank you sincerely for your cooperation and extend to you my congratulations upon the successful presentation of this case, to which you contributed in no little degree.

With expressions of my kindest personal regards, I am

J. Edgar Hoover
Director

Hyde was more to the point and more self-effacing in his appreciation of Urschel's role: "The credit goes most to Mr. Urschel chiefly because of his courage and his ability to distinguish what was going on under a blindfold," he said. Years later, he would laud Urschel as a "wonderful witness."

"It was nothing to my credit," Hyde added. "Any young lawyer could have tried it as well."

Meanwhile, Hoover went to work to insure that in this, and in all future victories, he indeed would get the credit. Cummings's team was all over the papers and the airwaves after the verdict. Hoover felt his Bureau — particularly with himself representing it — should have been out front, in the spotlight and taking the applause.

He started courting friendly members of the press and stars of the new radio networks. He would lure them with exclusive tips and leaks in return for favorable treatment and able assists in building his myth of invincibility. First in the door was pulp magazine crime writer Courtney Ryley Cooper, who loved a good detective story and had the narrative skills to turn it into a great one, even if it meant sidestepping some of the messy facts of the matter. That summer he began a series of stories for *American Magazine* that would turn the androgynous, fussy bureaucrat into not just the most admired lawman in the country, but a national celebrity, as well.

11
ALCATRAZ AND THE IRREDEEMABLES

While Hoover and the Bureau of Investigation were busily hunting down the Kellys and the rest of their ring, Attorney General Cummings had been working a parallel track to create a prison strong enough to hold them and the rest of the criminal underworld they hoped to bring to justice. If they were to escape, yet again, it would undo all the trust they'd just won from the adoring public.

Bailey and Bates had been sent to Leavenworth Federal Penitentiary by plane, guarded by ten heavily armed officers. From the military airfield where they landed in Leavenworth, Kansas, they were taken by armored car to the prison. Leavenworth was just eight miles away from the Kansas State Prison in Lansing, which Bailey and eleven others had broken out of in spectacular fashion just four months earlier, on Memorial Day. The irony was not lost on anyone.

As the guards were escorting Bailey into Leavenworth, he looked up at the walls and dryly observed that they were "pretty high."

"Guess I'll have a pretty hard time making it," he quipped. Despite the humor in his remark, few doubted the seriousness of his intent.

On Friday, October 13, Kelly was placed in a barred, bulletproof prison coach hooked to the Katy Limited and carted off to Leavenworth guarded by eight Bureau agents, all wielding machine guns.

Kelly was more succinct than Bailey on his way in. He looked at his guards and announced, "I'll be out by Christmas."

After Kelly had been carted off to Leavenworth, Kathryn was forced to face the reality that she might never see him again. On the Saturday morning after his relocation, she sat down and wrote him a love letter.

My Dear Husband:
No doubt you are back at Leavenworth by now. I really had my misgivings yesterday tho' it being Friday, the 13th I was sure the train would wreck, or you'd get hurt. You know my superstitious nature. . . . I will be awfully glad when I leave here. Anything for a change, however two of the jailers here have been

awfully kind and nice to me, the others hate me, I suppose.

It is much more lonely for me Dear, since you left. Just the thought of you here in the building was worth a lot. I do hope I can be with mother to cheer her up. I am going to try my best to be a model prisoner with her, and perhaps she can make parole, if I can't later. As for me personally, I'd just as soon be inside as out without you, and you know that. So don't worry about me Honey. My life is so wrapped up with you I wouldn't enjoy my pleasures outside without you anyway Dear. I do hope you will try to be a good prisoner sweetheart. The cards are stacked against you, so be man enough to realize it and don't give them a chance to murder you, that's what they want. I know how good and sweet you are Dear, and I will always adore you, and that's all that really matters. You have been and will always be, the one great love of my life, and if it is God's will to separate us forever, that cannot destroy our love, and I don't believe that is his will for he alone realizes that you and I never harmed anyone and that we've helped hundreds of the needy and I think we will again be together in the future. None of the accused have been given Justice here, you know. And a very bad picture has been painted of us, and poor old sweet mother, but honey the public doesn't know so don't feel hard about it. I am glad you were man enough to keep the other two fellows out of it. Nobody likes a squealer and altho' they deserved it, let the smart guys figure it out if they can. They could have cleared me, but rather than talk, I'd rather be here. Think of me, Sweetheart, and I shall be thinking of you constantly. Try to be satisfied and don't worry. Just remember the happy hours we've enjoyed together. Nobody can take those away and we have been happier in the past three years than most people have through a life-time, Darling.

With a heart full of love, and a big Kiss, until death us do part, your very own,

Kathryn

The letter was intercepted and held as evidence because of its reference to the two other gang members whom Kelly had not given up. It was never forwarded to Kelly at Leavenworth.

■ ■ ■ ■

Hoover had just put the Bureau on the national map with its stirring arrest and conviction of Bailey, Bates, Kelly and his gang, and he wanted to make sure they didn't make a mockery of it by walking out of a federal prison only a few short months later. They had the money, the influence and partners on the outside that could easily make it happen.

Hoover wrote to Director of Prisons Stanford Bates and warned him not to compromise his finely crafted image of the Bureau's invincibility by letting their captives escape. He reminded the Director that Bailey, Bates and Kelly were "desperate and dangerous." He reminded Bates that their fellow gang members — Tommy Holden, Francis Keating and Frank Nash — had all escaped from Leavenworth, that Kelly and Bailey were both suspected in the Kansas City Massacre and that Kelly had "boasted that he could not be held in a penitentiary and that he will escape."

After Bailey, Bates and Kelly had been transferred to Leavenworth, Cummings wrote a cautionary letter to Warden Robert H. Hudspeth:

Because of the especially fine work of the Federal officers in capturing and prosecuting Harvey Bailey and (Albert) Bates and the notoriety given to the case . . . I consider that it would be a shock to the country should either of these men escape. I shall expect, therefore, that you give personal attention to these men. I am informed that you have ample means to keep them in confinement. I shall hold you personally responsible for their safekeeping.

Director of Prisons Bates sent special instructions about Kelly to the warden, ordering that he "should be held incommunicado and no messages or letters should be delivered to or from him. He should be permitted no visits, not even from lawyers, except with the special permission of the Attorney General. He may be seen by the Doctor or by the Chaplain if in your judgment that is wise and safe. I suggest that he be placed in one of the cells in the segregation building; that he be permitted under no circumstances to communicate with other prisoners or to mingle in the yard. He will, of course, be given exercise but in the small exercise yard connected with the segregation unit. He will have regular food, tobacco, books and newspapers but no other privileges."

Hoover still worried about his trophy captures and sent agents into the prison to check on the conditions. He was not impressed. He sent a scolding letter off to Director of Prisons Bates, who, taking umbrage, fired back, "Who's running the prison anyway?"

Hoover, Cummings and others at the Department of Justice knew that the only way to control and punish the celebrity gangsters they hoped to round up was to create a new facility where influence peddling and special privileges did not exist. And, most especially, a prison that was escape-proof.

What they had in mind was something akin to the notorious French prison known as Devil's Island, a brutal penal colony located off the coast of French Guiana in South America, surrounded by fast currents and shark-infested waters.

Cummings had the perfect spot in mind. On October 13, two weeks after Kelly's conviction, he announced that the federal government was building a new prison on Alcatraz Island, off the coast of San Francisco, which had been used as a military prison since the days of the Civil War. The barren island, known even then as The Rock, fit perfectly with the militaristic theme of Cummings's War on Crime. He would describe and promote it in such a way as to counter the public's image of the coddling of gangsters in the federal prison system. He wanted the public to believe that the most dangerous criminals in the prison system were being sent to a brutal penal colony where they would be punished inhumanely and from which there was no escape possible.

Hoover held special contempt for the country's penal system, with its coddling wardens, loosely purchased pardons and — the worst sin of all — parole. He had a litany of phrases to describe them that he would throw around whenever he got the chance: "criminal coddlers," "shyster lawyers," "convict lovers," "legal vermin" and "swivel-chair criminologists."

The island prison, said Cummings, would be for convicts with "advanced degrees in crime." It would house the "habitual and incorrigible . . . the irreclaimable." Consequently, the prison staff would waste no time on rehabilitation. The prison would exist solely to punish its inmates and deter others from joining their ranks. It would be reserved for less than 1 percent of the prison population — the worst of the worst.

"Here may be isolated the criminals of the vicious and irredeemable type . . . so that their evil influence may not be extended to other prisoners who are disposed to rehabilitate themselves," he said. This was the place where he said he hoped to lock up the likes of Harvey Bailey, George Kelly and Al Capone.

Less than a year later, he would.

The assistant director of Alcatraz Federal Penitentiary, William Hammack, believed the prisoners ought to be sent to the island in large groups on special trains — heavily guarded, armored and moving in secret. He was convinced he could make his plan work, but it would require tight coordination and the cooperation of the railroads. He outlined his plan in a memo to Director of Prisons Bates.

The railroads agreed not to stop the special train at regular stations, and in fact the only occasion for stopping the train would be to change the crew, take on water or fuel, or perform some regular service. This would be done in the yard or at some point distant from the regular passenger station. Nobody but the train crew would know where the stops were to be. To safeguard this phase the railroad companies have agreed they will have [a] sufficient number of special agents and detectives in the yard or at the service station to insure no unauthorized person even approaches the train.

It would be impossible for anybody to know who was on the train unless the information was given out at Washington or at the institution from which the transfer originated. If the prisoners were selected beforehand, the train placed in the prison yard, carefully searched, the prisoners moved in and properly shackled, the entire party could move without anybody knowing anything about it except the officers inside the institution.

On September 4, 1934, Bailey, Bates and Kelly were removed from Leavenworth to be transferred with 101 other incorrigibles to Alcatraz on the heavily guarded railroad train. The plan was as audacious as it was precedent-setting. More than one hundred of the most dangerous and violent criminals in the federal penitentiary system would be loaded collectively onto a single train and transported across the Western badlands to an island prison in San Francisco Bay. The opportunities for mishap, escape and assault from outside forces were multitudinous. Still, it was decided that it would be safer to move the group collectively, rather than one at a time.

Hoover assigned Gus Jones to guard the cargo.

Kelly and company were on the largest — and last — run of the Alcatraz Express. Two other shipments of "furniture" (code for the inmates) had preceded them as the Bureau of Prisons tested its transportation plan with smaller loads of less-dangerous celebrity prisoners. They feared the dire consequences of losing the likes of Kelly or Bailey in some calamity — a rescue attempt, a train wreck or an outright assault. The Bureau also feared loose-lipped railroad workers or the eminently bribable rail yard guards who might assist the gangster crowd to somehow free the whole bunch or divert the train into some trap.

Although the first trains had delivered their cargo without incident, they were less successful in eluding the press. Photographs of the Alcatraz Express had been taken and stories about its cross-country trip published. Jones told his guards that this, the last trip, would be the most dangerous of all.

"We got away with the first bunch because they didn't have any idea of what we would do. But now they know it will be a rail move and they'll be ready for us if they intend to make an effort to break these men out," he said.

"There well could be an attempt because these men we are taking are connected into every bandit, stickup, and kidnapping gang in the country. Anywhere along the line they could derail this train . . . and hope their men would live through it and they could get them away — and they have damned little to lose if they don't."

The cross-country train ride was a special torture itself. There were to be sixteen guards accompanying each shipment. The ends of each car were enclosed with a metal mesh sheeting and the windows were barred and locked closed. The inmates were shackled together in pairs. They remained in their seats for the entire four-day trip, drinking water from pails with dippers and eating in their seats. The only time during the trip they were permitted to leave their seats was to use the restrooms, which they would do while bound to their partners. The trains raced across the country, with rail switchers clearing the tracks ahead of them. They refueled and changed crews in the rail yards rather than in the stations. The yards were cleared and guarded by armed guards until the trains could tear out and resume their journey.

As Jones walked through the railcars with his finger on the trigger of his submachine gun, surveying the scene, he thought of an incident from early in his career as a Texas Ranger, when he and his partner were about to enter a seedy Mexican bar to arrest a cattle rustler. His partner had turned to Jones and said, "If trouble starts in there just pull your pistol as fast as you can and shoot everybody in sight except me — they're all bound to be guilty of something."

Good advice in his present situation as well, he thought. And these men all really *were* guilty. He'd personally arrested a good number of them, and knew them all by name and reputation.

As Kelly's train raced through the drought-plagued Midwest he watched the wastelands of the territory he used to plunder fly by. The parched wheat fields, the rotten corn, the carcasses of dead cattle that had starved in the heat and were left rotting in the fields. The wind blew the dust off the barren fields and into the railcars on the rare occasions when Jones would allow a door to be cracked open for some brief ventilation. The dirt caked on the sweaty faces of the inmates until they were almost unrecognizable. When the train would stop, the heat in the car would rise. Rivulets of sweat carved tracks in their dusted faces, and the stench intensified as the men cursed and threatened their tormentors.

Kelly's train arrived at 6:00 a.m. at Ferry Point on the East Bay. From there, the prisoners were taken by barge to Alcatraz Island escorted by a Coast Guard cutter and a prison launch. The final 103 pieces of "furniture" had arrived. The Alcatraz population of 210 was complete.

The press had foiled the Bureau's attempts to keep the shipments secret, and each of their arrivals was greeted by throngs of reporters wanting to know who was on the trains that required such heavy protection, and who was being shipped to Alcatraz.

Each time, Warden James Johnston, reading from the Bureau's playbook, told them essentially the same thing.

"No one is going to know the identity of the prisoners housed here, nor even the numbers they go by. . . . We are not even going to let the outside world know to which duties they have been assigned . . . [the inmates] are not even going to have an opportunity to know what goes on outside. . . . These men were sent here because the government wants to break their contacts with the underworld. That is going to be done."

Once on the island, Kelly and the rest of the inmates were marched into a yard and taken two by two inside, where they were allowed to shower. They were then inspected by the medical staff, which probed and prodded, looking for evidence of contraband and drugs. They were given clean clothes, their prison numbers and marched off to their cells.

After their days-long ride through the Midwest and the western plains in the beastly hot railcars, the prisoners were freezing in the damp, windy weather on the island. When they assembled for their first meal, they were locked into the mess hall, where machine-gun-wielding guards walked the catwalks above and tear-gas canisters hung above the tables ready to be triggered if trouble broke out. They were allowed to eat, but not to talk.

Among Kelly's new neighbors were Al Capone, five members of Roger Touhy's gang, two from Bugs Moran's, five from Dutch Schultz's, ten from the Barker-Karpis collective and guys who'd ridden and worked with John Dillinger, George

"Baby Face" Nelson and Bonnie and Clyde. Among the notables was Gordon Alcorn, who'd kidnapped Charles Boettcher. Union Station massacre conspirators Frank Mulloy, Richard Galatas and Herbert Farmer were there. So were Jim Clark, who had busted out of the Kansas State Pen with Harvey Bailey, and Tommy Holden and Francis Keating, who Kelly had sprung from Leavenworth.

The old crowd was back together, but their life in Alcatraz would be decidedly different from their previous incarcerations. Alcatraz was the prison for the inmates that society had given up on. There was no effort made at rehabilitation, because the country had decided that the people sent to Alcatraz were irredeemable and, thus, they never were wanted back in the general population. Alcatraz was simply about punishment and confinement.

The prison strove to isolate its population from the outside world under a level of security theretofore unseen. Their interaction with the outside world would be virtually eliminated. All prisoners were equal and anonymous. There was no way to curry favors or game the system.

The guards were new and newly trained. They and their families were required to live on the island, but in the midst of the Depression, the Bureau of Prisons had little trouble finding men willing to live in such a godforsaken place.

The Justice Department imposed the rules at Alcatraz, and they were draconian and unambiguous.

Escape would be virtually impossible. Inmates would be deprived of opportunities for interaction with one another that might provide opportunities for collusion. There would be no special accommodations for rich celebrity prisoners. Information in and out of the prison would be strictly controlled. The regimen at Alcatraz would represent real punishment. In effect, the government was saying that it did not care if the inmates there were ever returned to society. In fact, they would prefer that they weren't.

The inmates at Alcatraz were informed that they were entitled to food, clothing, shelter and medical attention. Anything else was a privilege that had to be earned. On Alcatraz there were no newspapers or radios; there was no commissary where inmates could select items to purchase, like candy or cigarettes. Their days were regimented to the minute.

For the rebellious, there was solitary

confinement in the prison's "dungeon."

Life in the dungeon was a special form of hell, completely unknown to the outside world until it was described in testimony by inmate Harry Young, who was accused of murdering another prisoner with a home-made shiv:

Its size was approximately that of a regular cell — 9 feet by 5 feet by about 7 feet high — I could touch the ceiling by stretching my arm . . . You are stripped nude and pushed into the cell. Guards take your clothes and go over them minutely for what few grains of tobacco may have fallen into the cuffs or pockets. There is no soap. No tobacco. No toothbrush. The smell — it is like stepping into a sewer. It is nauseating. After they have searched your clothing, they throw it in to you. For bedding, you get two blankets around 5 in the evening. You have no shoes, no bed, no mattress — nothing but the four damp walls and two blankets. The walls are painted black. Once a day I got three slices of bread . . . I got one meal in five days and nothing but bread in between . . . In the entire thirteen days I was there, I got two meals.

He described the air fouled by the stench of human waste in the metal bucket that serves as the cell's toilet, and damp air from the large vent through which the winds blow constantly, making it impossible to stay warm.

Standing in your stocking feet on that concrete floor is not conducive to health . . . I tried to huddle in the corner and took my coveralls off and used them to try to keep my shoulders warm. Then I shifted and wrapped them around my legs to try to keep my legs warm. That went on day after day . . . I have seen but one man get a bath in solitary confinement, in all the time that I have been there. That man had a bucket of cold water thrown over him.

The monastic regime and hellacious conditions drove some inmates insane, but others learned to accommodate and accept it. They adapted and survived. George Kelly was among those in the latter group.

He entered Alcatraz at age thirty-four, and he would never again walk the earth as a free man. He was resigned to his fate. Initially, he would support the other inmates in their hunger strikes and fruitless protests for easier conditions. But after a few tours in the dungeon, he gave up on that and tried to make the best of the situation and live his life as well as he could. He would "do his own time" in the parlance of the inmates, enjoying the few breaks in the work routine, when he could play cards and dominoes in the prison yard with Bailey and Bates, Keating and Holden and some of the other bank-robbing pros from his gang days.

The prison psychiatrist described Kelly favorably in his reports, saying he fully accepted responsibility for his criminal actions, was smart, insightful and did not display signs of resentment. On the Stanford–Binet tests given by the prison, Kelly scored as "highly intelligent." The doctor wrote that he "shows a fairly normal reaction to a difficult situation . . . does not appear to worry too much." The doctor did not consider him "psychotic in any way."

For Kelly, the torture of Alcatraz was not the spartan conditions, the monotonous routine and the lack of any special privileges, but the deprivation of news from the outside world — the lack of newspapers, radio and correspondence. To keep his sanity he enrolled in several correspondence courses from the University of California, checked out books from the prison library and read constantly. (Al Capone, an accomplished mandolin and banjo player, convinced the warden to allow him to start a prison band. He recruited Kelly to play drums and Alvin Karpis to play guitar. Years later, Karpis would be released to the maximum security federal penitentiary in Washington state, where he taught fellow inmate Charles Manson how to play.)

Bates took a similar tack, consuming three to four books of nonfiction a week and outperforming Kelly in friendly competition in their correspondence courses. In fact, one of his teachers noted that his work in grammar and composition was "probably the best submitted at this institution thus far."

But Bates, whose take from the kidnapping was still largely unrecovered, was constantly being hounded by prison officials and federal agents for information about its whereabouts. With the agents constantly making a public show of pulling him off work details and out of his cell for interrogations, Bates feared he might be marked as a stool pigeon by the other inmates, who might assume that he was giving up information about them or their partners on the outside. And that was a particularly dangerous reputation to have in a federal prison, especially one housing known murderers and assassins.

Ultimately, he refused to meet with any agent unless he could bring Bailey with him as a witness. Bailey's reputation among the inmates was so stellar that if he vouched for Bates, that was good enough. Bailey would never violate the prisoners' code. He practically wrote it.

Annoyed with the constant harassment, Bates wrote to the warden complaining that he'd been having "unwelcome visits" that were causing him apprehension:

> I endeavored to impress upon the first visitor that I have no desire to discuss any phase of my affairs now or in the future with the Dep't of Investigation. I have never, since being in their custody, encouraged them to believe that I could or would divulge any information that would be of the slightest interest or benefit to them, nor has anything occurred since my arrival here to alter my attitude . . . I would appreciate very much if you will please enforce the order that you made known to me upon my arrival here Sept 4th, that I would be allowed no visitors.

While the Bureau of Prisons was filling Alcatraz with incorrigibles, Hoover's men continued their pursuit of other Public Enemies.

They would never get the man whose reckless act had started the whole crime war with his bold slaughter of lawmen in the parking lot in Kansas City. The "heat" had simply gotten to Verne Miller. Hoover's men found themselves racing against the forces of organized crime, who were also hunting Miller to eliminate him in the hope of getting the feds off their backs as they tracked him through his usual network of criminal hideouts and safe havens. Miller had planned to leave for Europe after saying farewell to Vi Mathias in Chicago when the Bureau's agents botched his attempted capture. The Bureau's subsequent hunt, and the problems it was creating for organized crime up and down the East Coast, had made him a marked man.

Agents had interviewed gang leader Louis "Lepke" Buchalter, head of Murder Incorporated, one of the nation's most notorious killing syndicates and one of Miller's earlier employers. He told the feds that "no one will have anything to do with Verne Miller now . . . If Verne Miller shows up you will know about it." In other words, we are hunting him too. If we find him, you won't have to worry about any legal technicalities.

On November 29, 1933, a motorist discovered a naked, mutilated, unrecognizable body on the side of the road on the outskirts of Detroit and notified the authorities.

They determined that the dead man had been struck in the head thirteen times with a hammer. His skull was crushed and flattened. His cheeks and face had been punctured multiple times with an ice pick. He'd been choked with a wire.

The body was so pummeled and mutilated that police had to identify it using fingerprints. It was Miller.

His body was shipped back to his hometown in South Dakota, where he was buried with full military rites, his casket draped with the American flag. Uniformed servicemen carried his casket through the overflowing crowd that had flocked to his funeral.

Hoover had concluded that Miller's partners in Kansas City had been Pretty Boy Floyd and his partner, Adam Richetti. The search shifted to them and the nation's new Public Enemy Number One, John Dillinger. With his bold and bloody bank robberies and daring jailbreaks, he'd become the new fascination of the nation's headline writers.

After his release from Indiana State Prison on a minor robbery conviction, Dillinger robbed his first bank in June 1933, about a month before the Urschel kidnapping. Then he and his gang went on a tear, robbing a half-dozen more before being arrested and jailed in Lima, Ohio. Members of his gang broke him out, shooting a sheriff in the process. Purvis and his team bungled an attempt to trap him at a gangland "resort" called the Little Bohemia in northern Wisconsin, resulting in a wild shootout and Dillinger's escape. Purvis and his Chicago agents later redeemed themselves in the public's mind when they famously shot and killed Dillinger while he was leaving the Biograph Theater in Chicago.

Purvis and his men also tracked down Pretty Boy Floyd and shot him in an Ohio farmer's field as he tried to escape. As he lay on the ground bleeding to death, they tried to extract information and a confession for the Kansas City Massacre.

"Fuck you!" was all he would say.

Agents captured and convicted his partner, Adam Richetti, who would be executed in 1938 for his alleged role in the Kansas City Massacre. He maintained his innocence to the end.

Doc Barker, Harry Dutch Sawyer, Volney Davis and Bill Weaver drew life sentences for the kidnapping of Edward Bremer Jr., the heir to the Schmidt Brewery fortune, and had joined Kelly on Alcatraz. So had Alvin Karpis. (Ma Barker and Doc's brother Freddie were killed in a six-hour gunfight with federal agents in Florida.)

Purvis solved the Charles Boettcher II kidnapping, the one that had inspired Kathryn Kelly, when he tracked down and captured Verne Sankey and his partner, Gordon Alcorn, in February of 1934, interrupting their plans to kidnap Babe Ruth and Jack Dempsey. Sankey hung himself in a Chicago holding cell. Alcorn pleaded guilty and was sentenced to life.

The days of criminals racing across state lines into the friendly protection of mobbed-up towns had ended. There was a new sheriff, and he sat behind a desk in Washington, DC. But his agents were seemingly everywhere, and, for the most part, were incorruptible. Empowered by new laws, courtesy of Attorney General Homer Cummings and the Roosevelt administration, the Bureau of Investigation had tamed the Wild West after eighteen hectic months of on-the-job training. The spate of high-profile kidnappings of wealthy individuals by gangsters and racketeers virtually disappeared, and although no reliable records were kept, kidnapping in general was reduced by an estimated 80 percent.

While his agents were busy rounding up and shooting down America's outlaws, Hoover was busy ramping up an extraordinary publicity machine to exploit their triumphs — and his.

Hoover continued to use his expertise at planting stories with friendly members of the press, who would use their "exclusives" to further the Bureau's glory. On the advice of one of his favorites, national columnist Drew Pearson, Cummings hired respected Washington correspondent Hugh Suydam from the *Brooklyn Eagle* to establish the Bureau's public affairs department.

Meanwhile, Courtney Ryley Cooper had been grinding out magazine stories about the Bureau's heroic exploits, all orchestrated by its brilliant director, who got star billing in all accounts. Hoover loved Cooper's work so much that Suydam decided to bring him in-house and put him to work ghosting stories that would go out under Hoover's byline. Simultaneously, Cooper went to work on what would turn out to be a masterpiece of agency propaganda, a book called *Ten Thousand Public Enemies*. Its dust-jacket copy read: "a detailed account of American crime — where criminals come from, what they do and how they are caught."

Hoover wrote the introduction, and in it he laid out the complications of bringing the bad guys to justice:

Primarily, there is the maze of politics, ranging from the vote-getting influence of a resort owner, which sometimes encompasses life and death, to the man who controls the election destinies of a crime-ridden city. There is the impediment thrown up by well-meaning but non-thinking folk who believe that crime is none of their business and that it is not their duty to aid those entrusted with the task of law enforcement. There is the morass of ineffectual laws, many of them created in legislatures by those directly concerned with the fortunes of the criminal. There is the innate urge of human nature to picture the widely publicized criminal in the role of a Robin Hood when the facts reveal him as exactly the opposite.

In 1935, Hoover was seeking a more distinctive name for his bureau. There were several Bureaus of Investigation and Divisions of Investigation in the various government departments. He and Cummings went to the President with a suggested name change, something that would mark the agency as the nation's premier law enforcement arm. FDR liked the idea, and later that year, on March 22, Congress officially recognized the Division as the Federal Bureau of Investigation, the FBI. Hoover's expert branding efforts continued to fall into place.

Hoover's experience with the newsreel depictions of the Urschel kidnapping and the Kelly trial had convinced him that, more than anything, the nation's attitudes were shaped by what people saw in movie theaters. As long as Hollywood was making charismatic heroes out of gangsters, lawmen would remain as their simple foils. Hoover, himself a movie fan, started a personal campaign to turn movie lawmen into the heroes and gangsters into the villains.

In April 1935, the movie *G-Men,* starring James Cagney, was released with great fanfare and public acclaim. Four years earlier, Cagney had starred in the hit movie *The Public Enemy,* in which he played a Capone-style gangster. Hoover had complained personally to Cagney, who he thought was glorifying major criminals and helping to make them popular heroes. Hoover threw his support in with the Catholic Church and other moralists and social critics who were trying to ban depictions of violence in movies, along with a host of other sins. The negative reaction to *The Public Enemy* was so strong that Hollywood panicked. Fearing that censorship and legal bans were impending, the industry instituted its own code in 1934, which, among other admonitions, banned gangster films entirely. But Hoover and Cummings worked the back channels to help carve out an exemption for the studios that were suddenly prohibited from producing one of their most profitable products. Studios would be allowed to continue making a small number of gangster films as long as an FBI agent was portrayed heroically. Hoover added his own rider to the exemption. No portrayals of FBI agents would be allowed unless he got a look at the script first.

Cagney, and the studios he worked for, had gotten the message, and they pursued the exemption with a vengeance. In *G-Men,* Cagney played a brilliant lawyer-turned-tough FBI agent who does battle against dangerous kidnappers of the criminal underworld.

G-Men was so successful that it spawned a series of a half-dozen imitators, which Hollywood rushed onto the market by the end of 1935, including *Let 'Em Have It,* starring Richard Arlen as an FBI agent who tracks a kidnapper who snatched his girlfriend. Hoover had harnessed the power of the motion picture industry and turned it into his personal propaganda machine.

But the *G-Men* screenwriters had also inadvertently given Hoover's career an added boost. They wrote the role of the attorney general out of the script. So Attorney General Homer Cummings, the man who launched the nation's War on Crime, wrote the legislation to expand the number of federal crimes and empower the Justice Department's army to enforce them, all but disappeared. Overnight, Hoover became more famous than his boss, and would quickly use that fame to make himself more powerful, as well.

Ten Thousand Public Enemies was published right on the heels of *G-Men* and shot to the top of the bestseller lists.

The G-Man brand was established, and J. Edgar Hoover was anointed as the nation's top cop. FBI agents were the heroes, and the outlaws and gangsters who once fascinated the public were denigrated to "dirty rat" status.

Convinced that he'd never escape Alcatraz and that there was no one left on the outside who could spring him or buy him out, Kelly decided to use his rhetorical skills in pursuit of greater freedom. In February 1936, Kelly hatched a wild-card scheme to get himself off the island by offering to do scientific research at some remote post owned by the government. He wrote to Attorney General Cummings on February 3.

Dear Sir:

I am writing you regarding a plan I have had in mind for several months. I realize it is unusual and that no precedent has ever been set for such issue but I understand that as Attorney General it is within your power to designate the place a Federal prisoner must serve his sentence.

As you know I am serving a life sentence for kidnapping, without any possible chance of ever being paroled.

The United States Government has uninhabited Islands in the Pacific, smaller than Wake or Midway. There is Admiral Byrd's abandoned camp at the South Pole, also extremely isolated outposts in Alaska. I feel certain there is at least one of these or some other place where the Government would like the atmospheric conditions studied over a long period of time. I know with the proper instruments and books I could make a meteorology survey of such a place that would be of benefit to science and the government.

My idea is, that such a place that has never been thoroughly studied, would be too lonesome and desolate for any free man to care to stay there longer than a few months even if he had company.

I could be taken from here secretly, placed on a boat in the Bay and transported with what supplies I would need. This could be managed in such a way that the crew need never know who I was or even that I was a prisoner from Alcatraz. Some kind of arrangements could be made for a boat to stop say every year or two, leave supplies and take back what data I had accumulated.

By this method I would be doing some useful work, serving my sentence and I believe by the time I was eligible for parole I would be shown some consideration.

With rapid strides that aviation is making, wind conditions and air currents will have to be studied all over the world. Two years ago the Islands the China

Clipper is using on its flights to Manila were practically useless, but today they are the stepping-stones to the Orient, and Meteorology conditions must be known at such places, and lots of time and money would be saved by knowing these conditions in advance.

This may seem like a hair-brained [sic] proposition to you, but I think it altogether feasible.

Hoping something can be done along these lines, I remain yours truly,

Geo. R. Kelly — #117

The attorney general's office, not accustomed to receiving relocation requests to conduct research in Alaska or the South Pole from jailed gangsters, dismissed the offer out of hand as completely loopy and bizarre. They had Kelly right where they wanted him.

Where Kelly got such an idea is unknown, as is any reason why he thought it might have any chance for success. But he was desperate and bored and, like most literate inmates, enjoyed writing letters, especially from Alcatraz, where so little information from the outside world was allowed into the prison.

What he craved was news from Kathryn.

When he landed on The Rock, he was not allowed to correspond with her for the first three months, and after that only two letters a year, each only three pages long. No other inmate suffered such a restriction, and Kelly protested constantly.

It was not until November 1935 that Kelly's contact with Kathryn was increased to once every two months. A year later, it was upped to once a month, and he was permitted to write on both sides of two of the three pages he was allotted. All of his correspondence, of course, was heavily edited and censored.

This particularly irked Kelly, who bristled at having his eloquent and romantic prose reduced to sloppy drivel by the prison censors.

At one point, he wrote to Kathryn proposing that they discontinue their correspondence because he could no longer stand having their letters abused so, and that the interference left him angry and depressed for days. He longed for the time when they wrote lengthy tomes to one another while he was doing time in Leavenworth before their wedding.

Do you remember the twelve and fourteen page letters you used to write me daily when I was serving that other "bit." I even recall one that was twenty pages long, and every page as sweet as you are.

It is almost needless for me to repeat how much I love you. To me you are the grandest girl in the world, and I will love and adore you if I live to be a hundred. I hope you get transferred this month and have a pleasant trip. Give Ora my love and don't forget the one who worships you. All my heart will always be yours, angel. Lots of hugs and kisses. As ever, your very own, Geo.

But, even though they were separated by thousands of miles, prison walls and restricted communication, the couple was still capable of a grand marital fight. Despite the sweetness of the letter, Kathryn snapped back an angry response, upbraiding him for going soft and letting the situation frustrate him so. If he didn't want to write to her anymore, fine. She angrily suggested they should get a divorce and he could do like Bailey and Bates, who just forgot about their women on the outside.

The threat and the scolding panicked Kelly, who couldn't respond because he'd used up his quota of letters allowed to go to Kathryn. He enlisted the prison chaplain,

Roman Catholic priest Father Joe Clark to intercede on his behalf to keep Kathryn from taking any precipitous action on divorce before he had a chance to explain himself.

Kathryn, who had no restrictions on her correspondence, wrote back a letter of contrition and assurance.

Sept. 11. 1940

Mr. Dearest, Bear:

I have thought in vain of how to word a reply to you that would express exactly how I feel about "us." And I find that it is most difficult to do. Your letter touched my heart. In fact I cried when I read it as I expected quite a different wording. I shrink from hurting you. That is the farthest desire of my heart.

Naturally, I did not think that you would be very hurt, as long as you had cancelled your correspondence to me . . .

She went on to explain that if she were freed from prison she would live the straight life and give up her cravings for the lifestyle of the rich and fashionable, and urged him to do the same.

I know you thoroughly honey, so don't think I'm harsh. What you need to do is forget "Machine Gun" Kelly and what he stood for and interest yourself in being plain, kind George who is just another "con" like myself. I have shared all the lead with you I intend to. We are not kids, we're quite aged . . .

Take care of yourself and think a few things over, and tell me, whether you are nourishing any hair-brained *[sic]* schemes, in that brain of yours to further spoil our peaceful old age together, or not? You should have found your true honest self by now. You were never bad, we both simply "thought wrong." . . . I will write you on the 1st, so keep smiling, and try to see our problem as I see it. . . .

Now don't worry, and be sweet; and let's do this bit of time with the best of grace and cheerfully . . .

Wish I could see you, I do, I do . . . Now settle down and be happy heart of my heart.

Devotedly,
Your Katrinka

In the spring of 1940, Director of Prisons James V. Bennett visited Alcatraz and sought out Kelly for a chat. Bennett explained how he had been in contact with Urschel and noted that Urschel seemed to bear no personal hostility toward Kelly. Had he ever considered writing to Urschel, Bennett asked.

Inmates at Alcatraz lived under a strict prohibition against writing to anyone but family members. Given the extraordinary difficulty Kelly was having getting correspondence through the censors, even to his imprisoned wife, he certainly had not considered writing Urschel — particularly since most of his earlier correspondence to Urschel involved threats to kill him.

Bennett told Kelly that if he — or Bates — decided they did want to correspond with Urschel, his office would arrange for the letters to get through. Bennett's motivation was somewhat driven by the fact that a good chunk of the ransom money had not yet been recovered. A dialog between the kidnappers and their victim might open an avenue of cooperation or reveal some clues as to the whereabouts of the money. Plus, in any eventual discussion of parole, Urschel's cooperation would be essential. This fact was not lost on Kelly.

On April 11, responding to Bennett's suggestion, Kelly sent a letter to Urschel through Bennett. Eloquent and insightful, it is considered to this day to be one of the most perceptive descriptions of the deprivations of prison life, and one man's effort to endure them.

Dear Mr. Urschel,

I hope I am not pulling a prize blunder . . . in writing to you. I have two reasons for doing so. First, I wish some information; second, I want to appease my curiosity. In respect to the latter, it all came about this way: Several months ago I had a talk with Mr. Jas. V. Bennett; in the course of our discussion, he mentioned that you had paid him a visit and asked me if I ever wrote to you. Of course my answer was no. Another of his remarks was: Mr. Urschel mentioned you and spoke well of you "considering the circumstances" — or something to that effect. I have pondered over his remarks quite a bit, and often wondered if for some unknown reason you did wish to hear from me.

He then told Urschel that he'd heard oil had been discovered in Wise County in the area where he and the Shannons had their farms — the very place where Urschel had

457

been held captive. He asked Urschel to get the "lowdown" on it and if it was true he'd be eager to sell oil leases on the land. Realizing that Urschel might not be willing to go into a business arrangement with the man who kidnapped him and threatened to kill his family, he tried to make amends.

Now before I go further don't think I am merely writing this letter to try to get in on your good graces. You can rest assured I will never ask you to do anything towards getting me out. Naturally I realize that your enmity could become a detriment in later years. So, to be truthful, I hope you do not feel too vindictive; although I hardly think that you are a person of malevolent disposition. After so many years, I must admit that I am rather ashamed of the grandstand play that I made in the courtroom. I was good and mad at the time. Need I remind you of the enthusiasm of the days during my trial. You and your friends shared in it; seemed to revel in it. What produced it? The Department of Justice's love of the dramatic? The public's desire for a good free show?

I feel that at times you wonder how I am holding up under my penal servitude, and what is my attitude of mind? It is natural that you should be infinitely curious. Incidentally, let me say that you've missed something in not having had the experience for yourself. No letter, no amount of talk, and no literary description in second-rate books — and books on crime cannot but be second rate — could ever give you the faintest idea of reality.

No one can know what it's like to suffer from the sort of intellectual atrophy, the pernicious mental scurvy, that comes of long privation of all the things that make life real; because even the analogy of thirst can't possibly give you an inkling of what it's like to be tortured by the absence of everything that makes life worth living . . .

Maybe you have asked yourself, "How can a man of even ordinary intelligence put up with this kind of life, day in, day out, week after week, month after month, year after year?" To put it more mildly still, what is this life of mine like, you might wonder, and whence do I draw sufficient courage to endure it. To begin with, these five words seem written in fire on the walls of my cell: "Nothing can be worth this." This — the kind of life I am leading. That is the final word of wisdom so far as crime is concerned. Everything else is mere fine writing. . . .

I suspect that there is in all of us, always, an obscure sense of fate, inherited from numberless ancestral misfortunes, which whispers: "We are not sent into this world to live too happily. Where there's nothing to worry us, it's not natural, it's a bad sign." A little misfortune gives us the assurance that we are paying our "residence tax" so far as this world is concerned — not much to be sure, but enough to ensure us against the jealousy and thunderbolts of Heaven.

A person in prison can't keep from being haunted by a vision of life as it used to be, when it was real and lovely. At such times I pay, with a sense of delicious, overwhelming melancholy, my tribute to life as it once was. . . .

I hope you will not consider my writing impertinence. If you do, just tear this letter up and forget it. Of course, I should enjoy hearing from you anytime. With best wishes, I am

Very truly yours,
George R. Kelly
Reg. No. 117

Urschel never responded to the letter, in part because virtually all of Kelly's share of the ransom had been recovered, and if he knew where the missing amount of Bates's share was, he'd never rat out his partner. He'd already been to the Shannon farm several times with Kirkpatrick and Vaught to talk to Armon to see if he had any idea where it might be. He told Armon he'd be handsomely rewarded if he could lead him to the money. But Armon didn't have a clue.

Instead of responding to Kelly, he wrote to Bates, telling him that no oil had been found in the vicinity of Kelly's farm. At Kelly's request, Bates had also written to Urschel to give him a strict accounting of his share of the ransom and where he had last seen it, but also to plead for leniency for Ora Shannon, who had no role in the kidnapping and was being punished harshly for not turning in her husband, daughter and son-in-law when she learned of it. Surely, this was not a crime punishable by life in prison.

"I, of course, feel terribly sorry for Mrs. Shannon," wrote Bates. "She is getting well up in years, in poor health, and after all, she took no active part in the crime — other than to carry out her husband's instruction to cook a dinner for you on Sunday while

Kelly and I were absent."

He told Urschel in the letter that he had received from Kelly $94,250, his cut of the $200,000.

I gave Bailey $500 out of my pocket and Kelly did likewise. I left the farm with $93,750. When we released you at Norman, Kelly and I separated. I drove via Chickasha to Amarillo, thence to Denver. My wife was in Portland, Oregon, where I communicated with her, advising her to return to Denver immediately. I put $50,000 in a bag with surplus clothes, locked it, and left it with friends to keep until my wife called for it. I left instructions in a letter addressed to her in my post office box for her to rent an apartment upon arrival and to leave the address in that box. . . . When I was alone in the apartment my wife had rented, I put $41,000 in the same bag with the $50,000. I probably spent about $2,000 all told and had $700 on me when I was arrested three days after returning to Denver. I told my wife when I left the apartment on the date of my arrest that there was over $90,000 in a locked bag in the clothes closet.

I did not authorize her to pay any money to anyone after my arrest, with the exception of $200 to a trusty by whom I sent a message warning her to leave.

He said he had no idea how much she spent, or was bilked out of, while she was on the road for sixteen months eluding capture, but that she had never been extravagant.

Because he had stopped communication with her after his arrest, Bates didn't know that Clara Feldman had led Urschel, Fitzpatrick and some law enforcement officers to three sites where she had buried portions of the ransom money outside Portland, Oregon, in Washington State and California. Her five-year sentence for conspiracy in the case was then reduced to probation. Nevertheless, nearly $60,000 was still unaccounted for.

In 1939, three hundred of Boss Shannon's neighbors in Wise County sent a petition to President Roosevelt seeking clemency, but Roosevelt denied it because Shannon hadn't served the ten years necessary to be considered for parole. Five years later, when he had, Roosevelt reduced his sentence and he was released from prison.

On his release, he continued to press his innocence with anyone who'd listen. He told reporters, "I'm just as innocent as that dog. I did what I did because I couldn't help myself. . . . Kelly and Bates, they're the ones who did the kidnapping. . . . We had to do what they told us."

He told reporters his wife had been writing to him every week and he was trying desperately to get her out, but was having no success. He said Kelly was writing him monthly. "At first, I thought I'd never answer him, but he's in there for life and will probably never get out. I can't hold anything against him.

"I never would have gotten out if it hadn't been for Mr. Roosevelt. Now there was a president for you. A fine man and close to the common people. I wrote him letter after letter, and I'll say this much for him. I never wrote one that he didn't answer," said Boss.

By the mid-1940s Al Bates's health was in serious decline. The lack of sun and exercise and the rich, fatty prison diet were taking a toll on his heart, as they would on many others on the island. He was experiencing chest pains, probably angina, and was taking daily medication for it.

Bates had a mild heart attack on March 24, 1948. He was then admitted to the prison hospital on Alcatraz. Two days later, he had a more serious attack, from which he was not expected to recover. The doctor told the warden to notify Bates's family, but Bates countermanded the order, saying that he wanted no one to be notified.

From his hospital bed, Bates clung to life for months, but his condition worsened. By June he was wracked with pain, pleading with the doctors for medication that would ease his suffering, but they declined to up the dosage.

Prison officials were hoping that on his deathbed, Bates might reveal the location of the still-unrecovered ransom money. In exchange for his promise to try to extract the information, Kelly was allowed to visit his old partner regularly, sometimes sleeping in a bedside chair to help him get through the night.

On July 4, Bates awoke at 3:30 a.m. in a tranquil, pain-free state. He asked the attendant for a cigarette. He smoked it calmly. Finishing it, he stubbed it out, closed his eyes, fell back asleep and died.

The headline on his obituary read, *Urschel Kidnapper Takes Ransom Secret to Grave.*

Ten years later, James Bennett would allow Kelly's transfer off the island back to Leavenworth, as his health had succumbed to the harsh conditions on The Rock. Even then, after eighteen years in prison, his reputation held, and any leniency in his case had failed to materialize. When word of his impending transfer was made public, the county attorney from Fannin County, Texas, protested that Kelly should not be transferred or paroled lest he be free to "further prey on the innocent citizens of this country. Never again do we want to see the terrible destruction that was wreaked on this nation by the gangsters of Kelly's ilk." He claimed that Kelly had robbed the Farmers and Merchants Bank in Ladonia, Texas, and during the holdup he "machine-gunned the town, leaving bullet holes which have not been erased."

The Oklahoma City sheriff reminded everyone involved in the case that he could still file charges against Kelly for robbery on the night of the kidnapping — taking money from Urschel and Jarrett — and those charges could still result in convictions carrying the death penalty. Kelly knew this was an empty threat because the statute of limitations had run out on that charge. Still, because the sheriff had filed detainers against Kelly, should he be released, they served as a hindrance to his possible parole.

Hoover wrote to the FBI office in Oklahoma City advising them to "be certain we watch closely and take steps to see Kelly does not get parole. We can expect anything from Bennett's outfit." Years earlier, Father Joe Clark had traveled to Washington to personally meet with Hoover and begged him to consider parole for Kelly. He was politely dismissed, but for his efforts he was put under the watchful eye of the Bureau's agents.

"Watch closely and endeavor to thwart efforts of this priest who should be attending to his own business instead of trying to turn loose on society such mad dogs," said Hoover.

Urschel notified the parole board that he wanted to appear at any hearing in which Kelly's parole was being considered. But he was selective in his vindictiveness. Years later, when Bailey petitioned for parole, Urschel supported him, as did Kirkpatrick, who told the parole board that Bailey had nothing to do with the kidnapping and everybody involved knew it. Bailey was paroled in 1962 and was immediately arrested by Kansas authorities for his role in the Memorial Day prison break that had occurred almost thirty years earlier, in 1933.

The governor pardoned him in 1965. He moved to Joplin, Missouri, where, using the skills he perfected doing time at Alcatraz, he went to work as a skilled cabinetmaker. Urschel and Kirkpatrick had arranged the job for him, as well as subsidized housing at the local YMCA. He lived an uneventful life there until his death at age ninety-one in March 1979.

Urschel's largesse also extended to Kathryn's daughter, Pauline. Left without parents or grandparents at the end of the kidnapping trial, Urschel arranged to pay anonymously for her schooling through college. Judge Vaught administered the account, never revealing the donor, whose identity did not come to light until years after his death.

On June 1, 1951, Kelly boarded a prison railcar with several other inmates from Alcatraz and made the journey back to Union Station in Kansas City, the scene of so many notorious activities of the gangster era nearly twenty years earlier. From there he was transferred, without incident, to Leavenworth.

After years of living in a single cell, he had trouble adjusting to life in Leavenworth with five cellmates.

He got a job as a clerk and was able to earn money for commissary items, which he saved up and sent to Kathryn. He was also allowed to write her longer letters, and more often.

And he could read uncensored news-papers and listen to the radio which he so loved, though the great jazz and blues which served as the soundtrack to his adventures in crime were increasingly being eclipsed by rhythm and blues, country western and something they were calling rock 'n roll, which the younger inmates inexplicably loved.

But the years on Alcatraz had ruined his health. He was in and out of the prison hospital with heart and respiratory prob-lems. On New Year's Day 1951, he wrote to Kathryn from his hospital bed.

I got up for about five minutes today but I was a lot weaker than I thought so I had to crawl back in bed. I think in another week I'll be able to go back to work. . . . Like you said, Angel, after this is over we will be immune to anything and nothing can hurt us . . . Excuse the poor notes lately, sugar, because your husband isn't up to doing a very good job of writing just now. I'll do better next week. I'll write as usual Sunday and in the meantime, I'll be thinking of you and loving you with all my heart. My love to your Mother and lots of kisses to my adorable wife.

Yours,
Geo

On July 17, 1954, Kelly was checked into the prison hospital suffering from chest pains and shortness of breath, most likely from a heart attack. The prison doctors gave him a shot of morphine and put him on oxygen. By midnight, the pains intensified. Shortly after, he began to vomit and suffocate. Twenty minutes later he was dead.

He was fifty-four years old. It was his birthday.

Leavenworth authorities notified Kathryn at the Alderson Reformatory for Women in Alderson, West Virginia, where she and her mother were being held. She arranged to have his body shipped to Boss Shannon, who was back at the farm in Paradise.

She wrote the warden asking for a keepsake from his personal effects.

"I thought you might be able to mail a few little keepsakes of his personal property home for me," she wrote. "I know he had a fountain pen he loved, which he wrote me with, that I would like to have."

Boss buried the infamous machine gunner in the family plot at Cottondale Community

Cemetery. His headstone was immediately stolen by souvenir hunters, as would several others that he replaced it with.

The news reports of his death and the obituaries that followed it described him as "the most notorious of the hoodlums who terrorized the Midwest," a man who could write his name on a wall with a machine gun, and who pleaded, "Don't shoot, G-men!" at his arrest in Memphis.

He would be remembered throughout history for something he never was, things he never did and words he never said.

EPILOGUE

After George Kelly's death, Kathryn and her mother continued to serve their time and protest their innocence from prison in West Virginia. Also serving time there was Mildred Sisk Gillars, who was convicted in 1949 of treason. Gillars was the notorious "Axis Sally" who had done radio broadcasts for the Nazis during the war.

Gillars introduced Kathryn to her attorney, James J. Laughlin, who went to work on her behalf seeking parole, which Hoover continued to oppose and Urschel continued to fight.

Laughlin then changed strategies and asked for a new trial, claiming that the government had used false evidence to tie Kathryn to the threatening letters that had been sent to Urschel. Laughlin also charged that during the trials, Kathryn and Ora Shannon suffered from "inadequate assistance of counsel, use of testimony known to be false, denial of compulsory service of process, and conduct of the trial in an atmosphere which prevented a fair and impartial trial."

Perhaps fearing that his files did contain evidence of false testimony, Hoover refused to release them. The government's case was further hampered by the inexplicable fact that no transcript of the original trial could be located.

Much to the surprise of Kathryn and her mother, the frustrated judge granted their request for a new trial and released them on a $10,000 bond on June 16, 1959.

A new trial was never scheduled, in part because the Justice Department and Hoover wanted to avoid embarrassment over the content of their files and their conduct in the case. So Kathryn and her mother remained free.

Kathryn took a job at the Oklahoma County Poor Farm, where she earned $200 a month, which she used to support her mother.

She continued to proclaim her innocence and that of her mother. She died in Tulsa in 1985. She was eighty-one. Ora had died five years earlier at age ninety-one.

Urschel went back to running his oil company and did everything he could to put the ordeal behind him and avoid publicity of any sort — and instructed his offspring to do the same. He continued to secretly fund Pauline's education through college, providing her with money for tuition, room and board and clothing.

He and Berenice traveled the world collecting antiques and fine art. He served on a number of boards and helped his stepson, Tom Slick Jr., establish the Southwest Foundation for Research and Education. The research center, now called the Texas Biomedical Research Institute, is one of the largest independent biomedical research institutes in the world.

Urschel died on September 26, 1970, four months after Berenice. He was eighty.

In 1958, the legendary B-movie filmmaker Roger Corman released his classic underground hit *Machine Gun Kelly*. In it, the murderous, machine-gun-wielding Charles Bronson, in his first leading role, is manipulated by his domineering wife into kidnapping the child of a millionaire. The film has little in common with the actual facts of the Urschel kidnapping, but it seared the image of a violent, psychopathic George Kelly into the popular consciousness that persists today. Made in just eight days, the film launched the career of Bronson, who for years was one of Hollywood's highest paid actors.

After coming so close to losing his job in 1930 at the hands of FDR's ill-fated first choice for attorney general, Thomas Walsh, Hoover hung on to his job with amazing tenacity. When he reached the government's mandatory retirement age of seventy in 1965, President Lyndon Johnson signed an executive order exempting him from compulsory retirement. Calling Hoover "a hero to millions of decent citizens and an anathema to evil men," Johnson noted that the nation could not afford to lose the services of the man who had created "the greatest investigative body in history."

On May 2, 1972, Hoover died in his sleep, still at the FBI after fifty-five years of government service, having served under ten presidents as its director. By then, his reputation had been irreparably damaged by his blackmailing of politicians, abuses of power and relentless hounding of individuals and organizations he suspected of having communist ties, ranging from Eleanor Roosevelt to Martin Luther King Jr. and the Southern Christian Leadership Conference, the Student Nonviolent Coordinating Committee, the Congress on Racial Equality and many of the leading civil libertarians of the time.

Even so, obituary writers and eulogists could not ignore his remarkable accomplishments in building the FBI into a law-enforcement agency that was both feared and envied around the world and promoting the idea of professionalism in American law enforcement.

Jack Anderson, the nationally syndicated investigative reporter whom Hoover had characterized as one of the "lowest forms of human beings to walk the earth," paid homage to him, noting that "when [Hoover] took over the FBI forty-nine years ago, it was loaded with hacks, misfits, drunks, and courthouse hangers-on. In a remarkably brief time he transformed it into a close-knit, effective organization with the esprit de corps exceeding that of the Marines." He also noted that "not a single FBI man has ever tried to fix a case, defraud the taxpayer, or sell out his country." That unblemished record would not last long.

The New York Times was equally impressed with Hoover's accomplishments, particularly those early in his tenure.

Hoover's power was a compound of performance and politics, publicity and personality. At the base of it all, however, was an extraordinary record of innovation and modernization in law enforcement — most of it in the first decade or so of his tenure.

The centralized fingerprint file (the print total passed the 200-million mark this year) at the Identification Division (1925) and the crime laboratory (1932) are landmarks in the gradual application of science to police work. The National Police Academy (1935) has trained the leadership elite of local forces throughout the country. Mr. Hoover's recruitment of lawyers and accountants, although they now make up only 32 percent of the special agent corps, set a world standard of professionalism.

The National Crime Information Center enables 4,000 local law enforcement agencies to enter records and get questions answered on a network of 35 computer systems, with its headquarters at the F.B.I. office here.

From the start, Mr. Hoover got results. His bureau rounded up the gangsters in the nineteen-thirties. It made the once epidemic crime of kidnapping a rarity ("virtually extinct," as the director's friends like to say). It arrested German saboteurs within days after their submarines landed them on the Atlantic Coast. And, in one of its most sensational coups, the F.B.I. seized the slayers of Mrs. Viola Gregg Liuzzo only hours after the civil rights worker's shotgun death in Alabama in 1965.

Mr. Hoover always understood the subtle currents of power among officials in Washington better than anyone knew him. Not a New Dealer at heart, he had nonetheless dazzled President Franklin D. Roosevelt with his celebrated success against kidnappers.

In catching the Kellys and hunting down the rest of their ilk — Dillinger, Floyd, the Barkers, Karpis and others — Hoover had launched one of the most remarkable careers in American government. His mastery of image-making and media manipulation turned the public's attitude on its head. No longer were outlaws automatically romanticized and admired. Lawmen gained new stature as heroes in the ongoing story of American criminality. He'd meticulously crafted their tough-guy confidence and their investigative invincibility until, in the public's mind, the FBI had become the elite force of American law enforcement. He'd made enlistment in that force the aspiration of millions.

In the eighteen months following the Kansas City Massacre, Hoover fought a war on Western outlaws and won. But Hoover was more a warrior of words than of weapons. And, as history is written by the winners, Hoover did not shy away. The story was as clear as it was long-lasting: The Wild West had been tamed and he, J. Edgar Hoover, was the man who tamed it.

SELECTED BIBLIOGRAPHY

Alix, Ernest Kahlar. *Ransom Kidnappings in America, 1874–1974: The Creation of a Capital Crime.* Carbondale, Illinois: Southern Illinois University, 1978.

Barnes, Bruce. *Machine Gun Kelly: To Right a Wrong.* Perris, California: Tipper, 1991.

Bjorkman, Timothy W. *Verne Sankey, America's First Public Enemy.* Norman, Oklahoma: University of Oklahoma Press, 2007.

Burns, James MacGregor. *Roosevelt, the Lion and the Fox, 1882–1940.* New York: Harcourt Brace and World, 1956.

Burrough, Bryan. *Public Enemies, America's Greatest Crime Wave and the Birth of the FBI, 1933–34.* New York: The Penguin Press, 2004.

Congdon, Don. *The 1930s: A Time to Remember.* New York: Simon & Schuster, 1962.

Cooper, Courtney Ryley. *Here's to Crime.* Boston: Little Brown, 1937.

————. *Ten Thousand Public Enemies.* Boston: Little Brown, 1935.

Cummings, Homer, and Carl Brent Swisher. *Selected Papers of Homer Cummings: Attorney General of the United States, 1933–1939.* New York: Charles Scribner's Sons, 1939.

Denton, Sally. *The Plots against the President: FDR, a Nation in Crisis, and the Rise of the American Right.* New York: Bloomsbury Press, 2012.

Egan, Timothy. *The Worst Hard Time: The Untold Story of Those Who Survived the Great American Dust Bowl.* Boston and New York: Houghton Mifflin Company, 2006.

Ellis, George. *A Man Named Jones.* New York: Signet Books, 1963.

Esslinger, Michael. *Letters from Alcatraz.* San Francisco: Ocean View Publishing, 2013.

Felt, Mark. *A G-Man's Life.* New York: Public Affairs, 2006.

Floherty, John J. *Our FBI: An Inside Story.* Philadelphia and New York: J. B. Lippincott, 1951.

Ganz, Cheryl R. *The 1933 Chicago World's*

Fair: A Century of Progress. Urbana, Chicago and Springfield: University of Illinois Press, 2012.

Gentry, Curt. *J. Edgar Hoover: The Man and the Secrets.* New York: W. W. Norton, 1991.

Hack, Richard. *The Secret Life of J. Edgar Hoover.* Beverly Hills: New Millennium Press, 2004.

Haley, J. Evetts. *Robbing Banks Was My Business.* Canyon, Texas: Palo Duro Press, 1973.

Hamilton Stanley. *Machine Gun Kelly's Last Stand.* Lawrence, Kansas: University Press of Kansas, 2003.

Haskell, Harry. *Boss-Busters and Sin Hounds: Kansas City and Its Star.* Columbus, Missouri and London: University of Missouri Press, 2007.

Hayde, Frank R. *The Mafia and the Machine: The Story of the Kansas City Mob.* Fort Lee, New Jersey: Barricade Books, 2010.

Helmer, William, with Rick Mattix. *Public Enemies: America's Criminal Past, 1919–1940.* New York, Checkmark Books, 1998.

Hoover, J. Edgar. *Persons in Hiding.* Boston: Little Brown, 1938.

Johnson, David R. *American Law Enforcement History.* Wheeling, Illinois: Forum

Press, 1981.

Karpis, Alvin, with Bill Trent. *The Alvin Karpis Story.* New York: Coward McCann & Geoghegan, 1971.

Karpis, Alvin, with Robert Livesey. *On the Rock.* Don Mills, Ontario: Musson/ General, 1980.

Kennedy, David M. *Freedom from Fear: The American People in Depression and War, 1929–1945.* New York: Oxford University Press, 1999.

Kessler, Ronald. *The Bureau: The Secret History of the FBI.* New York: St. Martin's Press, 2003.

King, Jeffery S. *The Life and Death of Pretty Boy Floyd.* Kent, Ohio: Kent State University Press, 1998.

Kirkpatrick, E. E. *Crimes' Paradise: The Authentic Inside Story of the Urschel Kidnapping.* San Antonio, Texas: Naylor, 1934.

————. *Voices from Alcatraz — the Authentic Inside Story of the Urschel Kidnapping.* San Antonio, Texas: Naylor, 1947.

Knowles, Ruth Sheldon: *The Greatest Gamblers: The Epic of American Oil Exploration.* Norman, Oklahoma: University of Oklahoma Press, 1978.

Maccabee, Paul. *John Dillinger Slept Here: A Crook's Tour of Crime and Corruption in St.*

Paul, 1920–1936. St. Paul, Minnesota: Minnesota Historical Press, 1995.

McElvaine, Robert S. *The Great Depression: America, 1929–1941.* New York: Three Rivers Press, 2009.

Medsger, Betty. *The Burglary: The Discovery of J. Edgar Hoover's Secret FBI.* New York: Alfred A. Knopf, 2014.

Miles, Ray. *King of the Wildcatters: The Life and Times of Tom Slick.* College Station, Texas: Texas A&M University Press, 1996.

Owens, Ron. *Legendary Lawman: The Story of Quick Draw Jelly Bryce.* Nashville: Turner Publishing, 2010.

Pegler, Martin. *The Thompson Submachine Gun: From Prohibition to World War II.* New York: Osprey Publishing, 2010.

Potter, Claire Bond. *War on Crime: Bandits, G-Men and the Politics of Mass Culture.* New Brunswick, New Jersey: Rutgers University Press, 1998.

Poulsen, Ellen. *Don't Call Us Molls: Women of the John Dillinger Gang.* Little Neck, New York: Clinton Cook Publishing, 2002.

Powers, Richard Gid. *G-Men: Hoover's FBI in American Popular Culture.* Carbondale, Illinois: Southern Illinois University Press, 1983.

———. *Secrecy and Power: The Life of J. Ed-*

gar Hoover. New York: Free Press, 1987. Carbondale, Illinois: Southern Illinois University Press, 1983.

Purvis, Melvin. *American Agent.* Garden City, New York: Doubleday, Doran, 1936.

Reddig, William M. *Tom's Town: Kansas City and the Pendergast Legend.* Philadelphia: J. B. Lippincott, 1947.

Schlesinger, Arthur M. Jr. *The Age of Roosevelt, Volume I, 1919–1933.* Boston and New York: Houghton Mifflin Company, 1957.

————. *The Age of Roosevelt, Volume II, 1933–1935.* Boston and New York: Houghton Mifflin Company, 1958.

Smith, James R., and W. Lane Rogers. *The California Snatch Racket, Kidnappings During the Prohibition and Depression Eras.* Fresno, California: Craven Street Books, Linden Publishing, 2010.

Smith, Richard Norton. *The Colonel: The Life and Legend of Robert R. McCormick, Indomitable Editor of the* Chicago Tribune. Boston and New York: Houghton Mifflin Company, 1997.

Sterling, Bryan B., and Francis N. Sterling. *Forgotten Eagle: Wiley Post, America's Heroic Aviation Pioneer.* New York: Carroll & Graf, 2001.

Strunk, Mary Elizabeth. *Wanted Women: An American Obsession in the Reign of J. Edgar Hoover.* Lawrence, Kansas: University Press of Kansas, 2010.

Summers, Anthony. *Official and Confidential: The Secret Life of J. Edgar Hoover.* New York: G. P. Putnam's Sons, 1993.

Theoharis, Athan. *J. Edgar Hoover, Sex, and Crime: An Historical Antidote.* Chicago: Ivan R. Dee, 1995.

Tuohy, John W. *When Capone's Mob Murdered Roger Touhy: The Strange Case of Touhy, Jake the Barber and the Kidnapping that Never Happened.* Fort Lee, New Jersey: Barricade Books, 2001.

Unger, Robert. *The Union Station Massacre: The Original Sin of Hoover's FBI.* Kansas City, Missouri: Andrews McMeel Publishing, 1997.

Wallis, Michael. *The Life and Times of Charles Arthur Floyd.* New York: St. Martin's Press, 1992.

Ward, David, with Gene Kassebaum. *Alcatraz: The Gangster Years.* Berkeley: University of California Press, 2009.

Whitehead, Don. *The FBI Story: A Report to the People.* New York: Random House, 1956.

ACKNOWLEDGMENTS

I am indebted to an army of friends and associates who helped make this book possible. Notably, my publisher, Andrew Martin, at Minotaur, whose enthusiasm for the project was both infectious and inspiring. Kathy Huck and Marc Resnick, my editors, who shepherded this book through the process and who taught me so much about the nonfiction narrative form. Hector De-Jean was masterful in getting the word out and getting the book noticed, no small task these days.

My agent, Wayne Kabek, believed heartily in the story and provided many brilliant insights and suggestions as it was shaped into a book.

Several of the descendants of the main characters in the story were most helpful, guiding me to sources and sharing their own collected resources and knowledge of the events. Kent Frates, a lawyer in Oklahoma

City and occasional golf partner of Charles Urschel, has spent a lifetime collecting material related to the case and has written extensively about it himself. He was generous with his time and resources and toured me through the stately federal courtroom in Oklahoma City, where the principals in the case were tried. Valerie Urschel Guenther, the granddaughter of "Big Charles," was kind enough to share her materials and recollections.

Research librarians at the Library of Congress and the Oklahoma Historical Society were enormously helpful and patient, as was Linda Lynn at the Oklahoma Publishing Company.

Several colleagues from my days in the news business provided valuable editing advice and encouragement, particularly Cathy Trost, Susan Bennett and Sharon Shahid.

I never could have written this book without the loving support of my wife, Donna, my daughter, Liz, and my son, Eric. Their wise counsel, editing and constant cheerleading were invaluable. I love them immeasurably.

Newspapers of the 1930s were coming of age during the Gangster Era, and their emerging professionalism and competitive zeal left us with a treasure trove of material on events and personalities that, if it wasn't for the reporters' and editors' fascination — and the fact that crime sells newspapers — might have been lost to history. E. E. Kirkpatrick, a principal in the Urschel kidnapping, was a former newsman, and if it hadn't been for his efforts to get the Urschel story down in print with his two books on the subject, many of the great details of this seminal crime would have been lost. Popular historians and journalists drew heavily on his accounts as they pursued the story in later years, adding great detail and context with their reporting and research. Among their writings, the work of Stanley Hamilton, Robert Unger, Bryan Burrough, Rick Mattix and Paul Maccabee were immensely informative — and great reads.

The FBI files on the era are informative and fascinating, and now, for the most part, readily accessible. Ironically, it would be those extensive files of the FBI's later years, kept so meticulously and obsessively by J. Edgar Hoover, that would ruin his reputation after a band of antiwar protesters broke into an FBI field office in Media, Pennsylvania, stole voluminous amounts of the agency's files and released them to the press in 1971. That event and its consequences are marvelously recounted in Sue Medsger's book, *The Burglary,* published in 2014.

ABOUT THE AUTHOR

Joe Urschel is Executive Director of the National Law Enforcement Museum in Washington, DC. Urschel is a former managing editor of *USA TODAY* where he also served as a senior correspondent and columnist and has worked for the *Detroit Free Press* as a reporter, critic and editor. His journalism honors include awards from the National Association of Newspaper Columnists, the National Association of Sunday and Feature Editors and an Emmy. He lives in Virginia.